Hand-Formed CERAMICS

Hand-Formed
CERAMICS
CREATING FORM AND SURFACE

RICHARD ZAKIN

CHILTON BOOK COMPANY
Radnor, Pennsylvania

Designed by Stan Green

Manufactured in the United States of America

Library of Congress Cataloging-in-Publication Data
Zakin, Richard
    Hand-formed ceramics : creating form and surface / Richard Zakin.
        p.   cm.
    Includes index.
    ISBN 0-8019-8505-6
    1. Pottery craft.   I. Title.
TT920.Z35   1995   95-10549
730'.028—dc20   CIP

1 2 3 4 5 6 7 8 9 0   4 3 2 1 0 9 8 7 6 5

Front cover, clockwise from center. *Vestige Structure II,* Joanne Hayakawa, USA,
stoneware, copper, graphite, and cement, 31×17×36 inches; the imagery of this piece is
monumental with strong architectural references; the drawing is spatial and goes well with
the three-dimensional clay forms; the rectangular forms in the lower front of the piece
contrast with the larger, more massive forms.

   Drape-formed platter, Matthais Osterman, Canada; the six-sided shape makes it unusual and appealing; note the carefully made rim with curved corners; this piece has its
roots in the European tradition of the decorative plate; photo by Jan-Thijs, © Jan-Thijs.

   Reopening the Window (see Plate 3 in the color section).

   Triad, Nancy Jurs, USA, maquette for a public sculpture in the Rochester Airport,
large segmented sculptural forms; Jurs often works in the large scale; she enjoys the freedom and the impact of large work and its sense of bravura and energy; photo by Marty
Czamanske.

   Sandblasted earthenware (see Plate 7 in the color section).

Back cover. See Plate 19 in the color section.

When I think of my parents, Ethel and Lester Zakin, I think of their strength and their optimism. They came to maturity during difficult times and their lives were not always easy. However, they believed they would prevail and live full, interesting lives. And that they have done. Furthermore, with the passage of time, they have retained their joy of life. Therefore, I want to dedicate this book to them.

CONTENTS

FOREWORD by William D. Parry xi

PART 1: HAND-FORMING BASICS

Chapter One
INTRODUCTION TO THE HAND-FORMING PROCESS 3
   A PICTORIAL HISTORY OF HAND-FORMED CERAMICS 4
   "LIVING INSIDE" HAND BUILDING 12

Chapter Two
WORKING WITH CLAY 19
   TOOLS 19
      All-Purpose Tools and Supplies for Hand-Forming 19
   THE KILN 20
   CLAY BODIES 21
      Choosing a Clay Body That Is Right for Your Work 21
      Assessing a New Clay Body 22
   MODIFYING THE CLAY BODY 23
      Additions to the Clay Body for Workability and Durability 23
   SPECIAL CLAY BODIES DESIGNED FOR LARGE-SCALE WORK 24
   PREPARING CLAY BODIES FOR HAND BUILDING 24
      Wedging 25
      Cutting 26

Chapter Three
BASICS OF THE FORMING PROCESS 27
   FORMS APPROPRIATE FOR HAND BUILDING 27
   ENCOURAGING STRUCTURAL INTEGRITY 27
   MAKING PRELIMINARY DRAWINGS AND MODELS 29

CONTROLLING MOISTURE CONTENT DURING THE HAND-FORMING
   PROCESS 31
WALL THICKNESS 31
JOINS 33
   Creating the Join 33
   Strengthening Joins 33
TEMPLATES 34
DEALING WITH FORMING PROBLEMS 36
   Warping 36
   Cracking 36
THE DRYING PROCESS 37
FINISHING 38
FIRING 39
HAND FORMING AND CLAY IMAGERY 40
   Methods for Creating Surface Imagery 40
   Stamped Imagery 44
   Sprigged Imagery 48
   Engraved Imagery 48
   Carved Imagery 49
   Combed Imagery 50

Chapter Four
METHODS OF FORMING AND FINISHING 51
PINCH FORMING 52
   Experimenting with Pinch-Forming Techniques 53
   Pinch-Formed Vessels 53
   Guest Artist: Kirk Mangus 53
COIL FORMING 55
   Forming Coils 55
   Building with Coils 55
   Efficient Coiling Methods 56
   Experimenting with Coil-Forming Techniques 57
   Guest Artist: Sue Abbrescia 59
   Portfolio of Coil-Built Pieces 61
   Guest-Artist: Eva Kwong 68
SLAB FORMING 68
   Using a Roller to Make Slabs 71
   "Throwing" a Slab 72
   Creating Tapered Walls 74
   "Seasoning" the Slabs 76
   Preshaping the Slabs 76
   Making Three-Dimensional Pieces from Slabs 76
   Experimenting with Slab-Forming Techniques 78
   Portfolio of Slab-Formed Pieces 85
   Guest Artist: Peter Beard 89
   Guest Artist: John Neely 89
   Guest Artist: Donna Nicholas 90
   Guest Artist: Jerry Caplan 91
DRAPE FORMING 93
   Experimenting with Drape-Forming Techniques 93

Rigid and Soft Drape Forms 93
Fired-Clay and Plaster Drape Forms 94
Plywood Drape Forms 95
Mixed Wood and Metal Drape Forms 95
Making Shapes with Rigid Drape Forms 96
Portfolio of Drape-Formed Pieces 103
Guest Artist: Yih-Wen Kuo 104
Making a Pillow Drape Form 105
Making a Hammock Drape Form 105

SOLID FORMING 108
Experimenting with Solid-Forming Techniques 108

CUT FORMING 111

MODULAR FORMING 112
Guest Artist: JoAnn Schnabel 112

COMBINING FORMING METHODS 113
Portfolio of Pieces Created Using Combined Forming
    Methods 114

MIXED-MEDIA TECHNIQUES 116
Mixed-Media Materials 116
Portfolio of Mixed-Media and Sculptural Pieces 118

PART 2: USING FORMING METHODS TO CREATE FINISHED PIECES

Chapter Five
VESSELS 123
FORMING METHODS FOR VESSELS 123
HOW USE INFLUENCES FORM 124
COIL-FORMED VESSELS 125
Portfolio of Coil-Formed Vessels 126
Guest Artist: Mary Barringer 127
PINCH-FORMED VESSELS 128
SLAB-FORMED VESSELS 128
Portfolio of Slab-Formed Vessels 129
DRAPE-FORMED VESSELS 132
Guest Artist: William Parry 132
MIXED-MEDIA VESSELS 134
COMBINING FORMING METHODS TO CREATE VESSELS 134
Types of Vessel Forms 135

A Hand-Formed Teapot—Barbara Frey 139
Guest Artist: Sandi Pierantozzi 140
Portfolio of Slab-Formed Teapots 142
TECHNICAL ASPECTS OF VESSEL FORMING 144
VESSEL FORM DETAILS 145
The Foot 145
The Lip 146
Handles 146
Covers and Lids 147

Chapter Six

CERAMIC SCULPTURE 149
AESTHETIC ASPECTS OF CERAMIC SCULPTURE 149
TECHNICAL ASPECTS OF CERAMIC SCULPTURE 150
SMALL-SCALE SCULPTURE (TABLE SCULPTURE) 151
MID-SIZE SCULPTURE 152
LARGE-SCALE SCULPTURE .152
BRACED FORMS 152
Metal Armatures—Jacquie Germanow 154
SCULPTURE FORMING 154
Pinch-Formed Sculpture 156
Coil-Formed Sculpture 156
Hand-Forming a Large-Scale Ceramic Sculpture—
    Virginia Scotchie 157
Guest Artist: Martha Holt 160
Guest Artist: William Steward 160
Portfolio of Coil-Formed Pieces 162
Slab-Formed Sculpture 164
Creating a Slab-Formed Sculpture—Aurore Chabot 164
Portfolio of Sculptural, Slab-Formed, and Mixed-Media Pieces 167
Segmented and Assembled Sculpture 171
A Segmented Sculpture—Ann Roberts 172
Guest Artist: Robert Arneson 174
Guest Artist: Douglas Baldwin 175
Solid-Formed Sculpture 176
Guest Artist: Bruce Taylor 176
Using More Than One Forming Method on a Single Piece 177
Guest Artist: Angelica Pozo 177
MIXED-MEDIA SCULPTURE 179
A Mixed-Media Piece—Thomas Seawell 180
Guest Artist: William Parry 181

Chapter 7

INSTALLATION ART AND WALL PIECES 183
INSTALLATION ART 183
WALL PIECES 186
Unsegmented Tile Pieces 186
Guest Artist: Neil Forrest 187
Segmented Tile Pieces 187
Two- and Three-Dimensional Imagery 189

Portfolio of Installation Art and Wall Pieces 191
Two Wall Pieces for Public Spaces—Dale Zheutlin 193

MAKING TILES 195
Flat Tiles 196
Shaped Tiles 196

INSTALLING WALL PIECES 199
Mastic, Mortar Cement, and Grout 199
Mounting a Large Tile Wall Piece—George Mason 199
Creating a Wall-Hanging Tile Piece—Richard Zakin 203
Portfolio of Wall Pieces 206

MOSAICS 207
Making Tesserae 207
Mounting the Piece 208
Mosaic Notes—Sally Michener 209

Appendix
SETTING UP A HAND-BUILDING STUDIO 213

GLOSSARY 215

INDEX TO ARTISTS 219

SUBJECT INDEX 221

FOREWORD

Richard Zakin was one of my first graduate assistants in 1965 at Alfred University. He has become a durable and rewarding friend. To students at that early time, he brought a sense of openness and search, as a result perhaps of his experience as a painter recently captivated by the craft of ceramics.

His career in teaching continues to enliven and instruct those around him. His writing gains in breadth and depth; it began with *Electric Kiln Ceramics* (Chilton, 1981), a practical guide to the use of clays and glazes employed in such firing and was succeeded by *Ceramics: Mastering the Craft* (Chilton, 1990).

His writing is generously characterized by its firsthand nature and comes directly out of his own experience and research; he is never far away in tone or direction. Like a devoted gardener or cook, he moves from one possibility to another, stopping to describe and demonstrate to his readers the nature of successful outcomes and their difficulties.

Zakin's keen observations are well served by his organization of the materials. He employs the research of history and materials science in his writing as naturally as they may have claimed his attention initially.

Hand-Formed Ceramics takes one procedure and focuses on it exclusively as the most ancient and rudimentary means of personal expression in clay (and in most aspects the least demanding in tools and equipment). This book becomes a testament to the imaginative variety of form and expression of the unique clay object as a one-of-a-kind adventure by which the mud is returned to its original rock-like nature. Zakin tells us engagingly and thoughtfully about that experience.

William D. Parry

PART ONE
HAND-FORMING BASICS

CHAPTER ONE

INTRODUCTION TO THE HAND-FORMING PROCESS

he first methods of forming clay were hand-forming methods. We have since learned to form ceramic pieces in other ways, using the potter's wheel, slip-cast molds, and extruders. Ceramists, however, continue to use hand-forming procedures and these procedures remain a primary way of creating ceramic work. Many great pieces have been made by ceramists who used hand-building strategies. For some of us there is no other way to create form that gives us the same feeling of enjoyment and accomplishment. As a hand-builder, it pleases me that the creators of many of our ceramic masterworks used hand-forming techniques.

Hand forming is more than a method or a group of methods—it is a way to create ceramic forms that centers only on the ceramist's hands and a few simple tools. The hand-forming ceramist shapes clay without the need for complex machines.

In this book I have brought together the various methods traditionally used for hand-formed ceramics. These are: pinch, slab, coil, modular, solid forming, and drape forming. Part One covers the basic forming methods of the hand-builder. In Part Two, I offer illustrated descriptions of the way in which ceramic artists go about creating their hand-formed work. This part is divided into three sections: vessels, sculpture, and wall pieces. The work in each category calls for the same basic techniques, but those techniques will be used in different ways.

Part of the appeal of hand building for the beginner is that the basic skills are easy and natural to acquire. In addition, only minimal equipment is required and that equipment is inexpensive. Even for the advanced ceramist, hand building can express the artist's skill as much as any technique in ceramics, and it can be extremely enjoyable as well. The pace in hand building is measured and steady, the mood a blend of the cerebral and the instinctive. Hand forming gives the ceramist the opportunity to try a great variety of forms. Its principal advantage, however, is in the directness and power of the forms it allows the ceramist to create. These forms speak of the nature of clay and reveal the process of creation.

Hand forming is not without its problems. Hand-formed pieces are prone to cracking and warping and achieving a finished look can be difficult. The hand-forming ceramist occasionally may have to deal with a common perception that the asymmetries and pieced-together character of hand-built work are "defects." Some critics may judge a hand-formed piece not as good as a mold-made or wheel-formed piece. On the other hand, many people like the direct way in which hand-built pieces evoke the character of the clay and the integrity of the building process.

The hand-building process can be awkward and inefficient, especially if the ceramist is trying to imitate forms that have been slip cast or formed on the wheel. Instead, the hand-forming ceramist must allow the work to *look* hand formed. Seams and joins will influence the way the piece looks and the form will be asymmetric. The committed hand-builder will enjoy these characteristics and see them as enriching the form.

I see the hand-forming process as exciting, challenging, and always evolving. You can lose yourself in it, and you can make surprising discoveries and reach difficult goals along the way.

A PICTORIAL HISTORY OF HAND-FORMED CERAMICS

Let us now look at hand-formed pieces made by ceramists from the distant and more recent past and explore the way these pieces were formed and ornamented. By looking at the past, we can learn a great deal from these processes.

The earliest ceramics were hand built and many of the great masterpieces were made using hand-building methods. Early in the history of ceramics, artists learned how to master their techniques and create pieces that were strong and expressive. Before the potter's wheel was developed, all early work was hand formed. These ceramics convey an atmosphere of intense intellectual excitement; for these ceramists, hand-formed clay was a state-of-the-art technology.

The later pieces show us how ceramists in the recent past worked with hand-forming techniques. I will discuss the work of ceramic sculptors active in the 1930s and traditional potters working in Nigeria.

Figure 1-1 was constructed with great precision. Its light weight is startling to a contemporary ceramist. The surface is smooth and the contours are taut and carefully designed. The handles flow smoothly into the main form and the base flows smoothly into the neck.

The piece is composed of a spherical base with low cylindrical neck. The ceramist who created this piece took advantage of the benefits of coil building, which allows full, bulbous forms. The spheroid base that makes up the lower part of the piece starts from a narrow foot, moves outward at a steep angle, and then moves inward again to the fairly narrow neck. The shoulder of the piece is gently curved. In the catalog *Asian Ceramics in Alfred Collections* (published in 1992 on the occasion of the exhibition of the same name), Margaret Carney Xie wrote: "The decoration of these pieces was always confined to the upper portion of the vessels. The lower portion of the urn was designed to be placed firmly into the ground." If I want to see this piece as its original owners must have seen it, I use the palm of my hand to block off the lower eighth of the base. Its proportions make much more sense to

Fig. 1-1. Neolithic, storage jar, Yang Shao, Gansu Province, China, 2700–2350 B.C., 11 × 10½ inches. Gansu (formerly spelled Kansu in transliteration) is a large province in north-central China. It was the site of a flourishing agricultural and pottery-making culture in China's neolithic period. In many ways this piece is typical of pieces made by potters in neolithic cultures. The potter made this piece from a buff-colored, low-fired, earthenware clay. It was coil formed and painted with a highly refined slip known as terra sigillata.

me when I do this. The placement of the two handles in their offset position is also interesting. This arrangement, rare but not unknown, is appealing in its asymmetry. I think the contemporary ceramist will respond to its appealing full form and the interesting logic of its asymmetric handle placement.

Figure 1-2, a coil-built work of the late Shang dynasty in China, is a low-fired earthenware clay body. The ceramist smoothed the surface of the piece, erasing all traces of the coiling process. The feet and body of the form are marked by a highly textured surface imagery created using a roller stamp. The ceramist flattened the coils on the neck and lip of the piece to produce a smooth surface. The most dramatic aspect of this piece is its tripod foot. The feet are mammiform in shape and ornamented with a roller-stamped surface. The lobed feet merge toward the middle of the piece to form a low arch. The shoulder curves inward to form a narrowed neck. The neck flares outward again to form a wide lip. The form has a wide stance, which gives it stability. This utilitarian object was probably made for daily use.

Fig. 1-2. li, Tripod vessel, late Shang or early Chou dynasty, China, c. 1523–1028 B.C., 6½ × 5 inches. Many of the earliest ceramic pieces were made by ceramists who used the coil method. Particularly important examples are from potters of the Jomon culture of Japan (7000–2000 B.C.), Susa in the ancient Middle East (5000–4000 B.C.), and the Shang (1523–1028 B.C.) and Chou dynasties of China (1027–771 B.C.). The work of these potters is similar in many ways and characterized by sophisticated forming and surface-creation skills. The coiling was well made and was finished with great care. These pieces are often exuberant, with taut shapes and inventive imagery.

Contemporary ceramists will enjoy this simple and direct form and the rich surface texture of this piece.

The large, robust, simply modeled figural sculpture in Figure 1-3 shows real understanding and love for the material. The piece was modeled swiftly and directly in a soft, coarse clay. The ceramist combed its surface to produce a rich texture. No slip or glaze was used. The fired color of this piece is a soft ocher. The basic form is derived from assembled cylindrical forms. The Haniwa sculptors used coil methods to produce these forms. Haniwa pieces can be quite large, usually 25 to 40 inches in height; this piece is 28 × 25 × 10 inches. The imagery is highly simplified and stylized. The simple cylinders that serve as the horse's legs are espe-

Fig. 1-3. Haniwa Horse, Japan, 5th–7th century A.D., The Herbert F. Johnson Museum of Art, Cornell University, Ithaca New York; Gift of Mary Palmer Rockwell. Haniwa ceramics are a product of the Old Tomb period of fourth- and fifth-century Japan. They are marked by the creation of large burial mounds and the large figural sculptures intended for placement upon them in a circle. The most common Haniwa pieces are simple clay cylinders, but the most striking pieces are given human or animal forms.

cially simplified. At first glance the piece seems almost childlike. Notice, however, the carefully and elegantly modeled harness and saddle. These details and the vigor of modeling and the intensity of feeling testify to a mature, sophisticated creation.

The Salado people were members of the Anasazi culture, precursors of the Pueblo culture, and lived in what is now central Arizona. They created coil-built vases and bowls that are especially noteworthy for their full forms and the richness of their coiled surfaces. Both are the result of how they used coil-forming tech-

Fig. 1-4. Corrugated ware, Salado (Anasazi culture, ancient Southwest, North America), ninth–twelfth century A.D., Everson Museum, Syracuse, New York.

niques. One of the best ways to achieve full bowl forms like this is to use coil techniques (see pages 55–56). The corrugated marks on the surface of this piece are the result of an effective coil strategy. Each indentation welds the top coil to the one below it, resulting in a strong pot wall. In this way the potter welded the coils together, strengthening the wall of the piece while simultaneously creating an appealing indented texture. The rich texture of this surface is the natural product of the coil-welding process. This piece is convincing and beautiful. I would recommend that every coil builder try it.

The mosaics in Figure 1-5 are made from colored glass. The rest of the modeling is in the form of clay ashlars (blocks) and highly stylized lions. The ceramic elements were made to look like cut stone. If this complex imagery had been sculpted in stone, however, it would have been expensive, difficult, and time-consuming to create. Modeled clay was the perfect material for Louis Sullivan's imagery. Sullivan created the designs, which his modeler, Christian Schneider, then executed.

In this design we see an elegant balance between the sensuous and the highly rational. Sullivan has made a specialty of the kind of imagery shown in the leaves in the bottom right-hand corner. The design seems random, yet Sullivan's drawings reveal that its underpinnings are logical and geometric. Note as well the blocks that run along the bottom of the frieze. These look especially stone-like but in fact are terra-cotta ashlars. Their ornament, with its vaguely Celtic character, is typical of Sullivan's work. Sullivan integrated the mosaics into this design to create a complex mixed-media composition.

Rosanjin Kitaoji made the set of small stacking trays in Figure 1-6 at the College of Ceramics at Alfred, when he visited the school on a trip to the United States in 1954. The trays are simple slab forms and are traditionally used for serving pickles. The edges are lively, irregular, and slightly curled. The contours of the forms are also irregular, and no two are alike. Many are concave, but a few are convex. The

Fig. 1-5. Louis Henri Sullivan, Peoples Federal Savings and Loan, Sidney, Ohio, 1917.
This detail of the main facade of a bank in Sidney, Ohio, is an example of the monumental terra-cotta facades that the great turn-of-the-century architect Louis Henri Sullivan designed for his buildings. Sullivan designed a simple rectangular frieze in terra-cotta and mosaic.

slabs are wider on one end than the other. The corners are slightly rounded and no two are alike.

These pieces have a slight glaze. Rosanjin created the marks in the center of the plates by placing grasses on the surface before the firing. The grasses contained fluxes that marked the clay. The result is set of pieces with an air of studied simplicity. The small irregularities are subtle, seemingly the result merely of the forming process, but in reality they are highly controlled.

These pieces show that a simple form can be executed boldly to produce images of great subtlety. They show us as well that we can interpret traditional forms in a way that looks very contemporary.

Until the 1930s very little ceramic sculpture was made by American ceramists. Then a number of American ceramists came under the influence of the Wiener Werkstätte, a crafts school in Vienna. In the mid-1930s a number of fine ceramic artists went to study at the school, among them Viktor Schreckengost, Karl Walters, and Ruth Randall. They all began to work in the Werkstätte's figural style, creating stylized and gently abstracted human and animal imagery. Their pieces were often humorous or satirical in mood. Work of this kind was popular up to World War II.

This piece is a free interpretation of the biblical theme of the lion and the lamb. The springing figure of the lion dominates the piece. The lamb perches demurely on the back of the lion. The rear part of the piece (the lion's flanks and legs) are raised from the base. The lion with its lamb "cargo" is placed on an oval, rounded mound of earth.

Viktor Schreckengost used contrasting elements in his work and liked to play one element against the other. Here he contrasted the highly textured lion's mane

Fig. 1-6. Rosanjin Kitaoji (1883–1959), Japan, The Museum of the New York State College of Ceramics at Alfred, New York, 9½ × 3½ inches. Rosanjin had an interesting and varied career. His original training was in calligraphy, but he became interested in antiques, especially traditional Japanese furniture. This led (in a circuitous way) to a long period when he ran a restaurant specializing in traditional Japanese cuisine. He wanted the bowls and serving pieces in his restaurant to emulate this tradition. Since he could not find what he had in mind, he hired potters to make pieces from his interpretations of traditional designs. His position in his studio was something like that of a movie director. Occasionally he would make hand-formed pieces, but in general he oversaw the design of the work of the studio, modifying the forms his assistants made. He would also execute the calligraphy we sometimes see on his pieces. Finally, he directed the glazing process, sometimes glazing the pot himself. The pieces from his studio were made only for the purpose of serving food. Photo by Brian Oglesbee.

against the smoother areas of the lion's body. He used a strong texture to create the lamb's coat. These textured areas are also glazed. He contrasted the shiny light-colored glaze with a mat brown slip. Schreckengost depicted the lion's body in action; it is taut, caught in a springing posture with its hind legs in the air. The artist also stylized the musculature and ribs to convey strength and action. The sheep also seems to be caught in mid-action. Its ears flap outward and its feet are extended and in the air. The lamb's airborne posture and the lion's curled tail contrast with the heavy forms of the lion's mane and flanks.

Schreckengost's use of contrasting surfaces and form elements has a strong relevance for contemporary ceramic sculptors.

Figure 1-8 is thick-walled with an open area in its central core. Its creator, Ruth Randall, seems to have enlarged the opening during the building process. It appears that she built the piece as a solid form and then hollowed it out. She probably used a wire tool to scoop out the clay from the interior of the piece.

The form is not marked by any abrupt joins. The surface of the clay is smooth, without texture or ornament. The feeling of space is strong but not exaggerated. The contour flows smoothly from section to section. In this piece Randall created an imagery in which she balanced stylization and realism. She not only captures

Fig. 1-7. *Spring,* 1941, Viktor Schreckengost (born 1906), figural sculpture, 15 × 30 × 7¾ inches. During the 1930s, Viktor Schreckengost created an important group of hand-formed ceramic vessels and sculptures. He created highly stylized but easily recognizable images depicting human and animal figures. These pieces appear to be molded mostly from blocks of clay. Schreckengost then hollowed out their centers and assembled the parts to create the piece.

Fig. 1-8. *Winter Weasel,* Ruth Randall (1898–1983), Everson Museum, Syracuse, New York, 10¾ × 4¾ × 9½ inches. Ruth Randall was noted for her hand-formed sculptural pieces. She studied at the Kunstgewerbe Schule of the Wiener Werkstatte in Vienna in 1933, working with Michael Powolny. She worked in the Viennese tradition, making moderate-size sculpture with stylized animal and human imagery. She created these pieces using slab- and solid-forming techniques and continued to work with these techniques throughout her long life. In the middle part of her career, she finished her pieces with painted glazes; she finished her later work with stains. Randall was the author of *Ceramic Sculpture* (Watson-Guptil, 1948), a useful book on the creation of hand-formed sculpture.

Fig. 1-9. Traditional coil-formed vessel, Nigeria. The work of the village potters of western Africa is an example of the survival of an ancient tradition. Most pieces are produced using thick coils. The potter then presses outward from inside the piece with an anvil-like tool while simultaneously paddling the outside of the piece, thus forming and thinning the vessel wall. The ceramist fired this piece at low temperatures and finished it in a monochromatic, carbon-darkened clay surface. In the hands of these skilled Nigerian potters (always women), this is an effective method for producing functional objects of great beauty.

the energy and sinewy character of the subject, but there is a strong feeling of movement and lively posture, as if the animal had been photographed in the wild. We can learn much from Randall's gift for characterization and her respect for the dignity of her subject.

The coil-formed covered jar (Fig. 1-9) is highly utilitarian, but at the same time the potter paid a great deal of attention to the design. The simple arc handle is striking. The ceramist placed the handle on a small hemisphere that elevates it. In turn, she placed the hemisphere on the gently curved lid. The body of the pot is a full curved form. The base mirrors the curve of the lid. It is unusually emphatic but at the same time is quite graceful.

The artist ornamented the surface of this piece with combed imagery, typical of the potters of this region of Nigeria. She made the parallel combed lines reinforce the form's shape.

These pieces have much to teach us. All the formal elements work together to create a harmonious and persuasive whole. Furthermore, we see in this piece an approach to utilitarian pottery that works well and that looks different from many of the utilitarian ceramic forms we are familiar with.

"LIVING INSIDE" HAND BUILDING

I am particularly interested in the work of those ceramists who have done most or all of their pieces using hand-forming techniques. I often refer to them as "living inside" hand building. It is interesting to see this work evolve over the years. In these examples we see how artists grapple with the problems of form as expressed in hand-built clay.

Nan and James McKinnell have been making pots since 1948. Much of their work is hand built. They have informed their work with a strong commitment to clay and have been true to the tradition of the studio potter. The McKinnells strongly influence each other as well as support and inspire each other in their work. We see in their work strong forms and expressive qualities. The result is a consistent continuum of production, from their early to their most recent pieces (Figs. 1-10–1-14).

Fig. 1-10. Nan B. McKinnell, USA, 1965–66, stoneware, 24″ in diameter. Photo by James O. Milmoe.

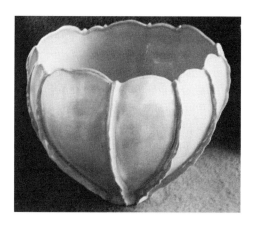

Fig. 1-11. Nan B. McKinnell, 1989, porcelain, clear matte glaze inside, semi matte glaze outside, 14″ × 15″. Photo by James O. Milmoe.

Fig. 1-12. James F. McKinnell, USA, 1965–66, stoneware, dark yellow-green glaze inside and occasionally on the lip, 19⅞″ × 27″ × 26½″. Photo by James O. Milmoe.

Fig. 1-13. James F. McKinnell, c. 1966, stoneware, 11¾″ × 11¾″ × 6½″. Photo by James O. Milmoe.

Fig. 1-14. James F. McKinnell, 1974, stoneware, 20" in diameter. Photo by James O. Milmoe.

Barbara Frey makes almost all of her work using hand-formed methods. Comparing her earlier work with her latest pieces (Figs. 1-15–1-18), one sees that her methods have remained the same, though the look of her pieces has changed. She builds now, as she has for many years, with slabs. We see the same concern in these older pieces with surface imagery as we see in her recent work. She produced much of the imagery in these older pieces using relief techniques, just as she does now. The mood of her pieces remains both thoughtful and playful.

Fig. 1-15.

Fig. 1-16.

William Parry has a restless approach to the creation of ceramic work. We see a great variety of form and imagery in his pieces. He has used slab forming and coil and mixed-media techniques to create them. The consistency between his older work and his most recent pieces (Figs. 1-19–1-23) is seen in the way he communicates a feeling of pleasure in the act of creation. The mood remains, from then until now, gentle, reflective, and engrossed in the artistic process.

I have used hand-forming methods from the beginning of my ceramic career. My natural curiosity has led me to try all the hand-forming methods and I like all of them a great deal. If you compare these earlier pieces with my latest work (Figs.

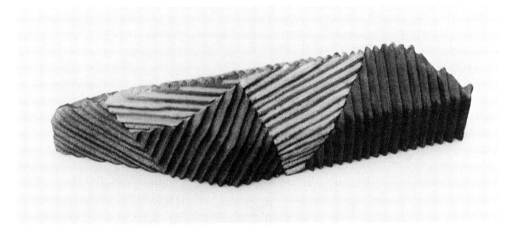

Fig. 1-17.

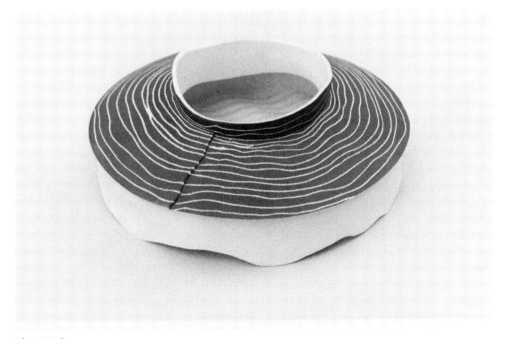

Fig. 1-18.

1-24–1-27), I think you will see that in all of it there is a concern for ideas. This, I hope, is what establishes the link of consistency from my earlier pieces to my most recent work.

Fig. 1-19.

Fig. 1-20.

Fig. 1-21.

Fig. 1-22.

Fig. 1-23.

Fig. 1-25.

Fig. 1-24.

Fig. 1-26.

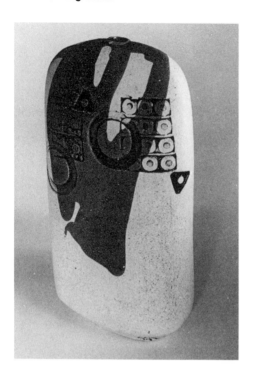

Fig. 1-27.

CHAPTER TWO

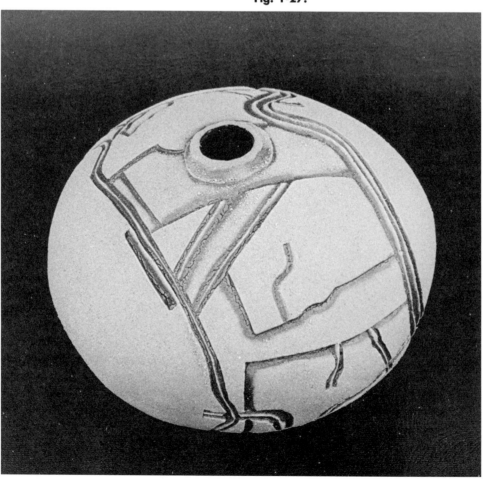

Fig. 2-1. Hand-forming tools used by the author.

WORKING WITH CLAY

TOOLS

One of the nice things about hand building is that the basic hand-forming processes require few tools; furthermore, these tools are usually inexpensive. In fact, you can make many of them quickly and easily and others you can adapt from different trades. Most hand-builders I know spend a good deal of time in hardware and cooking supply stores. Two of my own favorite tools come from unexpected sources—one is a scalpel with an exceedingly thin, sharp blade, purchased in a surgical pharmacy, and the other is a beautifully shaped spring-steel spatula that I found in the hardware department of a store in Paris.

Some tools are common to all hand-forming techniques. Others are used for one method only. I list these tools at the end of this section.

ALL-PURPOSE TOOLS AND SUPPLIES FOR HAND-FORMING

1. Heavyweight fabric: Pieces of heavyweight fabric can be useful for many processes. Use it for rolling out coils and slabs. For slab work, place the fabric between the clay and the wareboard. If you use two sheets of fabric, you can easily turn the slab to manipulate both of its sides. The best fabric for this purpose is a heavyweight canvas. Heavyweight felt is useful as well because it is smooth and therefore does not leave the pattern of a woven texture on the slab. Always keep several pieces of heavyweight fabric in the studio.

2. Wareboards: These boards serve to support slabs and hand-built forms during the process of building. I use Homosote, a material used in the building trades. It is a durable cardboard-like material about three quarters of an inch thick. Because of the rough texture and the absorbency of the material, the clay is less likely to stick to it than to the table surface. I prefer to keep as many as five wareboards in the studio.

3. A needle tool: Use this tool to cut clay. I use two needle tools—a strong, thick one for rough work and a very thin one for fine cutting and carving. Sharpened crochet hooks make fine durable needle tools. I always have extra needle tools on hand in case the one I am using breaks.

4. Knives: I use two types of knives—one has a heavy blade for coarse work and the other is a scalpel fitted with slim, sharp, replaceable blades. I use a scalpel for precise cutting and fine work. You can purchase a scalpel and blades at a surgical pharmacy or at a chemical supply house. Always keep extra scalpel blades in the studio because these blades will break.

5. A scoring tool: Use this tool to roughen the surface of the clay, especially when joining clay surfaces such as slabs and coils. A roughened surface will accept slip more efficiently and thus will produce a much better join. Combs or steel brushes work well for this purpose. You can find steel brushes at hardware stores and ceramic supply houses.

6. Cloth sheeting: Use cloth sheeting to encourage slow but even drying. You can use worn-out sheets or purchase cloth sheeting at a fabric supply house. I keep ten or twelve cloth sheets in my studio.

7. Plastic sheeting: Plastic sheeting will keep the work moist during the building process. Thin, transparent, impermeable plastic sheeting is available at hardware stores, or use plastic bags from the dry cleaners. I always have ten or twelve plastic sheets in my studio.

8. A cutting wire: Use this wire to cut through a lump of clay to break up lumps and improve the consistency of the mixture. The cutting wire may be hand held or permanently fixed. A hand-held cutting wire has handles at each end. A permanently fixed cutting wire is stretched between a vertical post attached to the front and back of the work table. To use a hand-held cutting wire, draw it through the clay; to use a permanently fixed cutting wire, push the clay through the wire.

9. A "banding wheel": This wheel is a freely turning stand on which sculptural and vessel pieces can be placed. Use it to work on and examine the piece from all angles. Banding wheels should be stable and heavy. A good banding wheel is a valuable tool and can be expensive. They are available from ceramic supply houses. One or two of these are useful in the studio. If you are handy with tools, you can make a banding wheel from new or used hardware parts.

You will also need specialized tools that are appropriate for particular formats (vessels, sculpture, and wall pieces) and for particular forming methods (coil, slab, drape, and solid forming).

THE KILN

The only expensive piece of equipment most hand-builders need is a good kiln. Hand-builders can use any type of kiln, large or small, fuel burning or electric, raku, salt, wood, or sawdust.

CLAY BODIES

Clay bodies should be workable and flexible enough to resist cracking. They should also be tough enough to stay together and resist warping during the building and firing processes. Clay bodies intended for hand building do not have to be as plastic (flexible and workable) as bodies formulated for work on the potter's wheel. Many hand-forming ceramists use a clay body that contains an aggregate material that encourages durability and workability at the expense of plasticity.

Most contemporary ceramists purchase prepared clay bodies from a supplier. This easy and reliable way to obtain a clay body is popular because many ceramists find the process of making clay bodies a difficult and dusty enterprise. You may find, however, that purchasing prepared clay bodies requires that you compromise on your requirements. For example, your supplier may not have exactly what you want. Because your supplier cannot keep a great number of clay body types on hand, you should decide what your needs are and grade them according to their importance. Then you can make an informed choice among the clay bodies the supplier carries or you can decide to keep searching for an appropriate clay body.

CHOOSING A CLAY BODY THAT IS RIGHT FOR YOUR WORK

Keep the following characteristics in mind when you choose your clay bodies:

> **firing temperature**
> **workability**
> **durability**
> **color**
> **shrinkage rate**
> **warp resistance**
> **moisture absorption**

First you must decide what *your* needs are: what firing temperature you want to use, what color you want in the clay body, what working qualities you need, and whether clay body absorption is a significant factor in your work.

For most ceramists the most important characteristic is firing temperature. Do you need the durability of the high fire, the reliability and economy of the mid-fire, or the color response of the low fire? Next in importance is clay body color. Do you want the brilliance of a white body or the richness of a darker, warmer color? The working qualities of the clay body must be compatible with the way you work. Do you want to work with curved volumes? If so, you will need a clay body that is plastic and bends readily. If you work with angular forms made from straight-sided slabs, you will not need a plastic clay body. If your clay body is very plastic, you may have to put up with a high shrinkage rate. Clay bodies that have a lower plasticity will shrink less.

Warp resistance is important to some ceramists. If you work with straight-sided pieces, warping will be obvious and you will want to avoid it; if you work with curved surfaces, warping will be less obvious and probably less important to you. Clay body texture varies a great deal. Some clay bodies are rough and coarse; others are smooth and fine textured. If you make large, monumental pieces, you should probably choose a coarse clay body. If you make small pieces and delicate forms, a fine textured clay body is the most appropriate. If you make utilitarian pieces, absorption will be an important characteristic. A highly absorptive clay body will diminish the durability and usefulness of the piece. Choose a clay body that has a low absorption at your chosen firing temperature. If your work is purely decorative, absorption may be of little or no importance.

Many ceramists want a clay body that is especially formulated for their needs. You can have your supplier mix your own recipes or you can do it yourself. I have included a group of recipes for specialized clay bodies for each firing temperature (see the recipe section on page 23). If you want to have your supplier mix one of these recipes, you may do so without worrying about copyright infringement.

Your supplier may mix your clay bodies in de-airing mixing machinery. This kind of clay does not need to be wedged. The de-airing process is as effective as wedging because it eliminates air bubbles and thoroughly mixes the materials in the clay body. De-aired clay bodies often have a smooth buttery texture and can be highly workable.

Always test a new clay body as soon as possible. Even the best suppliers will sometimes produce a bad batch of clay. Make testing a regular part of your work rhythm and you will avoid many problems.

ASSESSING A NEW CLAY BODY

The following procedures for assessing a new clay body are informal and take little time. Although they are quick and somewhat subjective, they will tell you a good deal about the new body clay. They will help you check for workability, body color, and resistance to cracking, warping, shrinkage, and absorption.

Assessing workability: Create a small piece using the same techniques you use in your normal work. Observe the body's bendability and working character.

Assessing warping and cracking: Create a form that you use in your normal work and dry the piece in your normal manner. Examine the piece for warping and cracking.

Assessing body color: Fire a test piece and examine the results.

Assessing shrinkage:

1. Make a test tile 13 centimeters long.
2. Draw a 10-centimeter line along its surface.
3. Dry the tile.
4. Fire the tile and measure the length of the line. Use the difference between the length of the unfired line and the fired line to compute shrinkage. For example, if the 10-centimeter line is now 8.5 centimeters, the difference, 1.5 centimeters, gives you a shrinkage rate of 15 percent.

Assessing warping:

1. Make a test tile 13 centimeters long.
2. Dry the tile.
3. Place the tile in the kiln and support each end with pieces of broken kiln shelf, leaving an unsupported span 10 centimeters long.
4. Fire the tile and examine it. If it has sagged a great deal, then the clay is likely to warp excessively.

Assessing absorption:

1. Using a fired test tile, place a few drops of a nonoily staining substance on the tile. Fountain pen ink is useful for this task.
2. Wait an hour for the substance to dry.
3. Wash off the substance.
4. If the surface of the clay body is stained, then the body is absorbent. The darker the stain, the greater the absorbency.

MODIFYING THE CLAY BODY

ADDITIONS TO THE CLAY BODY FOR WORKABILITY AND DURABILITY

Adding material that will modify the character of the clay body may have a strong and positive effect on the quality of your work. These additions make the clay either more robust and less rubbery (aggregates) or stickier and more bendable (colloids); either or both may be added. They will help the clay body withstand the rigors of the building and firing processes. The body becomes more workable before firing and more durable after firing.

You can add these materials to the clay body during the wedging process or during the mixing process. Some clay body suppliers will add special materials to the mix and will charge little for doing so.

Aggregates

Aggregates are coarse particles or thread-like fibers. The particle size of aggregates is much larger than the particle size of the clay and nonclay materials that make up most of the clay body. Therefore, their presence introduces a valuable characteristic—particle-size variation. This characteristic lessens the "rubbery" feel that marks clay bodies whose particles are all of a similar size. Aggregates allow the hand-builder to work with the clay with much greater freedom than would be possible otherwise.

Some aggregates burn out during the firing and some do not. The materials that burn out during the firing leave a network of cavities that can enrich the surface of the piece, lighten it, and make it less brittle. These materials include sawdust, coffee grounds, and chopped nylon. I have found chopped nylon (nylon filaments cut into short lengths) to be especially useful. Chopped nylon seems to "knit" the unfired clay together, making it strong, and helps it to resist warping and cracking.

I also enjoy working with Perlite. Perlite does not burn out; instead, it shrinks radically during firing. Perlite is made from mica particles that have been "popped" so that they take on a greatly expanded form. They return to their original size during the firing and leave only a tiny bit of mica. Perlite-loaded clay bodies are light and their surfaces are marked by the cavities left when the mica shrinks back to its original size.

The other type of aggregate is nonburning, which means it does not shrink or burn out during the firing. Since these aggregates do not shrink, they have the valuable property of controlling shrinkage. Additions of up to 10 percent are common; if a clay body contains 10 percent of a nonburning aggregate, the body shrinkage is reduced by 10 percent. This makes a significant impact on the way the piece looks after firing.

The most commonly used nonburning aggregate is made from fired clay. It is called *grog* in the United States and Canada and *chamotte* in England and Europe. It comes in various grain sizes from very fine to quite coarse. All sizes are useful and reliable additions to the clay body; the choice between one or another is dictated by personal needs.

Another type of nonburning aggregate is sand. Common sand contains significant impurities and, unfortunately, these will often cause bloating during the fire. White sand or silica sand is free of impurities and thus is much more reliable.

Colloids

Colloids are the direct opposites of aggregates in that their particle size is extremely tiny. Like aggregates, they encourage particle-size variation and enhance workability.

Also, they are "sticky," ensuring good joins between clay elements during the building process. Colloids therefore are especially useful as additions to clay bodies that are low in clay or contain only coarse clays. While these characteristics are valuable for all kinds of hand building, they are especially useful when added to coarse-particled, low-shrinkage sculpture bodies. The best-known colloidal material is bentonite, a very fine-particled clay. Bentonite is usually added as a dry powder to a clay body during the dry mixing process. A two percent addition of bentonite in most clay bodies will significantly enhance plasticity. Up to six percent may be required for very low clay bodies and porcelains.

SPECIAL CLAY BODIES DESIGNED FOR LARGE-SCALE WORK

Large-scale pieces are more prone to problems than small-scale work. The ceramist must choose work methods and materials carefully when working with large pieces. The ceramist who wishes to work on a large scale will usually use hand-forming methods, which lend themselves far more readily to the particular demands of large work than do wheel or cast forming.

Since ceramists will encounter cracking and warping often in large-scale work, clay bodies must be chosen carefully to avoid these problems. Ceramists have developed a whole class of clay bodies useful for large-scale hand-formed work. Generally these recipes contain coarsely ground, large-particle clays. Clays of this sort resist warping and excessive shrinkage. Aggregates (coarse particles) are often added to the body as well, for they too will effectively control shrinkage and warping. The clay content of these bodies ranges from 80 percent to 100 percent. These are excellent recipes and help keep the inevitable problems involved in making large-scale work to a minimum.

Theoretically, it should also be possible to control cracking and warping by limiting the amount of clay in the body recipe. Such bodies would contain 15 percent to 25 percent clay (much lower than the 80–100 percent clay content of normal sculpture bodies). To some extent, this compromises workability. However, the addition of colloids can compensate for the body's lack of plasticity. With careful building methods, clay bodies of this sort can be useful to ceramists who work on large-scale pieces.

PREPARING CLAY BODIES FOR HAND BUILDING

Most clay mixing processes result in a clay body that is not quite ready to use for creating forms. Clay straight from the mixer will usually be inconsistent and may contain air bubbles. To complete the mixing process, the clay must be wedged and cut. Wedging is the process of pushing a lump of clay back into itself. Cutting is the process of slicing the clay to break up lumps and improve its consistency. In the wedging and cutting process, the ceramist improves the workability of the clay body and prepares it for the rigors of the forming process. Doing this ensures that the clay is uniform in consistency and free from air bubbles. If a hand-builder avoids wedging, the attendant problems will not be so immediately apparent as they would be to the ceramist who works on the wheel. This is because air bubbles are not so obvious during the hand-forming process as they are during the throwing process. Air bubbles disrupt the throwing process and spoil the form. Hand-builders, on the other hand, may not notice anything wrong: before firing, the only sign that the clay has not been wedged and cut may be a small bubble on the surface of the piece. Air bubbles, however, will cause bloating and blistering during the firing and may ruin an otherwise excellent piece.

WEDGING

To carry out the wedging process you will need clay, a low table, and a large plaster block or a wareboard.

I will discuss two methods of wedging clay: *dog's-head wedging* and *spiral wedging.*

The first of these methods, dog's-head wedging, is easy to learn, but it works well only on small lumps of clay. It takes its unusual name from the characteristic look of the wedged lump of clay, which closely resembles a dog's head.

The second method, spiral wedging, works best with large lumps of clay. We call it spiral wedging because the wedged section moves in a spiral fashion from one section of the lump to the next. Spiral wedging takes some practice and is not as easy to learn as the dog's-head method. Most ceramists learn the dog's-head wedging method first and progress to spiral wedging.

Dog's-Head Wedging: Wedging a Small Lump of Clay (two thousand grams or less)
1. Take a lump of clay the size of a grapefruit from its container.
2. Form the shapeless lump of clay into a spheroid.
3. Grasp the spheroid in both hands.
4. Simultaneously press inward and downward. Literally push the clay into itself.
5. Turn the clay in your hands so that the narrowest point of the lump rests on the table.
6. Again press the clay into itself.
7. Repeat the process at least forty times.

At first the process will be halting and irregular, but after a short time you should develop a steady rhythm.

Spiral Wedging: Wedging a Large Lump of Clay
1. Take a lump of clay the size of a grapefruit, or larger, from its container.
2. Form the clay into a spheroid.
3. Grasp the spheroid toward its bottom with your hands offset.
4. Press hard with your right hand and not so hard with your left hand. A small section at the bottom of the lump will be compressed.
5. Continue the process.
6. As you continue, the lump turns. In time you will wedge every part of the lump.
7. Repeat the process at least forty times.

This process is more awkward and harder to learn than dog's-head wedging. At first the process will seem unnatural and will be halting and irregular, but after a time you should develop a steady rhythm.

CUTTING

When combined with wedging, cutting enables you to homogenize the clay lump and eliminate its inconsistencies. To cut the lump of clay, slice it randomly and reassemble it. When you combine cutting with wedging, large inconsistent masses in the clay will be broken down and the clay will then be easier to wedge. This process takes only a few minutes to learn.

Using a Cutting Wire

1. Take a lump of clay from its container.
2. Slice the clay into thin sections.
3. Combine the slices in a random order.
4. Wedge the clay.
5. Repeat the process two or three times.

CHAPTER THREE

BASICS OF THE FORMING PROCESS

FORMS APPROPRIATE FOR HAND BUILDING

Most of the ceramic forms we use today originated early in the history of the craft and far predate the invention of slip-cast techniques and also the invention of the potter's wheel. Few forms, therefore, are inappropriate for the hand-forming ceramist. In hand forming, however, the ceramist's intent is not to imitate the look of thrown or mold-formed pieces; such imitations always look awkward and unnatural. I am especially struck with the special identity of hand-formed work when I deal with the question of symmetry. Hand-formed work is usually asymmetric in character. Even spherical coil-formed pieces have subtle asymmetries. Thus it is important to understand that these asymmetries enrich the form. The successful hand builder will accept the asymmetric nature of hand forming and make the most of it.

ENCOURAGING STRUCTURAL INTEGRITY

Just as the ceramist may make the mistake of designing hand-formed pieces without keeping the character of the process in mind, so too the ceramist must be wary of creating pieces that ignore the nature of clay. Compact forms made in clay are

Bad   Good   Good

Fig. 3-1. Casserole designs.

strong and durable, while overextended, unsupported forms are weak. Weak, unsupported, and overextended forms cannot stand the rigors of the drying and the firing processes. In Figures 3-1–3-4 I show examples of these problems and discuss ways of dealing with them.

Figure 3-1 shows a group of casserole designs. The first is an example of a design that will not work in clay because the top is too wide and flat. In this case the clay will crack. In the next two examples I have domed the lid. These two designs will work because dome-shaped clay elements are strong.

Figure 3-2 shows a group of footed-jar designs. The first design will not work because the clay feet are elongated and unsupported. In the second design I retain the long feet, but now they are less meager. In the third design I have kept the feet narrow, but now, because they are shorter, will support the weight of the pot.

In Figure 3-3, a group of platter designs, the first design will not work because the foot is too small to support the width of the platter. The platter will warp and crack as a result. In the second design, the foot is wide and substantial and will support the platter well. In the third design, I replaced the foot with three feet. This design recalls the lightness and airiness of the first, but the placement of the three feet gives the platter form effective support.

Figure 3-4 illustrates sketches for a sculptural piece. In the first piece, the extended element at the top is elongated and unsupported. The form is exciting, but it is unlikely that it will survive the fire. The top piece will warp and crack. In the second design, I reposition, support, curve, and shorten the top element. Curved elements are more structurally sound and stronger than straight ones. In the third sketch, the top element is curved and supported at both ends. Although the top element in this design *still* may crack, it is far less likely to do so than the same element in the first sketch.

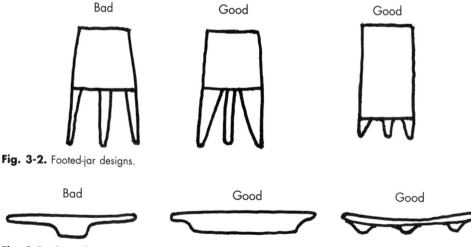

Bad   Good   Good

Fig. 3-2. Footed-jar designs.

Bad   Good   Good

Fig. 3-3. Platter designs.

Fig. 3-4. Sketches for a sculptural piece.

MAKING PRELIMINARY DRAWINGS AND MODELS

The hand builder often finds it useful to plan the piece before building it. This may be done by making preliminary drawings or creating small models (maquettes). Both procedures are useful, but they are at their best when combined. Start with a series of drawings. Then move on to a group of maquettes to see how the character of the piece will evolve into its three-dimensional form.

Using preliminary drawings is especially important if the piece will take a long time to complete. The drawings may help you anticipate problems before they oc-

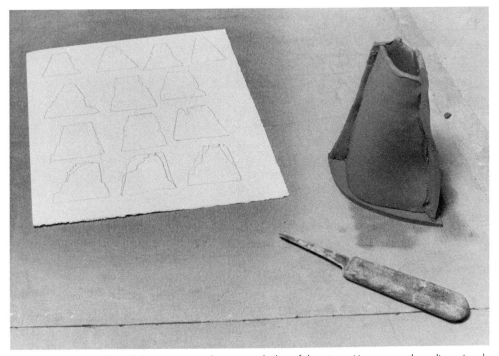

Fig. 3-5. A group of small drawings provides a partial idea of the piece. However, a three-dimensional model is needed to really understand what the piece will look like. Furthermore, the model helps to anticipate some of the problems encountered when creating the full-size piece. Photo by T. C. Eckersley.

cur. For example, to create a complex segmented wall piece composed of many slabs, the following strategy might be useful:

1. Make a group of small drawings of the proposed piece.
2. Choose the basic form and make more drawings to focus on the details.
3. Now make a small model of the piece; take special care with the details of forming.
4. If you encounter problems, try to work them out with the help of more drawings and models. Otherwise, begin work on the piece.

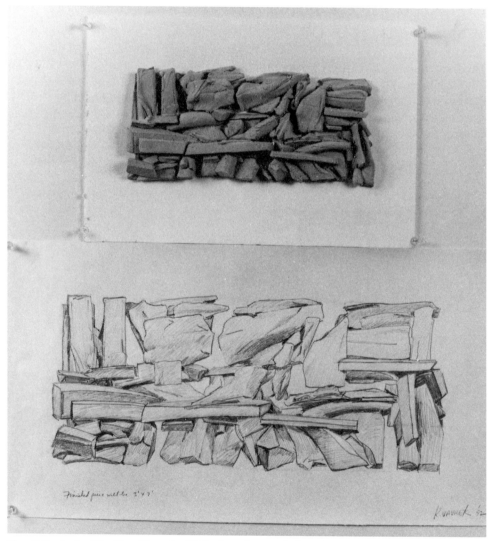

Fig. 3-6. *As in Life*, Ken Vavrek, USA, drawing and clay sketch. Vavrek works with high relief to create his pieces. Using a maquette gives him a better idea than a drawing does of the space and volume of the final piece. It also allows him to make changes more easily than he could on the piece in its final state (see Fig. 4-53). Photo by the artist.

CONTROLLING MOISTURE CONTENT DURING THE HAND-FORMING PROCESS

Keeping track of the moisture content of the piece is important during the hand-forming process. You must control the amount of moisture in the clay to ensure a consistent moisture content.

Many hand-formed pieces do not make it through the building process because they have an inconsistent moisture content. If one part of the piece is dry while another is wet, the pieces will probably crack and come apart. When you are not working on the piece, wrap it in plastic bags or plastic sheeting. The plastic will keep the piece from drying and will ensure a consistent moisture content throughout all of its segments. A great deal of moisture can escape from the piece, especially if the piece is resting on an absorbent work board. Therefore, do not forget to cover the underside of the piece. Do not, however, leave the piece tightly sealed for long periods (longer than a week); moisture may gather in the lower parts of the structure and damage it.

During the building process the entire piece or parts of it can dry out too much. You may need to moisten all or part of the piece. To moisten sections of the piece, spray with a plant atomizer. The clay will more readily accept a watery mist than a stream of water. Repeat the process if necessary. To moisten the whole piece, spray the piece and then spray the inner surface of a plastic bag. Place the piece in the moistened bag; the piece will slowly absorb the moisture from the surface of the bag.

At times during the building process, you will need to allow the piece to become more firm. You must encourage a slow, carefully controlled rate of drying. You can accomplish this in many different ways. Leave the piece uncovered for a few hours or create small openings in the plastic covering, or cover the piece with cloth rather than plastic.

If the piece is compact and will not dry unevenly, uncovering the piece can be effective. Be sure to examine the piece periodically to ensure that it *is* drying evenly but that it is not becoming *too* dry.

Leaving openings in the plastic covering can be quite effective, especially for a slow overnight drying.

A cloth covering allows slow and even drying without the buildup of moisture. I encase the piece completely in multiple layers of cloth to ensure a slow but steady evaporation process. This method is also effective for a slow overnight drying.

WALL THICKNESS

We rarely think much about wall thickness, but it strongly influences the physical and aesthetic character of the piece. The walls of most ceramic pieces vary in thickness from an eighth of an inch to half an inch. You may want to consider using walls thicker than this—walls an inch or even an inch and a half thick. The choices you make here are important. You must make these choices based on the size of the piece, the way in which you build it, how you will use it, and the clay body you use to make it.

Most ceramists consider an eighth of an inch a thin wall for small and moderately-sized pieces (up to half a yard tall). A quarter of an inch is a moderate thickness and half an inch or more is considered thick. Larger pieces require thicker walls.

Thin walls are appropriate for many types of utilitarian pieces because these pieces will be handled frequently in the course of use. Utilitarian pieces must be light and invite handling, especially those intended for serving food, such as dinner plates, pitchers, bowls, and cups. The creators of traditional food-serving shapes understood the necessity for thin walls when they made their shapes. Small-scale, elegant, decorative pieces (in both vessel and sculptural idioms) are also usually thin walled. Nonutilitarian pieces often work best if the walls are made moderately thick. Thick walls are appropriate for sculptural vessels and for sculpture.

Those ceramists who work with thin-walled pieces must use a clay body that is mature and dense when fired. Dense stoneware and porcelain clay bodies are appropriate because they ensure good durability. Ceramists who work with walls with a moderate or thick diameter can use a wider variety of clay bodies, including those that are soft and immature.

The hand-former will find that thin-walled pieces can be difficult to form. They are, however, easy to dry and fire. Fired pieces do not have the durability of thicker-walled pieces, but they are lightweight and easy to handle.

Coil-built pieces can be effective when used with thin-wall strategies. The coil-built pieces from the Pueblo culture of the American Southwest are thin and light, as are the coil-built vessels in the Yang Shao style from neolithic China. In fact these pieces are so light and thin that they are frightening to pick up the first time because they seem so fragile. These pieces take great care during building and finishing.

Thin-walled slab and drape-formed pieces share many of these attributes. They too are more difficult to form and require skill and patience. You must carefully condition the slabs before beginning the building process. Build the piece carefully and make sure that the piece does not dry too quickly. Although these processes are time-consuming, the elegance of the finished work will be amply rewarding.

Pieces of moderate thickness are quite durable both before and after firing. It is easier to work with walls of moderate thickness than with thin walls. Such pieces can be utilitarian or nonutilitarian as long as they will not be handled or cleaned a great deal. However, they are harder to dry and fire than thin-walled pieces.

Thick-walled forms are very durable. Many forms are at their best if the ceramist constructs the piece using thick walls. Contemporary ceramists rarely create pieces whose walls are thicker than one centimeter. I feel, however, that many hand-formed ceramic pieces are *too* thin. There is no need to make pieces thin if they will rarely be handled.

Using thick-walled forming techniques has many advantages. During the building process the ceramist will have few problems with sagging, warping, and cracking. A thick-walled piece will be much more durable than one with a moderate wall thickness.

Thick-walled forming methods are not without their disadvantages, however. They must be dried and fired very carefully. If the walls trap moisture, the piece will crack or explode. If a piece is more than a meter high and its walls are thick, it will be heavy. Tall or large thick-walled pieces are difficult to handle during the building process. After firing they are difficult to transport and may be difficult to place as well.

The coil method lends itself to thick-walled work. Thick coils are easily formed and easy to build. The use of thick coils accelerates the building process. The slab method is also appropriate for thick-walled pieces. Some of the problems associated with slab forming are lessened if you work with thick slabs. Thin slabs cannot always hold their shape, especially if they are moist, but thick-walled slabs hold their shape well. Thick walls aid the building of drape-formed pieces. Use a strong drape form and leave the piece on the form for a little while longer than you would a piece of normal wall thickness.

JOINS

Most hand-forming methods require that you join elements (such as coils or slabs) to create the form. Take great care with these joins. The joins can strengthen the piece or they can open and become subject to stress and cracking.

Work the joins together carefully to ensure a strong piece. First score the joins using a sawtooth tool or a comb with coarse teeth. Then apply slip, water, or vinegar to the scored areas.

Slip is a wet, soupy mix of clay and water. You may also add vinegar to the slip, which creates a sticky mixture that binds the parts together effectively. As it dries, however, slip may leave a slight ridge at the join. Therefore, some ceramists prefer plain water or vinegar to slip. These liquids are not as sticky as slip, and they leave fewer traces of their use. Ceramists who make highly refined pieces often prefer them to slip.

Once you form the joins, work the edges together. Run a stiff brush or an appropriately shaped wooden smoothing tool along the inside of the join to strengthen the bond between the elements. You can also paddle the joins to strengthen them and force the elements together.

CREATING THE JOIN

1. Score the joins with a sawtooth tool.
2. Apply water, vinegar, or slip to the scored area.
3. Force the join together.
4. Paddle the join.
5. Clean the outside of the join with a wooden or metal rib.
6. Finish the inside of the join with a stiff brush or a wooden smoothing tool.

STRENGTHENING JOINS

Reinforcing joins is especially important if the join connects large elements, such as two slabs. The joins are subject to great stress and will otherwise pull apart during the drying or firing process. I reinforce joins in one of two ways: by placing a coil of clay behind the join or by folding or thickening the join.

If I want to strengthen the join by adding a coil of clay, I let the join set for a few hours. I can then force the coil into the join and weld the two elements together. The method is simple and takes only a few minutes if you have good access to the joins.

In the second method of join reinforcement, I squeeze and lengthen the join area, creating vane-like elements along the corners of the piece. This method is easy and quick, but you must use it with care. The joins will be highly visible and can become an intrusive design element instead of a valuable part of the design. When they are done well, however, these joins are visually exciting and strengthen the piece. This method of reinforcement is particularly useful if you do not have good access to the inner surface of the joins.

Using a Clay Coil to Strengthen the Join

1. Score and slip the surfaces you wish to join.
2. Press the two elements together.
3. Smooth the inside of the join with a stiff brush or a wooden tool.
4. Paddle the join.
5. Allow the join to become firm for two or three hours (or let it sit overnight under plastic sheeting).

6. Make a coil from soft clay the length of the join.
7. Force the coil into the join.
8. Smooth the coil with a stiff brush or wooden tool.
9. Smooth the outside of the join.
10. Place the piece under plastic for a day or two.

Lengthening the Join to Create a Strong Bond

1. Score and slip the surfaces you wish to join.
2. Press the two elements together.
3. Pinch the join area to lengthen the join surface. You will create vanes along the length of each join.
4. Smooth these elements with a sponge.
5. Smooth the inside surface of the join with a stiff brush or a wooden smoothing tool.

TEMPLATES

One of the hand-forming ceramist's most important tools is the template. Templates are particularly useful as patterns for cutting clay forms. I keep many templates of different shapes in my studio. I use rectangular, rectangular with rounded corners, oval, and round templates for making plates and bowls. I use round templates for making spheres and templates of various shapes for making segmented wall pieces. I have come to rely on them a great deal because they make forming and cutting more precise.

Templates are especially useful when I want to create pieces of similar size and shape. For example, when combined with drape forming, templates help me make consistent plate and bowl sets. With a template I can cut a series of similar shapes, and with the drape mold I turn the slabs into three-dimensional shapes of the same form.

Although I have used cardboard sheets to make templates, I have come to prefer templates that do not fray when exposed to the moisture of the clay. Therefore, I use the thin metal sheets that are made as plates for the offset printing process (Fig. 3-7). The sheets can be purchased inexpensively from commercial printing shops. They are easy to cut with scissors and are durable and unaffected by the clay's moisture. In Figures 3-8 and 3-9 Anna Calluori Holcombe uses tar paper for her templates. Like metal sheets, tar paper will not fray when exposed to the moist clay.

Cutting and Shaping a Template

1. Choose a form.
2. Draw the outline of the form on the metal sheet.
3. Cut the template from the metal sheet.
4. Smooth the edges of the template with a file or with emery paper.

Using a Template to Cut a Platter Shape

1. Make a clay slab.
2. Place the template on the slab.
3. Rest the needle tool on the edge of the template. Run the needle tool along the template and cut into the clay.
4. Free the platter shape from the template.
5. Trim and clean the platter shape.
6. You are ready to finish the forming process.

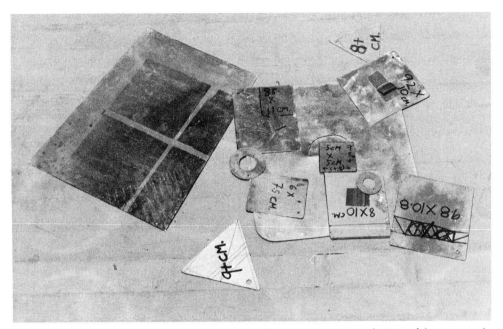

Fig. 3-7. This is a group of templates that I use as guides in creating my work. Most of them are made from thin sheet metal.

Fig. 3-8. Most of Anna Calluori Holcombe's work is in the wall-piece format. She uses templates to develop the forms and tar paper to make the templates. Tar paper has many advantages: it is heavy and durable, water-resistant, and easy to shape. Photo by Jim Dusen.

Using a Template to Cut Tile Shapes

1. Make a large clay slab.
2. Place the template on the slab. Try different placements to see which one is the most efficient.
3. Rest the needle tool on the edge of the template. Run the needle tool along the template and cut into the clay.
4. Repeat the cutting process until you have made the desired number of tiles.
5. Free the tile shapes from the templates.
6. Trim and clean the tile shapes.

DEALING WITH FORMING PROBLEMS

WARPING

One particularly vexing problem for the hand builder is the shrinkage that clay undergoes during the drying process. Most hand-built pieces have points of stress and these points cause some areas to shrink more than others. The uneven shrinkage causes the piece to twist and warp as it dries. Surfaces change shape and take on unexpected curves and swoops. Unfortunately, these changes make the form look awkward and weak. Warping is difficult to eliminate entirely, but there are many ways to minimize it.

- Consider using a clay body especially tailored to the needs of the hand builder. Clay bodies with large amounts of very fine particles (especially ball clays) are likely to warp. Make sure that your clay body contains only a small percentage of ball clay (10 percent or less). Also, make sure that the body contains 60–70 percent stoneware clays. These clays with their high percentage of medium-size particles (and some coarse particles as well) discourage warping. Also make sure that the clay body contains a reasonable proportion (10–20 percent) of very coarse clays (such as fire clays). You may also want to add some aggregates in the form of coarse particles to your clay body. The aggregates will help the clay body resist warping. The most common aggregates are made from fired clay. In North America, aggregates are known as grog, and chamotte in many other places. They are often used in amounts up to 5 to 10 percent. These fired materials do not shrink and therefore enhance warp resistance (see page 23 for material on aggregates).
- During the building process, reinforce the piece at points of stress. This is especially important at the edges and joins of the piece for it is here that warping will be especially noticeable. For directions on reinforcing your pieces, see page 33.
- During the building process and immediately after, it is important to achieve a uniform level of moisture. During the drying process, you will want to achieve a slow and even loss of moisture. See page 37 for complete directions on these procedures.

CRACKING

Do not be surprised if you find a crack in one of your pieces during the building or drying process. Even if you take the greatest care in building and drying, cracks will occur in your ceramic work. Check for cracking frequently during the drying

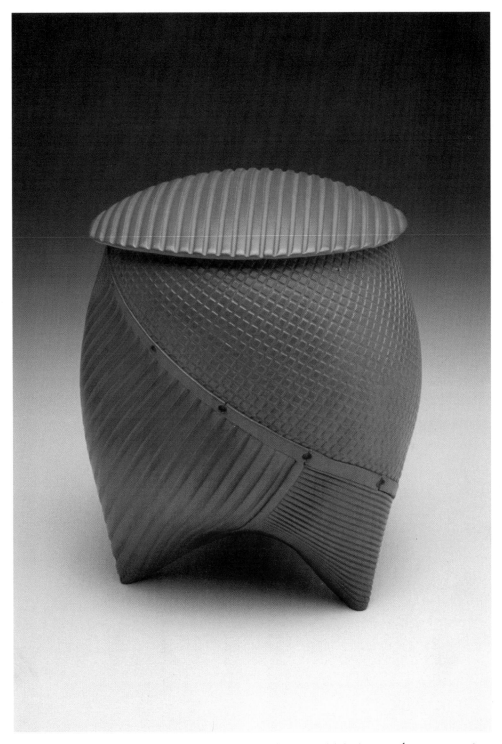

Plate 1. *Red Covered Jar*, **Sandi Pierantozzi, USA, earthenware, slab-built vase, 7½ x 6 x 6 inches.** Pierantozzi has built this piece from a slab into which she pressed a highly textured surface to create the strong relief pattern. She then went on to form the piece with a strong top and foot. *Photo by John Carlano*

Plate 2. **Roy Cartwright, USA, sculptural piece with mosaic surfaces, pinch and coil formed, 32 x 44 x 30 inches.** The mosaic elements create a beautiful surface finish for this form. Cartwright uses the mosaic surface as an alternative to paint as a way of establishing a strong postfired surface. *Photo by Jay Bachemin.*

Plate 3. *Reopening the Window,* Aurore Chabot, USA, sculptural form, earthenware, 20 x 11 x 15½ inches. In this piece Chabot juxtaposes a simple, dark-colored, "outer skin" with a brilliantly colored imagery on the inner surfaces of the piece. The strong textures on these surfaces include clay inlay and calligraphic imagery. *Photo by Chris Arito.*

Plate 4. *Envision,* Elyse Saperstein, USA, earthenware, terra sigillata, 25 x 12 x 8 inches. Saperstein has studied the totemic sculpture of neolithic artists and has fallen under their power. She places one figure on top of the other to create a kind of tower. The figures, mostly of animals, are stiff, schematic, and dramatic in pose. They do not relate to each other; rather, each one is a symbol-laden form unto itself. They are not domesticated but instead are powerful and mysterious symbols.

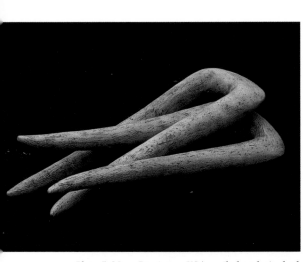

Plate 5. **Mary Barringer, USA, coiled and pinched sculptural form, stoneware, 3 x 6 x 16 inches.** This sculptural piece has a mysterious character. Its form hints at a figure or figures. The natural quality of the modeling is important. The pinched and coiled imagery has much in common with the natural growth processes of forms in nature. *Photo by Wayne Fleming.*

Plate 6. *Passion Fruit*, **Eva Kwong, USA, sculpture, coil built, saltglazed stoneware, 48 x 22 x 15 inches.** Collection Syntex Corp. This is a sculpture with vessel connotations. Its shape is simple and reserved with an elegant curve. The taut contour of this coiled piece is natural to the coil method. *Photo by Kevin Olds.*

Plate 7. **Graham Marks, USA, sculptural piece, coil construction, sandblasted earthenware, 31 x 31 inches (below).** Marks built this piece using coil-forming methods. It is on the border between the vessel and sculpture forms. Its form is simple, compact and strongly volumetric. The sandblasted surface is rich and highly textured, reminiscent of eroded earth. *Photo by Tim Thayer, courtesy of the Perimeter Gallery.*

Plate 8. *Flower Holder*, Deborah Black, Canada, slab-formed vessel, earthenware, slips, glazes, terra sigillata, 15 x 7¼ x 3½ inches. This piece is meant to be used and is at its best when it contains flowers. Black has softened the regularity of the four sided slab form by segmenting the form and giving the contours a pleasing irregularity. The piece has a soft, organic character. *Photo by Ed Gather.*

Plate 9. *Motor and Fires*, Neil Forrest, Canada, panel piece, stoneware and Egyptian paste, 18 x 15 x 4 inches. This tile wall piece by Neil Forrest is unsegmented and freely movable. It hangs on the wall in the same way as a painting, drawing or print hangs on the wall. Forrest has combined stoneware with Egyptian paste in this piece. Thus his work can have the strength of stoneware and the color and surface response of Egyptian Paste. *Photo by the Artist.*

Plate 10. *Forest Shrine: Penumbra*, Angelica Pozo, USA, terra-cotta on wood, 93½ x 68¾ x 13½ inches. In this piece the artist has combined a vessel form with a large tile piece. The whole structure is oriented to the wall and can be considered a wall piece with some sculptural elements. The character of images also varies a great deal, from soft and cloud-like to crisp and angular. Reminiscent of an altarpiece, it has strong ceremonial associations. *Photo by the Artist.*

Plate 11. *Bessie Lived in Cooperville*, Deborah Groover, USA, slab-formed vase. The form of this oval piece is loose and relaxed. Note the softly curved dips and rises at the lip and the simple handling of the foot. The broad expanses of the long walls of this piece are made for imagery. Groover uses an imagery that has the same relaxed attitude as the form. The two go together very well.

Plate 12. *Neostia*, Amara Geffen, USA, sculptural form, earthenware, coil built, 39 x 22 x 18 inches (below). In this piece Geffen places rock-like forms in the depression in the center of the pod like form. Geffen's pieces speak strongly of nature. *Photo by Bill Owen.*

Plate 13. *Water Tower Teapot*, Dan Anderson, USA, sculptural vessel form, slab formed with combed surface, 12 x 6½ x 5 inches. Anderson combs these slab-formed pieces in order to achieve a richly textured surface. *Photo by Joseph Gruber.*

Plate 14. *Round Trip Teapot #29*, Barbara Frey, USA, porcelain, 6½ x 9 x 4½ inches.
The form of this piece is simple and understated. Frey uses it to carry a

complex surface imagery in which she uses a great variety of images. The low-relief pattern on the side of the piece contrasts with the sculptural relief on the lid and the painted imagery on the handle and spout. *Photo by T. C. Eckersley.*

Plate 15. *Spiritstone, Winged Tail*, Ann Roberts, Canada, sculpture, 68.8 x 51.5 x 41.3 centimeters (below). Ann Roberts constructs her large clay sculptures as hollow forms made of coils, strips, or slabs. She used an evocative abstract shape at the top of the piece to suggest a shroud. She has then added painted imagery in the middle of the form to suggest clothing details. She has combined relief and painted imagery to define her imagery.

Plate 16. *Hold*, Virginia Scotchie, USA, 26 x 22 x 19 inches (above right). Virginia Scotchie makes sculptures using geometric forms. She relieves the starkness of the imagery by working with brilliant color and softly textured surfaces. In this piece Scotchie has made a strange, machine-like device of unknown purpose.

Plate 17. *Envelope Vase*, Judith Salomon, USA, 22 x 14 x 9 inches (below). Salomon gently curves her slabs in this four lobed elliptical piece. She created a complex contour at the lip by having each lobe join the next in the middle of the piece. The rounded feet mirror the elliptical shape of the piece. Of particular interest are the forms at the ends of the piece. Salomon has cut them to give them a wave-like contour. She often emphasizes the corners and edges of her forms. *Photo by Nesnadny and Schwartz.*

Plate 18. **Ric Hirsch, USA, coil-formed sculpture.** In this piece Hirsch has placed a strong vessel-like form on top of a monumental base. Then he placed a horizontal, angular element at the top of the vessel form. A good deal of energy here comes from the strong silhouette he has created.

process. Wrap the piece in plastic sheeting to encourage slow, even drying. Carefully remove the wrapping and check the whole piece carefully under good light. Be especially careful in areas where you have joined pieces together. Cracks often occur along a join.

If you do find a crack, deal with it as quickly as possible. Usually you will be able to heal it. The most useful strategy in healing a crack is to apply vinegar to the cracked area. Vinegar will wet the crack more effectively than water and will shrink less upon drying, making recracking less likely. Once you have soaked the cracked area with vinegar, press into the crack with a metal tool, such as a spoon. You will now see a groove where the crack was. Wet the groove with vinegar and smooth out the rough area. Carefully wrap the piece again. After an hour or two, unwrap it and check the worked-over area. The crack may reappear (though it will usually be smaller). If the crack does reappear, repeat the repair process. You may have to repeat the process three or four times before the crack is fully healed.

If you have placed too much stress on the piece during the building process, the crack will keep reappearing. In this case it may be best to destroy the piece and try the form again. Usually, however, you will be able to heal cracks, and since the process is not very demanding, it is always worth trying to save the piece.

THE DRYING PROCESS

The drying process can be quite demanding and complex especially for those pieces that have many joins, which are natural points of stress. At the beginning of the process, keep the piece wet for a few days to ensure a consistent moisture content. Once this is done, let the piece dry. Allow the drying to proceed slowly and evenly. Finally, at the end of the process, you must make sure that the piece is completely dry.

It is very important to maintain a consistent moisture content in all parts of the piece *before* you begin the drying process. If you do not do this, some parts of the piece may dry before others. Inconsistent drying will stress the piece and cause cracking, especially in pieces made in segments and assembled at the end of the process to form a whole. These segments, made at various times and using various building methods, rarely have a uniform moisture content. You can achieve a consistent moisture content by completely encasing the piece in thin plastic sheets. Those parts of the piece that are quite moist will lose some of their moisture to other parts that are drier. This process requires at least two days; for complex, segmented pieces, allow about five days.

At this point you can begin the drying process. You must use a strategy that will allow for a slow and steady rate of drying. Plastic sheeting is not appropriate for this process. If you completely seal the piece under plastic, there will be little moisture loss. This defeats the purpose because you want the piece to dry. Furthermore, because plastic sheeting is impermeable, you cannot leave the piece under it for long periods. Moisture will collect and form puddles on the inner surface of the plastic sheet. Parts of the piece will become wet and these areas will then be prone to softness, cracking, deformation, and the gathering of salts (which will resist the glaze).

On the other hand, you must not let the piece dry rapidly. A piece that dries too quickly will be especially vulnerable to cracking. Drying your work slowly and evenly will lessen the likelihood that sections of the piece will pull apart and crack.

Cloth sheeting allows slow and even drying without the buildup of moisture. Therefore, I switch from plastic to cloth sheeting when the piece is ready for drying. I encase the piece completely in multiple layers of cloth to ensure a slow but steady evaporation process. In this way I avoid moisture concentrations associated with the prolonged use of plastic sheeting and yet can control the rate of drying.

Once the piece feels dry to the touch, I remove it from the cloth sheeting and let it dry in the open air. To make sure that the base dries along with the rest of the piece, I place the piece on a raised drying rack or on layers of newspaper.

To ensure complete drying, wait for a while after the piece seems dry before putting it in the kiln. For most work of normal wall thickness, a few days to a week will be sufficient. You can test the piece by placing it against your cheek. If it feels cool, it is still moist; give it more time to dry.

Complex, thick-walled, and solid forms require extremely careful and thorough drying procedures. For a piece with thick walls, I often wait a month or more before firing. This is especially true of pieces with complex interior bracing, thick-walled forms, and solid forms. Solid pieces thicker than 5 centimeters should be pierced with a metal rod to create outlets for moisture and steam to escape.

You may want to be sure that pieces that are difficult to dry are ready for the firing by using special drying tools. You can place a light bulb inside a hollow piece after its surface has dried to ensure that the interior is also dry. Another effective technique is to use the kiln as a drying tool. If you are using an electric kiln, place the piece in the kiln, set the heat on low, and leave the door ajar. With a fuel-burning kiln, leave the pilot on and the damper open. Leave the piece in the kiln for a while to dry thoroughly. The drying process should last from a few hours to a day or two depending on the wall thickness of the piece.

FINISHING

The finishing part of the hand-building process is extremely important. Finishing takes only a small amount of the time required to make the piece, but it is a most significant part of the process because it ensures that the piece is convincing. This process most clearly separates the adept hand builder from the hand builder whose work is weak. During the finishing process you can clarify edges and define the form so that you can make a strong visual statement. You can also fill in and smooth surface marks that are incidental to the creation of the piece.

Unfortunately, finishing is the part of the hand-building process that is the most easily ignored. Finishing requires that you return to the work one final time right before you begin drying the piece. It takes place at that crucial point when the clay is firm but before it has had a chance to harden and become inflexible. This part of the process is easy to skip. However, even if you spend only a small amount of time in the finishing process, you will vastly improve your work.

When the piece is complete except for the finishing process, do the following:

1. Fill grooves and pits in the surface.
2. Sponge the surface of the piece.
3. Scrape the surface of the piece with a wooden or metal rib (Fig. 3-9).
4. Sponge the surface of the piece again.
5. Sponge and smooth the edges.
6. The finished piece is ready for the drying process.

Fig. 3-9. Finishing the base of a piece. Photo by T.C. Eckersley.

FIRING

Hand-formed work, especially work constructed from separate pieces, is more likely to crack and warp than forms that have been cast or thrown. Always fire hand-formed work slowly to lessen the chances of warping and cracking. Follow the firing chart below to ensure a very slow and careful firing. Especially prolonged are the preheating and soaking cycles.

A SCULPTURE FIRING, CONE 3 (1168° C–2134° F)

1:00 P.M.	Set the kiln on a low setting with the door left ajar.
5:00 P.M.	Close the kiln door and allow the kiln to fire overnight.

Next Day

9:00 A.M.	The interior of the kiln is quite hot (over 580° C, 1070° F). Turn up the temperature setting to medium.
10:00 A.M.	Turn up the temperature setting to medium-high.
12:00 P.M.	Turn up the temperature setting to high.
2:30 P.M.	The color inside the kiln is a light pink-orange as it reaches maturation temperature. Turn back the heat setting to low and begin the soaking period.
6:00 P.M.	Turn off the kiln.

Next Day

1:00 P.M.	Open the kiln door about 3 centimeters.
5:00 P.M.	Open the kiln door completely.
10:00 P.M.	Unload the kiln.

FIRING CHART

A Sculpture Firing, Cone 3 (1168° C–2134° F)

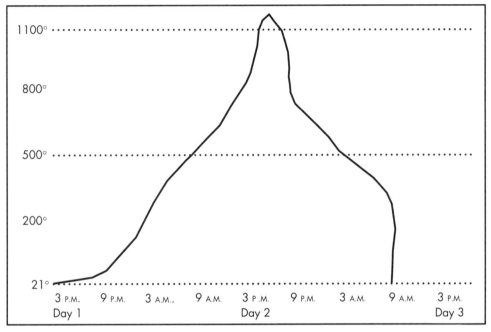

HAND FORMING AND CLAY IMAGERY

Clay can be used effectively to create imaginative imagery on ceramic pieces. You can create clay imagery by cutting, pressing, or carving into the clay or by adding clay elements to the surface of the clay. Using clay imagery, you can create simple textures or complex pictorial images. These techniques are appealing because you make them right before or shortly after you form the piece. There is little or no separation between the forming and the image-creation procedures.

Hand forming lends itself to the creation of rich clay surfaces during the forming and finishing process. As a result, it is far more typical to see clay imagery used with hand-formed pieces than with work formed on the wheel.

METHODS FOR CREATING SURFACE IMAGERY

> stamped imagery
> sprigged imagery
> engraved imagery
> carved (incised and excised) imagery
> cut (reticulated) imagery
> combed imagery

Stamped or pressed imagery (Figs. 3-10 and 3-11): Create this imagery by pressing into the clay surface with a textured material or a stamping tool. You can use any material that is hard enough to leave an impression in the clay. Stamps and textured materials will leave different kinds of impressions. By using the stamp repeatedly, you can ornament large surfaces of the piece. The edges will be hard and the imagery quite crisp. Textured materials encourage a softer imagery and softer edges. My favorite material for stamping tools is a plaster block. When I create imagery using textured materials, I am particularly fond of using crushed foil and suede leather. You can apply the stamped imagery to the slab while it is still on the workboard before you form the piece. Or you can apply the stamped imagery after you have formed the piece. The two strategies create imagery of a different character. The imagery you apply before forming will be precise and controlled. The imagery has little influence upon the shape of the piece. When you apply imagery after forming, you can also change the shape of the piece. The results will be less precise but more expressive.

Sprigged imagery: Press clay elements into the surface of the piece and attach them to the clay surface with slip. You may use elements of widely varying sizes and shapes. Once you have placed the sprigged elements, you can partially or fully blend the edges of the elements into the surface of the piece. As a result, when you use this strategy, you integrate surface and form. Rather than looking applied, the imagery will appear to come from *inside* the clay to erupt on the surface of the piece. You can add sprigged imagery to the slab before forming or you can add it to the piece after you have formed it.

Ann Cummings used sprigged imagery in Figure 3-12 to break the line of the lip and enhance the form. The sprigged forms are angular and go well with the angular geometric designs engraved in the sides and bottoms of the piece. The engraved

Fig. 3-10. *Floral Vessel,* **Kate Inskeep, USA, slab built, porcelain. Glaze surface: soda ash glazes and low-fire commercial glazes. Fired to cone 7–9 in a gas kiln.** Inskeep started this piece as a flat slab. She pressed the slab over a sheet of cardboard with cutout imagery to create a low relief on the surface of the slab. She then formed and finished the piece. Photo by Abbott Photo.

line in the piece has a strongly graphic character. Cummings first fired the piece to bisque. She then daubed a dark glaze over the surface and rubbed it off. The glaze remained in the interstices of the engraved lines.

For an interesting variation on normal sprigged imagery, try placing clay elements such as coils of small slabs on the *inside* face of the slab. Then flip the slab over, place it on the work surface, and press on the surface of the slab. The clay

Fig. 3-11. *Bud Vase,* **Sandi Pierantozzi, USA, slab built, terra-cotta clay body, terra-sigillata surfaces, fired to cone 2, 8¼ × 5 × 3 inches.** Pierantozzi pressed the slab into a highly textured surface to create the strong relief pattern. She then formed and finished the piece. Her forms are quite complex, and she had to be sure that she did not smear or mar the designs during the building process. Photo by John Carlano.

Fig. 3-12. *Miles Apart, Worlds Away,* **Ann Cummings, Canada, earthenware clay body, sprigged and engraved imagery, 3 × 22 × 11½ inches.** Photo by Paul Schwartz.

elements manifest themselves as gently raised areas. The indirect character of this method produces a tautly modeled slab surface.

Engraved imagery: Make engraved imagery by drawing a needle through the surface of the clay. The resulting linear imagery can vary greatly in width and depth and in line and visual character. You apply engraved imagery to the piece after you have formed it and allowed it to become firm.

Carved imagery (Fig. 3-13): Carved imagery is made by carving into the surface of the clay, either by incising or excising. You make incised imagery by cutting *inside* the drawn line; you make excised imagery by carving *outside* the drawn line. The difference between the two seems trivial, but their effects differ a great deal in appearance. In the incising strategy the effect is one of recessed imagery, while in the excising strategy the effect is one of raised imagery. You will find excised imagery especially useful for creating highly spatial bas-relief effects. You can create multiple layers of carved imagery by cutting the clay away in stages. You apply carved imagery to the piece after you have formed it and allowed it to become firm. See Figure 3-14 for an example of carved imagery.

Cut (reticulated) imagery: To make cut imagery, you cut *through* the wall of the piece. These cutout forms are limited in size, shape, and position only by the need to ensure the integrity of the piece during the firing. You apply cut imagery to the piece after you have formed it and it has become fairly firm.

Combed imagery: The simple strategy of combed imagery can produce fine results. Combed imagery takes various forms: it can be a simple overall textured surface or a parallel furrowed pattern. You can apply it to slabs either before or after you construct the piece.

Dan Anderson combs his slab-formed pieces in order to achieve a richly textured surface (Figs. 3-14 and 3-15). Note the way in which this stiff, nonflowing glaze reacts to the combed surface by collecting or flowing away from the grooved areas.

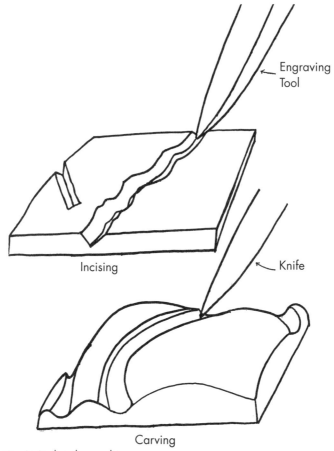

Engraving
Tool

Incising

Knife

Carving

Fig. 3-13. Creating incised and carved imagery.

Complex imagery: You can create complex imagery by lapping one image over the other and by combining image strategies. You can do this using one technique alone or by combining two or more of these techniques. Many variations are possible. By using complex strategies of this sort, you will have a chance to develop a personal and highly individual image signature.

STAMPED IMAGERY

You will need to make some simple tools before you can create stamped imagery. Stamps can be made from any material that is hard enough to leave an impression in the clay. Materials include plaster, fabric, crushed foil, bone, wood, rusted metal, rubber, and cork. I have used all these materials for this purpose.

Plaster stamps are easy to make and use. Carved plaster stamps leave raised and impressed patterns in the clay. To make a plaster stamp, you will need a chunk of hard (cast) plaster of paris, a small saw, a sharp knife, and clay.

1. Saw a small block from a chunk of hard plaster of paris (see pages 94–95 for directions on casting plaster in a plastic container).
2. Carve into the face of the block with a sharp knife.
3. Test the image by pressing the stamp into the clay (discard the clay at the end of the test; the plaster will make it unusable for building work).

4. Continue refining the stamp until you are satisfied with the imagery it produces.

You can also make a stamp from leather mounted on a wooden block. The rough side of a piece of leather is best for stamping because it has a pleasing texture and

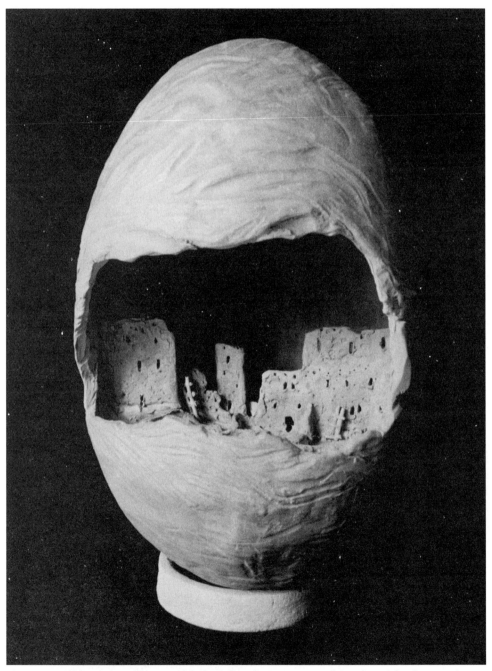

Fig. 3-14. *Zion Canyon Egg*, Cathie Murdaugh, USA, carved jar, burnished terra sigillata with mason stains and cone 06 glazes, 13 × 7 × 7 inches. Murdaugh carved the surface of this piece to create a texture that has strong desert landscape connotations. Photo by Fred McElveen.

Fig. 3-15. *Water Tower Teapot,* **Dan Anderson, USA, sculptural vessel form, slab formed with combed surface, 12 × 6½ × 5.** Photo by Joseph Gruber.

Fig. 3-16. *Water Tower Teapot with Cup,* **Dan Anderson, USA, sculptural vessel form, slab formed with combed surface.** Photo by Joseph Gruber.

will not stick to the clay. You will need a small piece of suede-finished leather, a wooden block, and glue.

1. Cut into the leather to create a design.
2. Press the leather into clay to check the design.
3. Once you are satisfied with the design, glue the leather to the wooden block.
4. The stamp is ready to use.

I especially like to convert everyday objects and found objects into stamps. Their shapes and textures can be complex and appealing.

Sheets of a textured material work well as stamps. It is easy to transfer the textures from the material to the surface of the clay. A particular favorite of mine is a flat sheet of crushed foil. Not only is it highly textured but the textures are natural looking and finely veined.

You will need a sheet of textured material, such as fabric, screening, or foil.

1. Choose a durable and highly textured material.
2. Cut or shape the material.

Bones make interesting stamps. Many types of bones used to make soup have interesting interior sections filled with a network of supporting structures. You will need a clean, cooked bone.

1. Make sure the bone is clean and free of all food particles.
2. Saw the bone to reveal the texture of its interior.

Small wood fragments make excellent stamps. The wood will not stick to the clay.

1. Saw the wooden piece to make the shape you desire.
2. Grind down any sharp edges.
3. Emphasize the wood grain with a wire brush.

Creating Stamped and Pressed Imagery

You can apply stamped imagery to the slab before you begin constructing the piece. After you have formed the slab but before you begin to build the piece, press the stamp into the surface of the slab. Because the slab rests on the workboard, the imagery will be clear and sharp.

You will need a clay slab, a plaster stamp, and a sponge.

1. Stamp the slabs with various stamping tools.
2. Assemble the slabs, being careful not to damage the imagery.
3. Carefully sponge and clean the imagery.
4. Construct the piece.

To press a textured material into the slab, lay the textured material on the surface of the clay. Press it into the clay using your fingers or a roller. You will need a sheet of textured material, such as fabric, screening, or foil.

1. Choose a durable and highly textured material.
2. Cut or shape the material.
3. Lay the material on the slab right after you have formed it.
4. Use a roller to press the material into the slab.
5. Form the slab into a piece.

You can also press imagery into the surface of the piece while you build it. The imagery will not be as sharp and clear as imagery that is pressed into the flat slab before construction, but it may complement the form more effectively. When you press into the wall of the piece during construction, support the wall by placing your hand on the inside of the piece. You will need a stamp and a sponge.

1. Place your hand as a support on the inside wall of the piece.
2. Press the stamp on the surface of the piece.

SPRIGGED IMAGERY

You can apply sprigged imagery before or during the building process and use it alone or in combination with pressed imagery. You will need clay elements (coils and thin slabs) for sprigging, a knife, a needle tool, a sponge, and a paddle.

1. Cut and form the clay sprigging elements.
2. Apply slip to the surface that will contact the form.
3. Press the imagery on the surface of the piece.
4. Lightly paddle the imagery.
5. Carefully sponge and clean the imagery.

To create sprigged and blended imagery, you lay down coils and sheets of clay, then smooth some or all of the edges into the surface of the piece. You will need a knife, a needle tool, a sponge, and a paddle.

1. Cut and form the clay elements you wish to apply to the surface of the piece. Coils are especially useful for this kind of work.
2. Apply slip where needed.
3. Press the sprigging on the surface of the piece.
4. Blend the edges of the sprigging into the surface of the piece.
5. Carefully sponge and clean the imagery.

To create sprigged imagery on the *inside* face of the slab, attach design elements only on one side of the slab. Then press on the other side of the slab to reveal the contours of these elements. The indirect character of this method produces a highly modeled slab surface.

1. Place clay elements such as coils or small slabs on the side of the slab that will be on the inside of the form.
2. Attach these elements with slip.
3. Flip the slab over and place it on the workboard.
4. Press your hand over the surface of the slab. The clay elements will appear as gently raised areas.
5. Use the slab (or slabs) for building a piece.

ENGRAVED IMAGERY

To create engraved imagery, you cut into the clay with a needle. Discarded dental tools can be adapted to make an engraver's needle tool. Use a grinder to reshape the tool. In order to be strong enough, the tool must move from a sharp point to a thick shank.

For engraving, use a clay body that is fine textured and free of grog. You can engrave into leather-hard and dry clay. The clay is soft and accepts the engraving easily. Engraving works best on completed pieces. You will need an engraving tool: a ceramist's needle tool or a dental tool will work well.

1. Draw linear imagery on the surface of the form.
2. When you are satisfied with the drawing, deepen the lines with the engraving tool.

3. Let the piece dry. Then scrape and smooth the engraving using a scraper and a scrubbing tool (a woven plastic scrubbing pad will work well).

CARVED IMAGERY

Carving is an effective way to create imagery on hand-formed pieces. As is the case with engraving, for carving it is best to use a clay body that is fine textured and free of grog. You can carve into leather-hard and dry clay. The clay is soft and accepts the carving easily. Carving is best done on completed pieces in their cheese-hard or leather-hard state.

You will need a knife for carving. Use a scalpel for precision work or a sharp knife if you require a stronger blade. You will also need wooden smoothing tools, a scraper, and sponges for blending and finishing the imagery.

I use scalpels with removable blades for precise carving. Scalpels are extremely sharp and blades are small and slim and thus do not get in the way of carving. Their one fault is that they are likely to break because of their slim profile. Therefore, keep extra blades on hand. Scalpels come in several designs: they may have a stainless-steel handle, a narrow plastic handle, or a wider plastic handle designed to fit the hand. I prefer to use scalpels with metal handles because the handles are almost as thin as the blade and do not get in the way of the carving. I also like scalpels with wide, molded plastic handles designed to fit the hand because they are comfortable to use.

Always smooth the sharp edges of the carved imagery with a simple smoothing tool—a small chisel-shaped tool made from a flat wooden stick or a flat piece of metal. To make a simple wooden smoothing tool:

1. Flatten the end of a small strip of wood (I use sticks from ice cream bars).
2. Sharpen the wood with coarse sandpaper to make a chisel-like form.
3. Use fine sandpaper to smooth the edge.
4. Apply some oil to the smoothing tool and it is ready to use.

The most common form of carved imagery is incised imagery. In this technique the ceramist carves the imagery into the surface of the piece.

1. Create and finish a form.
2. Draw imagery on the surface.
3. Carve *inside* the lines to give the appearance of sunken forms.
4. Use a wooden smoothing tool to blend the marks created during carving.
5. Finish the image with a scraper and a fine sponge.

Excising creates an image that is more complex than incising. In this technique you carve around the imagery so that it appears to be raised. Always use a smoothing tool when creating excised imagery; otherwise the imagery will not be effective.

1. Create and finish a form.
2. Draw imagery on the surface.
3. Carve *around* the lines to give the appearance of raised forms.
4. Use a wooden smoothing tool to blend the marks created during carving.
5. Finish the image with a smoothing tool and a fine sponge.

Highly complex imagery can be created by carving overlapping forms to create the impression of multiple layers. This kind of imagery requires patience and good problem-solving abilities.

1. Create and finish a form.
2. Draw imagery on the surface.

3. Overlap the images so that some appear to be superimposed over other imagery.
4. Carve *around* the lines to give the appearance of raised forms.
5. Carve around some of the images so that they appear to be under the others.
6. Use a wooden smoothing tool to blend the marks created during carving.
7. Finish the image with a smoothing tool and a fine sponge.

You may also wish to combine pressed, sprigged, and engraved imagery. Combining methods is another way to create complex clay ornament on the surface of your pieces.

For sprigging, you will need clay elements (coils and thin slabs), a knife, a needle tool, and a paddle. For stamping, you will need a stamp. For engraving, you will need an engraving tool and a sponge for finishing the piece.

1. Cut and form the sprigging.
2. Apply the slip where necessary.
3. Press the sprigging on the surface of the piece.
4. Lightly paddle the sprigged imagery.
5. Press stamps into the surface of the piece and the sprigged elements.
6. Cover the piece with cloth or with loosely wrapped plastic sheeting and let it become firm.
7. Draw linear imagery on the surface of the piece.
8. When you are satisfied with the drawing, deepen the lines with an engraving tool.
9. Carefully sponge and clean the imagery.
10. Let the piece dry.
11. Redefine the engraved imagery using an engraving tool.

COMBED IMAGERY

Combed surfaces are created by dragging a toothed tool across the surface of the clay. You may apply combed imagery to slabs before creating the piece or to the piece itself after you have completed its construction.

Combs have many sources. Some are ready-made, such as hair combs and toothed trowels. You can make combs from metal, wood, or plastic. Before you comb the surface of the clay, coat it with a slippery solution such as soapy water. The solution will help enhance the crispness of the combed imagery.

To apply combined imagery to a completed form:

1. Coat the area you will be combing with soapy water.
2. Dip the comb into the soapy water.
3. Begin dragging the comb across the surface of the clay.
4. After a minute or two, dip the comb again into the soapy water.
5. Complete the combed pattern.
6. Smooth the combed area lightly with a fine sponge.

CHAPTER FOUR

METHODS OF FORMING AND FINISHING

Hand building is not one method but rather a group of allied methods in which the ceramist shapes or forms plastic (workable) clay without using a potter's wheel. Instead, the ceramist shapes and joins clay elements, such as slabs or coils, to create the piece.

I will discuss the following forming methods:

> **pinch forming**
> **coil forming**
> **slab forming**
> **drape forming**
> **solid forming**

I will also discuss the use of modular imagery and mixed-media techniques in hand-formed ceramics.

Hand-forming methods require preparation and the acquisition of a set of complex skills. At first, hand-forming methods may seem quite simple and easy to learn quickly. However, using these methods to create truly accomplished work requires patience, a willingness to learn, and hard work.

It is easy to develop a rudimentary proficiency with hand-forming methods, but more than likely the beginner will at first create work that is weak and unpersuasive. The beginning ceramist should try to stay unsatisfied with these results; to know that better work can be done and to strive to create work that is strong and represents the true intent of the artist. In this book I would like to help ceramists master the forming skills necessary to produce persuasive hand-formed ceramic pieces of the highest quality.

PINCH FORMING

Ceramists have used pinch-forming methods for millennia. These methods are probably the most instinctive and natural for creating forms. If you observe young children working in clay, you will see that they instinctively create pinch-form pieces.

To begin the pinch-forming process, rest your fingers on the outside of the block of clay. Now thrust your thumbs into the clay and pinch your thumbs and fingers together to create a cavity. This simple action defines the shape in a natural way and with instinctive form. By exploring and experimenting, you will quickly see that you can create a variety of forms by making only subtle differences in hand pressure. Most pinch-formed pieces take the form of cups, bowls, or elongated cup forms.

The depth of a pinch-formed piece usually is that which you can achieve with the unaided hand. However, as you continue with the pinch method, you can make the piece larger and deeper. Extra wads or coils of clay can be added to the top of the piece and pinched to extend its height and modify its shape. You can also employ other forming methods in conjunction with pinch forming; for example, you can use slabs or coils to modify the form and create pieces unmarked by the limitations of the basic pinch-forming technique.

Pinch forming is simple and easy to learn and the results are often pleasing in their consistency and natural character. The tools are simple and the techniques are direct. Your hands and fingers are your primary tools.

We often see pinch forming as limiting the ceramist to a small repertory of forms and to only small objects. In the hands of a practiced ceramist, however, these limitations diminish in importance. I have seen large and complex pinched or pinched and

Fig. 4-1. *Bird Maidens,* **Eric James Mellon, England, pinch-formed figures. The tallest is 7 inches high. Fired in a raku kiln.** For Mellon, the pinch-forming process is liberating, allowing his imagination free play.

coiled pieces and have found them to be highly successful. We derive many of our ideas of the limitations of the method more from preconceived notions than from reality.

EXPERIMENTING WITH PINCH-FORMING TECHNIQUES

To begin to experiment with pinch forming, you will need clay, a paddle, and a fork or other scoring tool. Almost any clay will work with this method.

Building a Small Pinch Form

1. Wedge a lump of clay into a spheroid form.
2. Place your thumbs together on the surface of the spheroid.
3. Press into the spheroid with both thumbs.
4. Turn the sphere in your hands.
5. Again press your thumbs into the spheroid.
6. Continue to press and turn the spheroid until it begins to take on a hollow, bowl-like form.
7. Pinch the clay to raise the form up and out.
8. Continue to create and define the form.
9. Finish the lip with a sponge.
10. You may wish to use a rib and a paddle to define the form as well.
11. Allow the piece to become firm.
12. Create a base by adding a coil of clay to the bottom of the piece.
13. Weld the base into the form.
14. Smooth and finish the form.

Building a Large Pinch Form

Beginning with the basic pinch-forming method, do the following:

1. Add pinched-clay wall segments to the lip of the piece.
2. Weld the elements together using pinch methods.
3. Raise the wall as high as you wish.
4. Smooth and finish the form.

Building a Form by Combining Pinch Forming with Coils

Beginning with the basic pinch-forming method, do the following:

1. Add coils to the lip of the piece.
2. Pinch the coils to weld them to the lip.
3. Continue the coiling process, raising the lip as high as you wish.
4. Smooth and finish the form.

PINCH-FORMED VESSELS

Pinch forming lends itself best to small pieces that are marked with strong visual textures. Although pieces made with this technique are limited in size, their highly worked surfaces can have a strong personal character. Pinch forming lends itself most easily to vases, but you may use it as well for cups, pitchers, and teapots.

Kirk Mangus exploited the pinch method to create a vase in which he combined a strong surface texture and an expressive painting style.

Guest Artist: Kirk Mangus

Kirk Mangus pinches his forms from a single ball of clay. He retains and emphasizes the curves, dips, and raised areas that result from the process. These areas play an important part in defining the character of the piece.

Fig. 4-2. *Demon Vase*, Kirk Mangus, USA, pinch formed, earthenware, 6 × 9 × 5 inches. Using the pinch-forming method, Mangus has crated an energetic surface. The piece looks like the product of a natural phenomenon. Its surface is strongly molded with torn imagery in high relief. While such a surface might not seem promising as a ground for strong painted imagery, Mangus has developed an expressive painterly style of glaze application that works well with the form.

The part that movement and kinetic energy play in ceramics is difficult to describe but is very important. Many aspects of ceramics testify to the energy of the working process. When we see the piece, we see a form that is now solid and frozen. The artist, however, defined its character during the time it was soft and workable, as Mangus has done in this piece. The surface is energetic and restless; it expresses a feeling of movement and impacted energy. In the past many ceramists avoided pinch forming because they felt that the strategy resulted in surfaces that were too unruly and too difficult to control Mangus has instead turned these characteristics to his advantage.

Mangus describes the materials and processes he used to create these pieces:

> I used a red clay body made from 50 percent red clay, 50 percent fireclay, plus 20 percent sand. I use a high bone ash crawling and foaming glaze and then paint the surface with overglaze enamels.

> I wanted to make small, extremely direct pieces to go with this surface and wanted the pieces to look as if they had "just happened." I use pinching to get this effect. The emotion of creating a form in a short period of time by pushing and pinching is very intense. After I make the pieces, I study them for a long time, sometimes for days or even weeks, and keep the ones that still excite me.

> I fire only a few pieces at a time. I once tried to make about a hundred at the same time. After the first firing, however, the thrill was gone. I couldn't paint them or respond to them. I could only see the potential of a few ideas that were underdeveloped; painting them was futile. Now, I fire only six or eight at a time, work on them and study them, and then maybe make some more in a couple of weeks or months. Spontaneity takes a long time.

COIL FORMING

The ceramist makes coil-formed pieces by rolling a lump of clay into long, narrow, serpent-like forms. The ceramist then begins to form the wall of the piece by winding these forms one on top of the other in a spiral or coiling motion. We give the serpent-like forms the name of the process and call them "coils." Even though this term can cause some confusion, ceramists have become used to it and are not willing to change it.

Coil forming is an ancient method: some of the oldest ceramic pieces in our museums were formed in this way. Ceramists continue to employ this method because it produces such fluid surfaces and allows them to make such a wide variety of forms.

FORMING COILS

Most ceramists make coils in the following simple way:

1. Place a small lump of clay on the table.
2. Place your hands next to each other, palms facing down.
3. Roll the lump forward and back in a smooth rocking motion it takes on an extended, serpent-like form.

Small differences in the condition of the clay and the way you use your hands will make a big difference in the character of the coil. The clay should be moist and bendable. Avoid making short, choppy movements when forming the coil. Move your hands back and forth at least 10 inches. Relax your hand muscles. Otherwise the coils may be irregular and poorly made. Irregular coils may break easily or may form a coil within a coil that lacks structural integrity.

You can also make coils vertically without rolling them on a table. Many ceramists who specialize in coil building come to prefer this method. You can quickly form long, well-shaped coils. The ceramist Bruno LaVerdiere explains the process:

1. Take up a lump of clay about the size of an orange.
2. Roll your hands back and forth over the clay.
3. Hold the coil vertically in the plam of the hands, but never let it touch your fingers.
4. Turn the coil slowly and rhythmically, moving your hands like the balance wheel of a clock; never let the coil take more than a quarter of a turn.

BUILDING WITH COILS

Begin the coil piece by starting with a pinch-formed, press-formed, or slab-formed base. This base will serve as a strong, structurally sound foundation for your work. A base made from coils is liable to crack or open and will not be structurally sound.

Allow the base form to become firm. Place a coil on its lip. When the first layer is complete, begin the next layer, working in a spiral motion.

During the coil-building process, it is important to pause and cover the piece in plastic sheeting for a few hours. During this time the drier parts of the piece (at the base) will take on moisture and the wetter parts will become drier and firmer. Allowing the piece to become firm is especially important. If you do not allow the piece to become firm, the wet coils at the top may sag and fall, collapsing part of the wall with them.

Continue the process until the form is complete. To ensure that the coils do not crack or break during the firing, join them with slip (a soupy mixture of clay and water) or vinegar. To impart significantly greater strength, weld the coil layers together using a toothed tool. Do this on the inside or the outside or on both inner and outer surfaces of the piece. The tool scores the surface of the coils and creates a binding surface layer that discourages the coils from cracking apart.

EFFICIENT COILING METHODS

Coiling is often a slow process, though it need not be. Once you become an accomplished coil builder, you will be able to produce pieces fairly quickly. While the process itself can be slow, the most significant inefficiencies in the method derive from the need to stop from time to time to allow the piece you are working on to become firm. Some ceramists try to arrange their work schedules around other tasks and integrate these interruptions into their work methods naturally and easily. Most ceramists do not mind these necessary interruptions, while some find them to be problematical. If you are among those who find these interruptions annoying you can choose between two simple strategies to help you deal with them.

Forced drying: In the past coil builders made use of the powers of the sun and the wind to dry their pieces quickly. The contemporary ceramist, however, has access not only to these natural phenomena but to heat lamps as well. I have watched contemporary coil builders place heat lamps inside their pieces in progress. They build and dry their work simultaneously (and need only to leave an opening wide enough to withdraw the lamp at the end of the process).

Simultaneously forming multiple pieces: In a strategy that takes a natural approach, you can work on more than one piece at a time. Simply stop working on one piece and begin working on another. You can even work on two, three, or four pieces at a time in this way. While jumping from one piece to another at first may seem awkward, you will soon develop an effective working rhythm that you may find very natural. It is an especially useful strategy because the idiosyncrasies of one piece can play off the character of the others.

Coil-Forming Possibilities

Ceramists usually use coil-building methods to create simple symmetrical (or almost symmetrical) forms, such as spheroid vessels. While the coil-building method is effective for creating such forms, you can also use it to create complex, compound forms. Coil building has a great advantage when it is used to build forms. In fact, you can use the method to create forms that you cannot achieve with any other technique. For example, you can begin to make a piece starting from a simple base that branches into a complex structure composed of many small forms. When knit together, these branches in the end will become a single form again. Finally, coiling is useful for creating large forms. Many of the large pieces illustrated in this book were created using the coil-forming process (Figs. 4-3A and 4-3B).

Because ceramists can use coil building to create unique shapes and extremely large pieces, it is a valuable forming method. I find the freedom of the coil-forming process especially exciting. On the other hand, coil building can be slow, but with experience you will gain some speed.

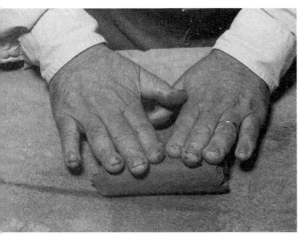

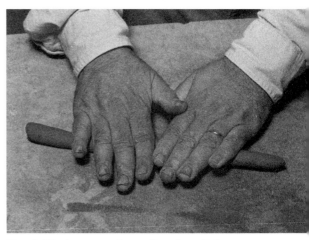

Fig. 4-3A. To make coils on a flat surface, place a small lump of clay on the work table. Place your hands next to each other, palms facing down, and roll the lump forward and backward into a thick cylinder.

Fig. 4-3B. As you continue rolling, the cylinder will take on a serpent-like form.

EXPERIMENTING WITH COIL-FORMING TECHNIQUES

EXAMPLE 1: A COIL-FORMED CYLINDER
1. Form a slab base in the shape of a cylinder.
2. Allow the base to become firm.
3. Score and slip the lip of the base.
4. Place a coil on the lip of the cylinder.
5. Apply slip to the exposed edge of the coil.
6. Continue adding coils to build up the wall of the piece.
7. Pause peridically to allow the wall to become firm and strong.
8. Score the inside or outside (or both) of the cylinder wall to weld the coils together. Paddle the form to refine it and to continue welding the coils.
9. Smooth the surface of the piece with a rubber or metal rib.
10. Strengthen the lip with a thick coil.
11. Smooth and finish the piece.

EXAMPLE 2: A COIL-FORMED SPHERE
1. Create a shallow, pinch-formed bowl to use as the base of the piece.
2. Allow the base to become firm.
3. Score and slip the lip of the base.
4. Place a coil on the top outer edge of the lip.
5. Apply slip to the exposed edge of the coil.
6. Continue the coiling (always at the top, on the outside edge of the lip) and build up the wall of the piece.
7. Pause periodically to allow the wall to become firm and strong.
8. Score the inside or outside (or both) of the wall to weld the coils together. Paddle the form to refine it and to continue welding the coils.

Halfway through the building process, change the direction of the wall. You will now move back toward the center of the piece.

1. Add the coils on the inside rather than the outside edge of the lip, redirecting the wall construction inward.
2. Pause again toward the top of the piece.
3. Complete the form.
4. Comb the surface to weld the coils.
5. Smooth the surface of the piece with a rubber or metal rib.

EXAMPLE 3: A COMPLEX, COMPOUND COIL-FORMED PIECE

1. Create three slab-formed cylindrical bases.
2. Allow the bases to become firm.
3. Score and slip the lips of the bases.
4. Place coils on the top outside edges of the bases.
5. Continue the coiling upward and outward.
6. Pause periodically to allow the walls to become firm and strong.
7. Score the inside or outside surfaces (or both) to weld the coils together.
8. Paddle the forms to refine their contours and further weld the coils.

You are now ready to join the forms.

1. Join together the lips of the cylinders using thick coils. The coils will reinforce the join, which will be subject to a good deal of stress.
2. Continue the coiling process.
3. Fill in the space in the middle that probably will occur between the base forms.
4. At this point, reinforce the edge of the piece.
5. Complete the form.
6. Smooth the surface of the piece with a rubber or metal rib.

EXAMPLE 4: A COIL-FORMED PIECE WITH AN IRREGULAR CONTOUR

1. Create an irregular curved base from slabs.
2. Let the base become firm.
3. Begin placing coils on the base.
4. Using the coils, begin to form areas that billow out and others that move inward. Try to create the feeling of movement.
5. Continue the process until the wall reaches the height you need.
6. Finish the piece.

EXAMPLE 5: CREATING A THIN-WALLED COIL PIECE

1. Form a base.
2. Allow the base to become firm.
3. Roll out a group of coils two millimeters in width.
4. Cover the coils with plastic to ensure that they do not become too dry.
5. Score and slip the lip of the base.
6. Place a coil on the lip of the cylinder.
7. Apply slip to the exposed edge of the coil.
8. Continue adding coils and build up the wall of the piece.
9. Cover the lower portions of the piece to ensure that they do not become too dry.
10. Pause periodically to allow the walls to become firm and strong.
11. Score the inside or outside surfaces (or both) to weld the coils together.
12. Paddle the form to refine it and to continue welding the coils.
13. Smooth the surface of the piece with a rubber or metal rib.

14. Strengthen the lip with a three-millimeter coil.
15. Smooth and finish the piece.

Guest Artist: Sue Abbrescia

Sue Abbrescia makes coil-formed pieces using a complex woven strategy. Notice the care she takes to ensure a smooth, taut contour.

1. Sue Abbrescia creates the base by placing a slab over a drape form (Fig. 4-4A).
2. She rolls her coil in the palm of her hand (Fig. 4-4B).
3. Abbrescia works in front of a mirror in order to monitor her progress. She builds the wall layer by layer (Fig. 4-4C).
4. She covers the vessel with a plastic bag for a few weeks to control moisture (Fig. 4-4D).
5. She cleans the piece and readies it for firing (Fig. 4-4E). See Figure 4-5 and Color Plate 38 for Abbrescia's finished pieces. Photo series by Marshall Noice.

Fig. 4-4A.

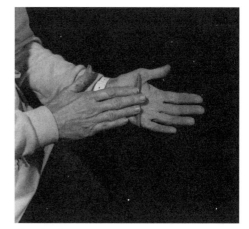

Fig. 4-4B.

Fig. 4-4C.

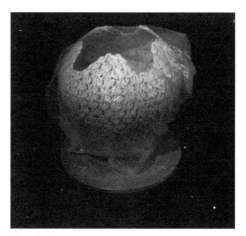

Fig. 4-4D.

Fig. 4-4E.

PORTFOLIO OF COIL-BUILT PIECES

Sue Abbrescia used the coil method to create the complex woven surface seen on Figure 4-5. The repetition of this woven texture over the surface of the piece gives it a natural quality. The feeling is similar to the one we get from looking at an object such as a wasp's nest. The form is simple, subtly asymmetric, and quite strong. The construction of the finished piece is illustrated on page 59.

Fig. 4-5. Sue Abbrescia, USA, coil-formed vase #0442, white earthenware, cone 06, 11 × 10¾ inches. Photo by Marshall Noice.

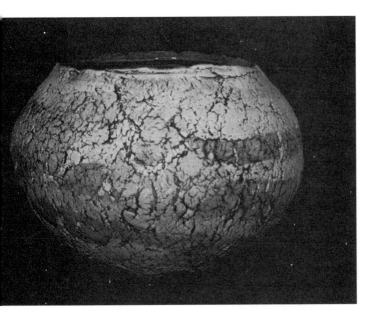

Marc Barr first coiled the piece shown in Figure 4-6, then pushed the surface outward from the inside. The result is a highly textured surface. The form is simple and natural and speaks of the clay. (Photo by the artist.)

Fig. 4-6. Marc Barr, USA, coil-formed vase. Photo by the artist.

Fig. 4-8. Jamie Walker, USA, coil-formed pitcher, 22 × 18 × 9 inches. The artist smoothed the coils in this piece to create a clean surface unmarked by texture. He uses coils not for their surface but for their flexible form-creation options. This piece with its abrupt changes in angle is quite remarkable for its posture. Photo credit by the artist.

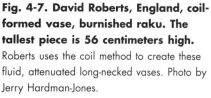

Fig. 4-7. David Roberts, England, coil-formed vase, burnished raku. The tallest piece is 56 centimeters high. Roberts uses the coil method to create these fluid, attenuated long-necked vases. Photo by Jerry Hardman-Jones.

Fig. 4-10. *Ndebele Form #5,* David MacDonald, USA, pit-fired earthenware, coil-formed sculpture with raffia and wood additions. MacDonald enjoys the subtle asymmetries and the full, gourd-like forms he can get from the coil forming. These pieces are strongly influenced by African vessels, both ceramic- and gourd-formed.

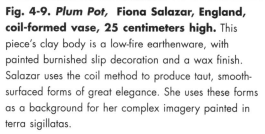

Fig. 4-9. *Plum Pot,* Fiona Salazar, England, coil-formed vase, 25 centimeters high. This piece's clay body is a low-fire earthenware, with painted burnished slip decoration and a wax finish. Salazar uses the coil method to produce taut, smooth-surfaced forms of great elegance. She uses these forms as a background for her complex imagery painted in terra sigillatas.

Fig. 4-11. *Stoneware Floor Bottle,* Nan McKinnell, USA, coil-formed vase, 17 × 20¾ inches. This piece, reminiscent of an insect boll, is full and strong. The lip and neck are particularly strong, as is the foot and the area just above it. This is a large piece with a monumental quality. The surface is simple and works well with the form. Photo by James O. Milmoe.

Fig. 4-12. *Wedge Top Bottle,* Lee Akins, USA, coil built, 19 × 12 inches. This form has a complex silhouette with an especially interesting top area. The double-sprouted form flows naturally from the body of the piece. This kind of visual unity, even in complex forms, is a hallmark of coil-built pieces. The strong texture on the surface of this piece is the result of partially scraping and smoothing the coiled surface. Photo by the artist.

Fig. 4-13. *Gateway,* George Kokis, USA, ceramic sculpture, coil formed with paper/ clay body, 19 × 15 inches. Kokis emphasizes the characteristics of the coil-forming process. Coil lines and soft forms play a significant part in the imagery of this piece. Photo by Tom Kearcher.

In Figure 4-14, we see complex, compound shapes made from coils. Liz Quackenbush scrapes and smoothes her forms to produce a smooth surface, which then serves as the ground for her elaborate painted imagery. She divides the piece into various formal sections. The line between each section is quite strong. During glazing she ornaments each section with a different painted motif. Figure 4-14 is interesting because we see the piece in use as a flower container. Many ceramists feel that only simple pieces should be used to hold flowers. Quackenbush shows us that a complex piece as well can work with flowers.

Fig. 4-14. *Chimney Vase,* **Liz Quackenbush, coil-formed terra-cotta, 14 inches high.**
Photo by John Sheldon.

Fig. 4-15. *Diplorhidsa,* **Amara Geffen, USA, coil-formed sculpture, earthenware clay body, 22 × 21 × 13 inches.** Photo by Bill Owen.

Fig. 4-16. *Arkhaiokurios,* **Amara Geffen, USA, coil-formed sculpture, earthenware, 22 × 17½ × 12 inches.** Photo by Bill Owen.

Amara Geffen's pieces are complex structures composed of full forms joined by tube-shaped forms, reminiscent of pods and insect structures. Coil forming is well suited to the creation of these pieces (Figs. 4-15 and 4-16).

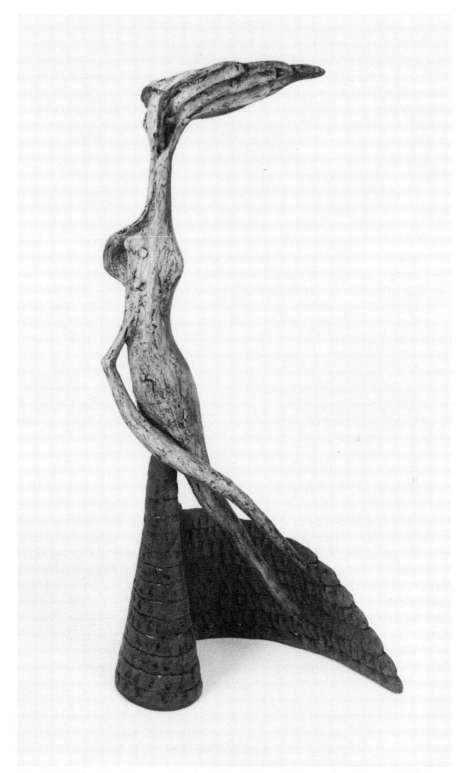

Fig. 4-17. *Shadow Dancer*, Martha Holt, USA, coil-formed sculpture, 41 inches high. The artist used the coil-forming process to create a large piece that is unusually delicate and attenuated. Holt skillfully used different surface textures to create a rich surface. Photo by the artist.

Guest Artist: Eva Kwong

Sometimes it is difficult to define the sources for the character of a ceramic piece. In its form, *Oosphere* (Fig. 4-18) is very simple. The lively surface derives its energy from the small irregularities produced during the coil-building process. These irregularities give the piece a natural energy. The body of the piece is strong and slightly heavy looking. The high domed lid is well proportioned and its curve is strong and surprising. The smooth curve of the lid contrasts well with the slightly heavy base. The lid is set into the base in a way that is quite pleasing. It protects the lid and emphasizes the lip of the base. The soft undulating lip is especially lively and satisfying. A smoother, straighter lip line would not have been as interesting or as successful. Attention to such details can greatly enhance the character of a hand-formed piece.

Eva Kwong says of this piece:

> *Oosphere and most of my other work was made out of a clay body of 50 percent red clay and 50 percent fire clay plus 10–20 percent sand. I use this also when I throw. The body is easy to mix and is inexpensive. I start most of my hand-built work by pounding out a slab with my hands. I pound both sides of the slab. I feel hand pounding makes for a denser slab than one made from a roller.*

> *I then make the base of the piece and add a thick coil (4–6˝) to it. I squeeze the clay between my palms to build, shape, and thin the wall of the piece. I can make the coils stretch in any direction in an organic manner. This method helps me create a taut surface. I feel it is a versatile way of construction. Every time I repeat this procedure, the piece gains 6 to 12 inches in height.*

SLAB FORMING

Clay slabs are simple sheets of clay that for many ceramists serve as the core of the forming strategy. You can use them to create vessels, wall pieces, and sculpture. In themselves they have no particular character or special identity, nor should they have. This lack of character gives them great flexibility because you can use them in many different ways. Their variability makes them hard to define; they can be thin or thick, wide or narrow, large or small. Slabs are a means to an end rather than an end in themselves. Most slabs range in thickness from a quarter of an inch to an inch. Slabs vary greatly in length and width as well, but a typical measurement is 15 by 20 inches.

Slab-formed work has a pieced-together quality. To make the wall of the piece, the ceramist will join together one or more slabs. Later the ceramist makes the lip and foot of the vessel and adds them to the form. Each join leaves its mark. The contour of the vessel breaks or changes direction at the point where one piece joins another. These seams and breaks in the contour easily enable us to distinguish slab-formed vessels. They have their own special character.

When working with slabs, you must be sensitive to the way the clay body handles. Some slabs are flexible, while others are quite stiff, depending on the moisture content and the particle size of the clay body. A low moisture content and coarse particles contribute strength but discourage the formation of curved surfaces. A moist body and fine particles discourage strength but *encourage* the formation of curved surfaces.

Fig. 4-18. *Oosphere,* Eva Kwong, USA, coil-formed vessel, low fire, 40 × 20 × 20 inches. This nonutilitarian covered jar is large and its form is simple. Small irregularities mark the contour. Eva Kwong says of this piece: "I start out with a flat slab for the bottom of the piece. Then I add large coils to build the vessel walls. I use fat coils; while building with them, I thin them out by pinching them as I place them." Photo by Kevin Olds.

The moisture content of a slab strongly influences its working character. Slabs are difficult to make from very wet or very dry clays. You must learn to judge when the slab is ready for forming with each new shape and building strategy. Slabs made from wet clays will waver and collapse during the building process. Slabs with a moderate moisture content will be workable and flexible and therefore easy to work with. They will be particularly useful for creating curved forms. Clay slabs with little moisture (leather hard) will readily lend themselves to the creation of flat-sided forms, but you will not be able to curve them without cracking.

You can enhance the usefulness of clay slabs by allowing them to rest under plastic for a day or two. During this time they will become more plastic and durable. We call this process *seasoning*, in which all clay particles in the body, even the finest particles, are moistened. Seasoning greatly enhances the workability of the clay. The slabs are still bendable, but they are stronger than freshly formed slabs and much easier to work with. You can shape the slabs easily and they will readily retain their shape. They will also be much stronger and less likely to sag or crack. This is a particularly useful strategy if you are creating large pieces.

To season slabs, encase them in thin, flexible, plastic sheets. Plastic sheeting is a good sealant and the sealed-in moisture migrates to all particles in the slab. I pre-

MOISTURE CHART

Clay State	Slab Forming	Piece Forming
Soupy	This is not an appropriate state for forming slabs; you cannot create form.	This is not an appropriate state for forming pieces.
Wet	This is not an appropriate state for forming slabs; the wet clay sticks to both roller and workboard.	This is not an appropriate state for forming pieces; the work collapses.
Moist	This is the most appropriate state for forming slabs. The clay easily forms into slabs.	It is easy to build forms with moist clay though they may be difficult to control in this state.
Cheese hard	This is not an appropriate state for forming slabs; the stiff clay resists forming.	It is difficult to curve cheese-hard slabs because they crack easily. However, it is easy to build with cheese-hard slabs. Form shapes with moist clay, let them harden to the cheese-hard state, and then build with them.
Leather hard	This is not an appropriate state for forming slabs; the stiff clay resists forming.	The leather-hard state is not appropriate for forming. It is, however, the most appropriate state for finishing the piece.

fer to allow a day or two for the seasoning process, but even an overnight seasoning will be useful.

Slab thickness varies depending on several factors. The most significant factor
is the size of the piece. Small pieces (5–10 inches in their largest dimension) should
be an eighth of an inch thick or more. Mid-size pieces (11–22 inches) should be a
quarter of an inch thick or more. Those ceramists who work with large pieces
(23–40 inches) should aim for a wall thickness that is three eighths of an inch or
more. Ceramists creating extremely large pieces will want to use wall thicknesses
of half an inch or more. Another factor that should play a part in your choice of
wall thickness is the intended use of the piece. Vessels that will be picked up during use should be lightweight and have fairly thin walls, while forms that will not
be handled can be (and often should be) heavy and thick-walled.

You can taper the thickness of the slab so that the wall of the piece will be
thicker at its base than at the top. This useful strategy encourages strong, durable,
stable forms that convey a sense of appropriate weight and balance. Also, this strategy allows you to refine the piece in a subtle but persuasive manner. Because it will
add another level of complexity, however, I recommend this strategy especially to
advanced hand formers. (See page 74 for directions on making slabs with tapered
walls.

Forming slabs can be physically demanding because clay is viscous and resists
shaping. Therefore, the shaping process requires strength and persistence. In addition, the process takes some care. The ceramist must ensure that the slab is free
from wrinkles, tears, and weak spots and that it does not vary too much in thickness. Making one slab is not such a daunting task, but making three or four requires
some effort. If you must make twenty or thirty slabs, you may find your strength
and patience severely tested.

I will discuss three of the many ways to create slabs: hand-rolled slabs, thrown
slabs, and slabs made on a slab roller.

USING A ROLLER TO MAKE SLABS

Many ceramists form their slabs by hand, using a rolling pin. We call this process
"rolling out the slab." The method is simple and foolproof, but it can be tedious.
Following are some useful tools for slab rolling.

Wooden Rollers

Rollers are long wooden cylinders made from pine or another soft and absorbent
wood. Roll them along the surface of the clay to flatten and smooth the slab.

Height Guides

Many ceramists use height guides as an aid to the slab-rolling process. These guides
can be made from wooden strips and placed at the edges of the slab. The guides
support the roller and dictate the height of the slabs, ensuring that they are of the
desired thickness. Purchase lath or furring strips of soft pine at a lumber yard and
cut them into strips approximately .3 to .5 centimeters thick.

Slab-Rolling Fabric

To ensure that the thin slab does not tear as you pull it away from the work table,
roll the slab on a piece of fabric. The fabric should be durable enough to withstand
the wear involved in the rolling-out process. It should be stiff enough to resist wrin-
kling; wrinkles will leave crease lines in the slab.

Transfer the slab from one piece of fabric to another. By doing this you can easily turn the slab over to work both of its sides. If you transfer the slab from one piece of fabric to another, you free it from the fabric. This makes the rolling-out process easier and will help you finish more quickly. After positioning the clay lump on the fabric, place the wooden height guides at the edges of the fabric. Roll out the slab as before. Now, however, you can make a slab that has a uniform, controlled thickness.

To roll a slab on fabric, do the following:

1. Wedge the clay.
2. Flatten the lump of clay by dropping it on the table.
3. Place the lump of clay on the piece of fabric.
4. Begin flattening the lump of clay using the wooden roller (Fig. 4-19A).
5. Lay another piece of fabric over the surface of the clay.
6. Flip the fabric and clay over so that the underside of the clay is now on top (Fig. 4-19B).
7. Peel off what is now the top fabric. It will peel off easily and allow for easier rolling to facilitate the flattening process.
8. Continue this process until the slab is uniform and of the desired thickness.
9. Trim the edges of the slab.

"THROWING" A SLAB

While rollers are useful for smoothing slabs and giving them a uniform thickness, they may not be the best tools for creating slabs. Because clay is dense and viscous, a clay lump is difficult to flatten when hand rolling a slab. Therefore, many ceramists use the "throwing" method for forming slabs. In this method the ceramist uses the forces of inertia to reduce the energy required to form a slab. When you throw a lump of clay against a board at the appropriate oblique angle, it will stick to the board for a second; inertia will cause the clay to spread and thin. If you repeat this action several times, you will quickly and easily form a slab. This process requires much less effort than hand rolling. I like to throw slabs onto Homosote boards (a thick cardboard-like material) because their textured surface encourages the thinning process. Furthermore, they are moderately absorbent, which allows the clay to release easily from the board.

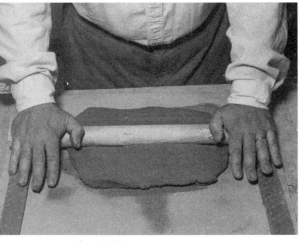

Fig. 4-19A.

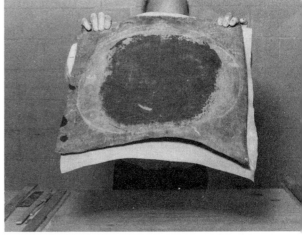

Fig. 4-19B.

1. Form the lump of clay into a fat bun-like shape (Fig. 4-20A).
2. Grasp the clay in both hands with your arms extended in front of you (Fig. 4-20B).
3. In a sharp snap, throw the clay downward and at an angle in the general direction of your body.
4. Repeat the process until the slab attains the thickness you need (Fig. 4-20C).
5. Trim the edges of the slab.

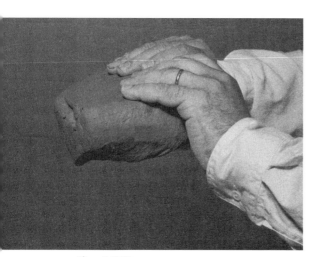

Fig. 4-20A.

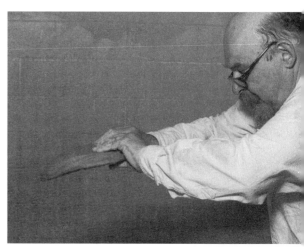

Fig. 4-20B.

Fig. 4-20C.

The process of throwing a slab will feel awkward at first. Most people want to throw the clay straight down upon the board. Instead, throw the slab at an angle so that the clay *skids* against the board. It is this skidding motion that thins and forms the slab. In a short amount of time you should master the process; it will save a good deal of your time and energy. If the resulting slab is not smooth and flat, use a roller to finish it. Because the slab is already of the appropriate thickness, this finishing process will require little mechanical effort.

Mechanical Slab-Rolling Devices

In recent years mechanical slab-rolling devices have become popular because they speed the process of making slabs and save energy. These devices work in a way that is similar to a rolling pin. The main part of the mechanism is a heavy metal roller. The gears or cables that drive the roller give you a mechanical advantage in that they lessen the effort required to move the lump of clay through the machine. Unfortunately, slab-rolling machines are expensive and bulky. While they are useful in the classroom, the rollers will often need repair when they are used by students who are unaware of their limitations. For the studio ceramist who makes six or more large slabs a week, slab rollers are almost a necessity.

Slab-rolling machines make a uniform slab. Some ceramists enjoy using these "perfect" slabs, but others find their mechanical regularity boring and take them off the machine and finish them by hand.

To use a mechanical slab roller, first prepare the clay for the rolling process by wedging it and then flattening it into a thick pancake shape. This will lessen the load on the machine and lengthen its life.

1. Set a piece of fabric on the bed of the slab roller.
2. Place the lump of clay on the fabric.
3. Place another length of fabric over the lump of clay.
4. Make sure that the fabric will not get caught in the mechanism.
5. Begin turning the handle of the slab roller.
6. Finish rolling the slab.

CREATING TAPERED WALLS

When using a roller to create tapered slabs, use height guides of different thicknesses. Place the narrower height guide on one end of the slab and the thicker one at the other end. The narrow side will be used for the top of the piece and the thick side will be used for the bottom.

To create tapered slabs using the slab-throwing method, throw a normal slab and then finish it using a wooden roller and height guides of different thicknesses.

The methods for creating tapered slabs using the slab roller vary depending on the nature of the mechanism. If your slab roller has screw-type adjusters to control slab thickness, adjust the screws so that one is higher than the other. Slabs are more difficult to taper in a slab roller in which shim boards control slab thickness. It is best to remove the slab from the machine. Then taper the slab using hand-rolling procedures and height guides of different thicknesses.

EXAMPLE

Make tapered slabs for a three-sided piece by throwing the slabs and then finishing and tapering them with hand-rolling methods.

1. Throw the clay to create a large slab (see directions on pages 72–4). Keep the slab a bit thicker than the thickness you want to end with.

Fig. 4-21A. This contemporary slab roller has a cable mechanism that pulls the roller over the clay. (Note the heavy roller and the large turning wheel.) Place a piece of fabric on the bed of the machine, so that you can easily remove the completed slab.

Fig. 4-21B. Place a top layer of fabric over the clay to keep the clay from sticking to the roller. When you have finished forming the slab, remove it from the machine and place it on the work table.

2. Place the slab on a stiff fabric.
3. Use a needle tool to cut out the three wall shapes you need for the piece.
4. Release the shapes from the fabric.
5. Place the shapes back on the fabric so that the bases of the wall shapes are at the bottom of the fabric and the tops are at the top.
6. At the top of the fabric, place a 4-millimeter height guide; at the bottom, place a 6-millimeter height guide.
7. Turn the fabric sideways so that you can roll out the slabs easily.
8. Using a wooden roller, roll along the wall shapes, tapering each shape so that the base is thicker than the top.
9. Remove the height guides and place a stiff fabric over the slab.
10. Flip the slab over and remove the top fabric.
11. Again, place the height guides. Be sure to place the higher guide next to the thick side of the wall shapes. Place the shorter height guide next to the thinner side of the wall shapes.
12. Repeat the rolling process.
13. Finish the wall shapes.
14. You are now ready to assemble the three-sided form (see page 80 for directions on making a triangular form).

"SEASONING" THE SLABS

EXAMPLE

To prepare slabs in order to create a three-sided piece (such as the one described above), use the following procedure:

Day 1: From a slab, create the three sides of the piece and a base. Lay the slabs on a sheet of plastic one on top of the other. Place a piece of newspaper between each slab to prevent sticking. Drape the ends of the plastic over the slabs, completely enclosing them.

Day 2: Twenty-four hours later, remove the slabs from their protective covering and place them on a workboard for a few minutes to allow them time to become strong and workable. You can now begin the building process with some assurance of a good result.

PRESHAPING THE SLABS

Often during the building process you will want to manipulate the slab and use it to create a shape. You may want to fill out its shape, giving it a slight curve, or you may want to give the slab a curved form. Do not try to do this when the clay is half dry; do it while the clay is still fairly wet. At this point, however, you cannot build with these forms because they are still too soft. Slab shaping and slab building should be done at two different times. Allow twenty-four hours between the shaping and building procedures to give the slabs a chance to set, which will facilitate the building process. Then you can construct the piece with your shaped forms.

MAKING THREE-DIMENSIONAL PIECES FROM SLABS

Slab forming is one of the most exciting and challenging forming methods in ceramics. The method is flexible and slab pieces can be made in a variety of shapes. These include rounded and angular, hard and soft, regular, and irregular or amorphous. Size varies too: slabs lend themselves to the construction of pieces of varying sizes, from tiny to more than a meter in height.

Fig. 4-22. Peter Beard, England, slab-formed vase, 34 centimeters long. Beard forms the basic shape from slabs and lets it set up. Then he assembles the pieces when the clay is fairly firm. He creates ripples in the slab while the clay is soft and assembles the slabs when they become firm.

You should know how to make the following basic shapes using slabs: cylinders, three-sided pieces, four-sided pieces, and ellipsoids. In the process of making these shapes, you will learn how to create a great variety of forms. If you know how to build these forms, you will have the basic tools needed to master the slab-building process.

Rounded shapes often have an organic, gourd-like quality. To create a rounded form, curve the slab and wrap the edge of one side of the slab to its opposite edge. In this way, you can make forms such as cylinders, ovals, and ellipsoids.

Angular shapes can appear crisp and taut. To make an angular form, join slabs at their corners. This contrast of slab and corner defines the character of angular pieces. The pattern of slab and corner, if well carried out, can serve to strengthen and support the piece. It can also enhance its aesthetic appeal. You can create triangular, rectangular, cube, rhomboid, or many-sided forms in this way. They may be symmetric or asymmetric.

I like to mix rounded and angular forms to create soft curves and angular corners. Their volume, size, and character vary, recalling the variety found in natural forms. In this way an infinite variety of slab-built forms are possible. These complex, compound forms are among the most interesting forms available to the slab builder. The results are always surprising and I never tire of them.

Slab building can require a great deal of planning. You can create a simple form without worrying too much about the shape of the slabs. However, before constructing a more complex form, you need to plan the shape of each slab. While a simple pen-and-ink sketch may sometimes be useful, it is best to make a small model of the piece in clay. Making practice forms can help you anticipate the character of the finished piece.

It is important that you experiment and develop your slab-building skills. Once you attain these skills, you will be able to create pieces that convey a feeling of rightness and assurance.

EXPERIMENTING WITH SLAB-FORMING TECHNIQUES

Building a Cylindrical Slab-Formed Shape

The following procedure will help you make a simple cylinder about 8 centimeters in diameter and 15 centimeters high.

You will need a rectangular clay slab at least 30 × 15 centimeters. See page 31 for appropriate wall thickness. You will also need a piece of stiff fabric, a scoring tool, a needle tool, and a sharp knife.

1. Place a piece of stiff fabric on the work table.
2. Place the slab on the fabric, with the wider dimension of the slab parallel to the table edge facing you.
3. Push down the two edges on the sides of the slab so that they taper and come to a sharp point.
4. Score and slip *one* edge.
5. Flip up the other end of the slab and score and slip the *underside* of the other edge.
6. Pick up the slab, set it on its edge, and curve it until both ends meet, forming a standing cylinder. The first time you do this you may be afraid that the cylinder will collapse, but be assured that this kind of form is quite stable.
7. Carefully press the tapered ends together to create a good join.
8. Make a base. Make it larger than the cylinder to ensure that it will fit well.
9. Score the bottom edge of the cylinder and paint it with slip.
10. Score a ringed area on the base where the base and the cylinder will join and paint it with slip. Place the cylinder on the base.
11. Trim the base so that it is flush with the walls of the cylinder.
12. Paddle the piece to define the form and further secure the joins.
13. Finish the piece.

Building an Asymmetrical Cylindrical Slab-Formed Shape

Start this piece in the same way as the simple cylinder. Take the process further, however, and cut into the cylinder wall. By doing this you can make a form that is asymmetric and spontaneous in character.

You will need a rectangular clay slab at least 30 × 15 centimeters. See page 31 for appropriate wall thickness. You will also need a piece of stiff fabric, a scoring tool, a needle tool, and a sharp knife.

1. Place a piece of stiff fabric on the work table.
2. Place the slab on the fabric, with the wider dimension of the slab parallel to the table edge facing you.
3. Push down the two edges on the sides of the slab so that they taper and come to a sharp point.
4. Score and slip *one* edge.
5. Flip up the other end of the slab and score and slip the *underside* of the other edge.
6. Pick up the slab, set it on its edge, and curve it until both ends meet, forming a standing cylinder.

7. Carefully press the ends together to create a good join.
8. Let the cylinder dry under plastic for a day.
9. Make two or three narrow V-shaped cuts, starting from the top edge of the cylinder.
10. Pinch the edges of the cuts.
11. Score and slip the edges.
12. Push the cut edges together to change the character of the form.
13. Trim and smooth the seams.
14. Place a bottom slab at the base of the form.
15. Trim the base.
16. Finish the piece.

Building a Cylindrical Slab-Formed Shape

1. Cut a large rectangular slab; this will serve as the wall of the piece. Cut a round slab; you will use this for the foot. Taper the edges on the right and left side of the rectangular slab (Fig. 4-23A). Score and slip these tapered edges.
2. Pick the slab up so that it rests on its bottom edge. Curve the slab (Fig. 4-23B).

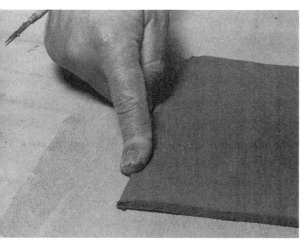

Fig. 4-23A.

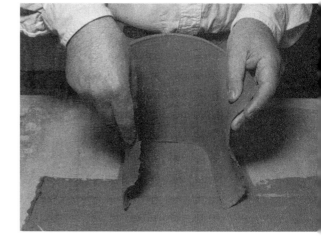

Fig. 4-23B.

Fig. 4-23C.

Fig. 4-23D.

3. Make both ends meet. Carefully press the ends together to create a good join (Fig. 4-23C).
4. Join the cylinder and the bottom slab. Notice that the bottom slab is a little larger than necessary to ensure a good fit (Fig. 4-23D).
5. Trim the edges of the bottom slab. Paddle the piece to define the form and further secure the joins (Fig. 4-23E).
6. Finish the piece.

Making a Four-Sided Slab Piece

You will need five rectangular slabs—four for the sides and one for the base. The sides should be at least 10×18 centimeters; the base should be 12×12 centimeters. (See page 31 for appropriate wall thickness). You will need a piece of stiff fabric, a scoring tool, a needle tool, and a sharp knife.

1. Prepare five slabs—four for the sides of the piece and one for the base. Let the slabs become firm. Score the join corners of two slabs and paint them with slip. Attach the first two pieces, pressing them together firmly to ensure that the join is strong (Fig. 4-24A). Because the slabs are firm, they will stand on their own.
2. Score the area where you will attach the next slab. Add this slab to the piece. Carefully join the slabs together (Fig. 4-24B).
3. Place the last slab and the foot and join them carefully to complete the structure (Fig. 4-24C).
4. Trim and sponge the wall joins (Fig. 4-24D).
5. Clean the lip (Fig. 4-24E).
6. If you wish, carve the lip (Fig. 4-24F).
7. Trim the base so that it is flush with the sides of the piece.
8. Clean the base and prepare it for drying and firing (Fig. 4-24G).
9. The piece is nearly in its finished state and I am about to prepare it for drying and firing (Fig. 4-24H).

Building a Triangular Form from Slabs

The following directions are for a three-sided form. You will need four rectangular slabs—three for the sides and one for the base. You may vary the width of the slabs to create an asymmetrical shape or you may make the base wider than the top for a more graceful shape. The sides should be at least 10×18 centimeters; the base

Fig. 4-23E.

Fig. 4-24A.

Fig. 4-24B.

Fig. 4-24C.

Fig. 4-24D.

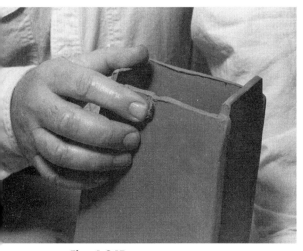

Fig. 4-24E.

Fig. 4-2FD.

Fig. 4-24G.

Fig. 4-24H.

should be $12 \times 12 \times 12$ centimeters. (See page 31 for appropriate wall thickness.) You will need a piece of stiff fabric, a scoring tool, a needle tool, and a sharp knife.

1. Form the slabs. Prepare the three sides and a base.
2. Let the slabs become firm.
3. Begin by joining two walls. Score the area where you will join them and paint them with slip.
4. Join the slabs together, pressing and manipulating them to make sure that the join is strong. If the clay is at the cheese-hard stage of dryness, the piece will stand on its own once you have joined the slabs.
5. Score the places where the joins for the last slab will go.
6. Place the third (and last) slab and join it carefully to complete the structure.
7. If you want to strengthen the joins (optional but useful), do this now.
8. Score and paint the bottom edges of the slabs and the base with slip. (Make the base a little larger than necessary to ensure a good fit.)
9. Add the base and join it securely to the rest of the piece.
10. Trim the base so that it is flush with the sides of the piece.
11. Paddle the piece to define the form and further secure the joins.
12. Finish the piece.

For a variation on this form, use shapes that taper and are wider at the bottom than at the top. The resulting form will be a pyramid shape.

Building a Complex Four-Sided Form from Slabs

In this piece you will combine angular and curved forms. Because you make one wall longer than the others, you must curve it so that it can work with the narrower walls. The resulting form is complex and asymmetric.

You will need five slabs—four for the sides and one for the base. The sides should be at least 10 to 12 centimeters high and should vary in width (make one slab much wider than the other three). Their shape should taper so that they are narrower at the top than at the bottom. The base should be at least 2 centimeters wider than the widest wall slab. (See page 31 for appropriate wall thickness.) You will need a piece of stiff fabric, a scoring tool, a needle tool, and a sharp knife.

1. Form the five slabs—four for the walls and one for the base.
2. Curve and shape the slabs.
3. Let the slabs become firm.
4. Begin by joining two walls. Score the area where you will join them and paint them with slip.
5. Join the slabs together, pressing and manipulating them to make sure the join is strong. If the clay is at the cheese-hard stage of dryness, the piece will stand on its own once you have joined the slabs.
6. Join the rest of the slabs using the same methods.
7. Since one wall is much wider than the others, you must curve it so that it can work with the others.
8. As you join the slabs, the formal structure of the piece will reveal itself.
9. If you want to strengthen the joins (optional but useful), do this now.
10. Score and paint the bottom edges of the slabs and the base with slip. (Make the base a little larger than necessary to ensure a good fit.)
11. Add the base and join it securely to the rest of the piece.
12. Trim the base so that it is flush with the sides of the piece.
13. Paddle the piece to define the form and further secure the joins.
14. Finish the piece.

Creating a Thin-Walled Slab Piece

When creating thin-walled forms, you have to make sure that the walls will not wobble and collapse during the building process. You do this by seasoning the slabs under plastic for twenty-four hours and then letting the clay dry to a cheese-hard state.

You will need slabs three millimeters thick to create the sides and the base of the piece. You will need a piece of stiff fabric, a scoring tool, a needle tool, and a sharp knife.

1. Form slabs three millimeters thick.
2. Prepare the sides and a base.
3. If you wish to shape the slabs, do so now.
4. Place the slabs under plastic for twenty-four hours to become firm.
5. Remove the plastic from the clay and let the clay dry to a cheese-hard state. If the clay is not cheese-hard, the thin slabs will not be strong enough for you to be able to build the form.
6. Score the area where you will join the slabs to form the walls and paint them with slip.
7. Join the slabs together, pressing and manipulating them to make sure the join is strong.
8. Strengthen the joins with a clay coil or by extending the join (see page 34).
9. Score and paint the bottom edges of the slabs and the base with slip. (Make the base a little larger than necessary to ensure a good fit.)
10. Add the base and join it securely to the rest of the piece.
11. Trim the base.
12. Paddle the piece to define the form and further secure the joins.
13. Finish the piece.
14. Keep the piece under plastic for a day or two to ensure an even moisture content before you let it dry.

Creating a Thick-Walled Slab Piece

Thick slabs are easy to build with because they have good strength and rigidity. You should brace the joins carefully to ensure that they can handle the stress created by the thick walls. Also make sure that the piece is thoroughly dry before firing (see page 37).

You will need slabs one and a half to three centimeters thick to create the sides and the base of the piece. You will need a piece of stiff fabric, a scoring tool, a needle tool, and a sharp knife.

1. Form slabs one and a half to three centimeters thick.
2. Prepare the sides and a base.
3. If you want to shape the slabs, do so now.
4. Place the slabs under plastic for twenty-four hours.
5. Remove the plastic from the slabs and let them become firm.
6. Join the slabs together, pressing and manipulating them to make sure the join is strong. These thick slabs are very strong; the piece will stand on its own once you have joined them.
7. Strengthen the joins with a clay coil (see page 34).
8. Score and paint the bottom edges of the slabs and the base with slip. (Make the base a little larger than necessary to ensure a good fit.)
9. Add the base and join it securely to the rest of the piece.
10. Trim the base.
11. Paddle the piece to define the form and further secure the joins.
12. Finish the piece.
13. Keep the piece under plastic for a day or two to ensure an even moisture content.
14. Dry the pieces carefully and thoroughly.

Plate 19. *Double Spout Bottle*, **Lee Akins, USA, coil built, 18 x 13 x 11 inches.** This coil-built form has a complex silhouette. The top area is especially interesting. This double spouted form flows naturally from the body of the piece. This kind of visual unity, even in complex forms, is a hallmark of coil-built pieces. The strong texture on the surface of the piece is the result of partially scraping and smoothing the coiled surface. *Photo by the Artist.*

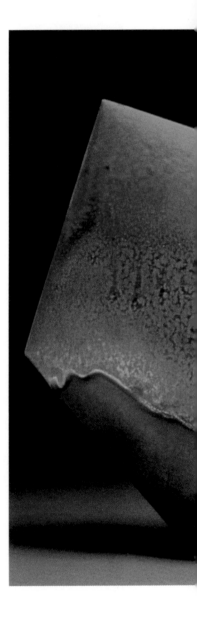

Plate 20. *Vessel XVII*, **Donna Nicholas, USA, cylindrical slab-formed vase, 26 x 7 x 7 inches.** This form is simple and austere. Its sides taper softly and its curves are subtle and highly controlled. Note the slight bulge in the contour of the sides. Note also the parallel, diagonal ridges, which give the form strength and break the line in an interesting way. These careful touches are very telling in this piece. *Photo by the Artist.*

Plate 21. *Dog Cup*, **Kirk Mangus, USA, pinch formed, 2 x 2 x 5 inches.** The surface of this piece is marked with strong textures. While such a surface might not seem promising as a ground for a strong painted imagery, Mangus has developed an expressive painterly style of glaze application that works well with the form.

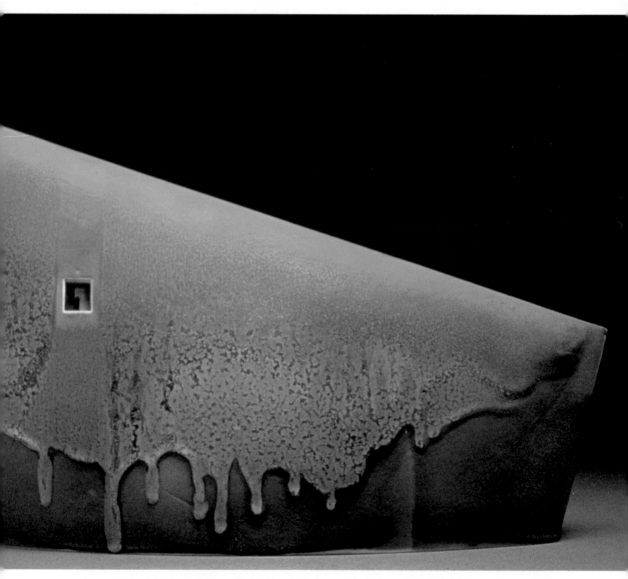

Plate 22. *Eternal Home*, **Yih-Wen Kuo, USA, drape formed, 14 x 26 x 6 inches.** This piece is a sculpture with many aspects of a vessel. This piece has a carefully judged and emphatic contour. Kuo has varied his sizes and angles; yet all work harmoniously with each other. The three small openings in the form break through the broad expanse of the form and open it up without weakening it either visually or in its structure. *Photo by Barry Stark.*

Plate 23. *Pod #1*, **Sylvia Netzer, USA, sculptural piece, coil formed, stoneware clay underglaze, fired to cone 6, 13 x 16 x 20 inches.** Netzer has created a form that alternately swells and recedes. This kind of form is particularly well suited to coil-building techniques. *Photo by Dorthy Handelman.*

Plate 24. *Metamorphic Spiral II*, **Jacquie Germanow, USA.** In this piece the artist has created an effective layered imagery. *Photo by Walter Chase.*

Plate 25. **Sue Abbrescia, USA, coil vase, 9 x 16 inches.** Abbrescia used the coil method here to create a complex woven surface. The repetition of this open woven texture and its subtle asymmetry give it a natural quality. The taut contour is strong and full. *Photo by Marshall Noice.*

Plate 26. *Pyramid IBM*, **Elizabeth MacDonald, USA, 54 x 42 inches.** The artist uses her rich ceramic color and the segmented format of the tile medium to create a simple but compelling imagery.

Plate 27. *Vase #713*, **Richard Devore, USA, 14¼ x 13 inches.** Devore has created a simple shape that reminds us of forms in nature, such as those growing at the edge of ponds. The lip is especially well thought out. Its curving contour is rich and unpredictable. *Photo by John Buffington and Eve Vanderweit.*

Plate 28. *Frigate*, **Jerry Caplan, USA, terra-cotta, paper clay, 18 x 25 x 9 inches.** Paper clay is a blend of these two media and its visual characteristics are very much a blend of both. The textured surface of this piece is quite appealing. Caplan has left it free of glaze so that we can fully appreciate its character.

Plate 29. **Lana Wilson, USA, slab-formed teapot.** Wilson plays with the teapot form to create a piece with strong ceremonial associations. She has enlarged the spout to the point where it dominates the form. The corded surface creates a unified image. *Photo by Martin Trailer.*

Plate 30. *Rain Forest Mural,* **Amanda Jaffe, USA, ceramic tile, 5½ x 8 feet.** Jaffe made this piece for the Staten Island Zoo. Not surprisingly, it refers to nature. She used the coat of a feline animal as the basis for the stylized and patterned imagery. The border around the piece unifies and dramatizes it.

Plate 31. *Monkey Wrench*, **Mitch Messina, USA, mixed-media sculptural form, 85 x 36 inches.** Note how the artist handles each of the materials in this piece quite differently. The wooden forms are angular and extended. The metal forms are thin, wiry, and extended. The clay is soft, highly textured, and volumetric. *Photo by Walter Colley.*

Plate 32. *Arbor Vitae #8*, **Martha Holt, USA, 59 x 37 x 3 inches, low-fire wall piece.** Martha Holt uses coil forming methods here. The highly stylized form suggests the image of a female figure. The complex surface is coil derived and highly textured. This is a fine example of a large wall piece with high-relief imagery.

Plate 33. *Journal*, **Thomas Seawell, USA, mixed-media sculpture.** Seawell is a printmaker who occasionally creates mixed media pieces. He constructed this piece using a clay structure with non-clay elements attached to it. Seawell plays the transparency of the clear plastic elements against the opacity of the low-fire clay. The subject is an abstracted treatment of the architecture typically found in small towns in America. *Photo by Stan Godwin.*

Plate 34. *Block Vase*, Peter Beard, England, slab formed, stoneware clay body fired to 1280°C. Beard formed a square piece from four similar slabs. The unevenly cut lip is an important feature of this piece. Also important is the raised foot with its curved edge.

PORTFOLIO OF SLAB-FORMED PIECES

Fig. 4-25. Barbara Frey, USA, teapot, 6¾ × 9¾ × 4¼ inches. The basic form of this teapot is simple and direct. Frey uses this simple form as a base for her complex imagery. The imagery is complex in part because Frey uses many strategies to create it. She presses the wavy, horizontal lines into the surface of the piece using a bisque roller. Using a scalpel, she carves into the surface of the domed top. She adds the sprigged rock forms to the surface of the dome. This piece is virtually an encyclopedia of ornament-creation strategies for hand-formed work. Note too that, notwithstanding the great variety of imagery and technique, Frey has imbued the piece with a sense of strong unity. Photo by T. C. Eckersley.

Fig. 4-26. Joe Molinaro, USA, slab-formed, porcelain, cone 10 reduction salt-fired, 14 × 20 × 6 inches. Elliptical forms are well suited to slab-forming strategies because they can be put together easily and naturally. The two sides are tense and taut and their curve is controlled and strong. The edges are sharp and clear. The large surfaces of these forms take the imagery well. Photo by M. S. Rezny.

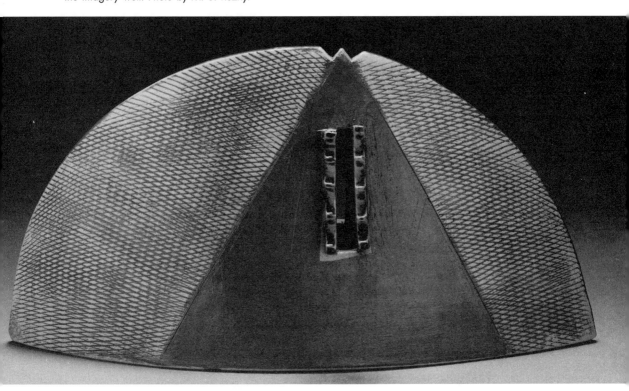

Fig. 4-27. *Triangular Tripod Vessel,* Michael Sheba, Canada, slab-formed with impressed textures, 16½ × 4½ inches. The artist has created a piece in which he repeats the triangular forms. The basic form of the piece is an up-ended triangle. The piece is supported by three triangular feet. The strong lip is triangular in shape. Sheba has taken this angular form and softened it by curving the edges of the triangle. The elongated feet lighten the form. Photo by Dale Roddick.

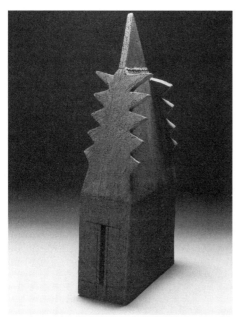

Fig. 4-28. *House Form,* Joe Molinaro, USA, slab-formed vase, terra-cotta clay body, fired at cone 2, 22 × 4 × 16 inches. Molinaro has created an architectural form using flat and sheet-like slabs. He exploited a simple four-sided form with flat planes and angular silhouettes to create this totemic piece. The angular edges and dramatic tilt of the slab at the top are the focal point. Photo by M. S. Rezny.

Fig. 4-29. Lisa Ehrich, USA, slab-formed sculpture, commercial glazes, fired to cone 06–05. Ehrich creates her pieces using flat slabs that are quite firm. She uses these slabs to create a crisp form with carefully cut contours. The contrast of a full, curved silhouette with smooth flat surfaces is the keynote of these pieces. Photo by Traci Hicks.

Fig. 4-30. *Moonhowl,* **Leslie Strong, USA, slab-formed sculptural form, terra-cotta, cone 06, 15 × 8 × 9 inches.** The artist created this piece from slabs that she assembled and then carved. The carving enriches the simple slab surfaces.

Fig. 4-31. *Structure—Landscape Series,* **Peter Valenti, USA, slab-formed covered vessel, raku-fired, 12 × 13 inches.** This piece is interesting for its details. The sides are softly curved. Note the carefully punched areas at the foot and on the handle. Both strategies soften the imagery. Photo © Courtney Frisse.

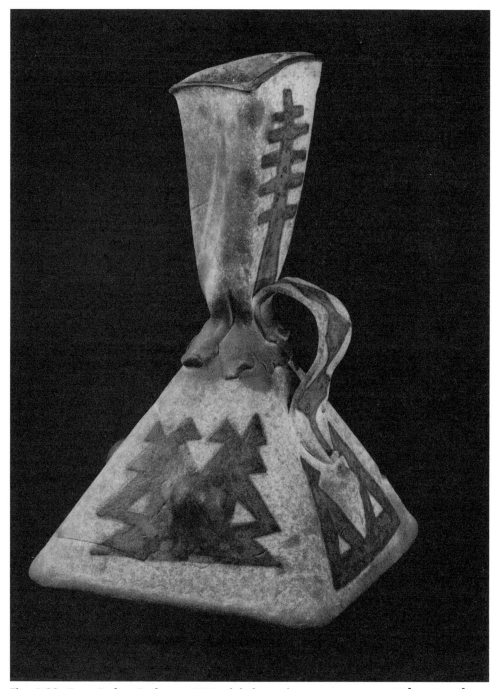

Fig. 4-32. *Tepe,* **Turker Ozdogan, USA, slab-formed vase, stoneware, 15½ × 9 × 9½ inches.** This four-sided piece was made in two parts. Note that the artist rounded and smoothed the edges and joins of the form, especially the four corners, the join in the middle of the piece, and the top and bottom edges. In this way he imbued the piece with a soft character.

Guest Artist: Peter Beard

Peter Beard has created a nice contrast between the soft curved walls and the hard edges where the slabs come together (Fig. 4-33). The softly curved forms of the slabs, the curved base, and the irregular curves taken by the lip relieve the boxy quality of the four-sided form. Beard has made every effort to soften the angularity of this rectangular form. The result is a rich effect in which the artist has fully exploited the plasticity of the material.

Fig. 4-33. *Block Vase,* **Peter Beard, England, slab formed, 34 centimeters long.** The English potter Peter Beard executed this simple rectangular form from thin slabs with care and intelligence. Beard allowed the slabs to dry to a point just short of leather hard (this state is often termed "cheese hard"). Working with paper templates, Beard cut the shapes he needed for the pot walls. He then curved and bowed the slab shapes and assembled the piece, joining the edges with a thick slurry. Excess slurry was smoothed over the seam in the inside joins to create the equivalent of a fillet. Beard then sealed the piece in plastic to season it. He then shaped it using a rasp (a coarse file) and allowed the piece to dry.

Guest Artist: John Neely

John Neely is highly aware of the different aspects of the building process. Of the process, he says "I assemble the bodies of my teapots using stiff, slab construction techniques and use other methods to make the added parts. I pinch and carve the lugs, make the spouts with press molding or throwing methods, and throw parts of the lids and the lid seatings. Once I have made all the pieces, I wrap them in plastic for a day or more before I assemble the piece. This eliminates drying problems that occur from differences in moisture content. I then assemble the pieces using a deflocculated slip. The slip shrinks less than the body and this enhances its filling ability and minimizes drying cracks. Once I assemble the piece, I again wrap it in plastic. In this way I ensure a uniform moisture content and allow the joins to harden slowly. I smooth the corners with a notched tool, which helps me maintain a constant radius. Finally, I clean the piece and prepare it for firing.

Fig. 4-34. *Teapot,* **John Neely, USA, slab formed, white stoneware with 48/60 mesh granite wedged in, cone 11.** This is a rectangular slab-formed teapot. While its aesthetic character is important (especially owing to a rich surface), it is essentially a useful pot.

89

Neely says: I use the following white stoneware clay body:

Pioneer Day Clay Body	cone 10–12
kaolin	45
light-colored fire clay	35
potash feldspar	20
white grog	10

To this recipe I wedge in a crushed local granite (60/30 mesh) for tooth and visual texture.

The joins in this piece are clear-cut, clean, and not smoothed out. The form is simple, direct, and understated. Making the various parts of a teapot work together can be difficult. Neely does not attempt to blend the forms or hide the joins. Instead, he keeps the parts separate and emphasizes the joins. The result is a piece whose virtues are strength, intellectual clarity, and honesty.

Guest Artist: Donna Nicholas

To create the two-part piece in Figure 4-35, Donna Nicholas used slab construction methods. As a construction aid she used a system of external cardboard supports. Nicholas developed this idea by drawing it full scale on butcher paper until she was satisfied with the proportions. She then transferred the shapes to a piece of cardboard and cut out the cardboard sections with a utility knife. Nicholas sponged each piece of cardboard with water on one side so that she could attach it temporarily to the dampened slab. Usually a gentle rubbing with the hand would attach the cardboard to the slab. She then cut around its edges with a knife to create the sides. She cut and beveled the edges and scored the surfaces that met and brushed them with water.

Nicholas first attached the back and bottom to one side, welding the inside seam. She then placed the three-sided forms upright. With the cardboard supporting them, they were able to stand alone. Holding the upright piece with one hand, she picked up the remaining piece, carefully aligned it, and with the other hand began pressing the seams together. Once she tacked the seams, she paddled them to ensure a good bond. Because the clay was soft, she could use the paddle to adjust the form's stance. When the second side

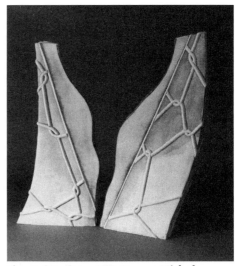

Fig. 4-35. *Gyre XIII,* **Donna Nicholas, USA, sculptural forms, slab formed, low-fire clay and glazes, talc body with 5% kyanite to resist heat shock during refiring, 27 × 25 × 9 inches.** Photo by the artist.

was in place, she could adjust their relationship. At this point she left the pieces on the studio table overnight to dry and become leather hard.

The next phase of the process called for strengthening the seams and making adjustments to the forms. Nicholas first needed to determine whether the piece was dry enough to remove it from the cardboard. She peeled back a few inches of the cardboard and pressed the clay with her finger to see if it was firm enough to continue. Nicholas peeled the cardboard off the pieces slowly. Once the object was out of the cardboard shell, she welded all exposed seams and cleaned the edges of the form with a metal rib.

Nicholas kept the pieces leather hard until she finished all of the detailing. She created her surfaces by layering colored slips and underglazes that she applied first at the leather-hard stage. She created the piece from clay elements in varying degrees of dryness. Then she kept the finished forms wrapped in plastic for a day or two so that the moisture content could even out. During this phase she studied the piece and adjusted its stance. The drying was done in stages—first loosely covered, then uncovered for a week or so. She added more layers of slip and underglaze color after she fired the piece and again after subsequent refirings.

In this piece Nicholas wanted to create a sculpture that transcended a strict verticality. The result is a form whose diagonal energy makes a strong statement.

Guest Artist: Jerry Caplan

In recent years some artists have begun to experiment with handmade paper and art objects made from that paper. Many ceramists have followed these experiments with interest and have concluded that paper and clay are indeed complimentary materials. As a result, a number of ceramists have begun combining paper and clay. The ceramist Jerry Caplan has produced an interesting series of hand-formed pieces using this combination of materials.

In *Nude with Window* (Fig. 4-36), Caplan bent a slab into four sections to create a kind of freestanding relief. He developed the surface using relief and engraved lines and used texture to good effect, contrasting the smooth and rough sides of the slabs to produce a strong image. The edges, too, slightly rounded and soft, show the effect of the paper pulp.

Fig. 4-36. *Nude with Window,* **Jerry Caplan, USA, slab formed, low-fire, paper/clay, 7 × 12 inches.**

The textured surface of this piece is quite appealing. As a result, Caplan felt no need to glaze the piece. He did use some stains and smoked imagery to modify the color without covering the surface of the clay.

Fig. 4-37A. Caplan combines paper in the form of linter with dry powdered clay. He adds water and mixes with a propeller. He places the mixture of linter, clay, and water on plaster bats to form slabs.

Fig. 4-37B. The completed slabs.

Fig. 4-37C. Caplan begins the slab-building process.

DRAPE FORMING

Drape forming is a building method in which you use simple forms or molds to create volumetric forms. Once you learn this forming process, you will find that you can create unusual and sophisticated pieces. Clay elements (either coils or slabs) are placed inside or outside the form and take on its shape. The clay is withdrawn from the form when it stiffens. Forms can be made from a variety of materials, such as wood, bisque-fired clay, fabric, and sheet metal.

EXPERIMENTING WITH DRAPE-FORMING TECHNIQUES

Drape-forming *will* impose some form limitations on your work. The method is limited to the creation of open forms, such as those for platters and bowls. However, these simple forms can be combined to make more complex pieces. For example, to make a closed form such as a sphere, combine two bowl forms. You can create a great variety of complex, compound shapes by combining simple drape-formed shapes.

The process of drape forming requires that you withdraw the piece from the form without stressing or deforming it. You cannot do this if your piece is closed or if it has bends and undercuts. To aid the withdrawal process, you must give the form a shape that encourages easy removal.

Although the drape-forming process is simple, it may take some time before you can exploit its possibilities effectively. The first time you try the drape-mold technique, you may find the process awkard and time-consuming. In fact, you may assume that the method is more trouble than it is worth because you will have to make the shape work once you remove it from the form. In addition, you may have to deal with clay that won't release from the form. In time, however, you will become more adept and learn how to finish these pieces successfully. Then the process will seem more natural and take less time.

Before you begin the drape-forming process, it is best to season the clay slabs overnight. Seasoned slabs will take on their new form easily; they will also release from the form easily and resist cracking.

Many ceramists have come to see the drape-forming method as an invaluable aid in creating hand-built forms. The method is on the frontier between hand forming and mold forming. I consider drape forming as a kind of extension of the hand-building process.

There are many types of drape forms and they vary a great deal. This variety is a real advantage, however, because it encourages a wide range of form possibilities.

RIGID AND SOFT DRAPE FORMS

Drape forms fall into two broad categories: those that are rigid and those that are soft. Each has its advantages and disadvantages, and each leaves its mark on the character of the ceramic piece. Both forms are easy to make and use.

Rigid Forms

The best materials for making rigid forms are bisque-fired clay, plaster of paris, wood, plywood, and sheet metal. These materials will give you excellent control over the shape of the piece. You can also control the wall thickness by varying the amount of pressure as you paddle against the form. These characteristics make rigid forms useful for creating compound forms. To make a compound form, you join two hemispherical forms together at the lip. The two pieces must mate effectively; you can accomplish this most easily using rigid forms. The control that characterizes rigid forms also makes them useful for making identical (or nearly identical) sets of plates and bowls.

Clay often sticks to the rigid form during the building process. Some drape forms are absorbent and have less of a tendency to stick, but even these forms will stick in time. Material such as newspaper may be placed between the clay and the form or you may use a clay that is "short" (gritty and nonsticky). You can do this by adding grog to the body. Adding grog is a good idea anyway, because it encourages rugged clay bodies. Drape forming requires a rugged clay body because it must withstand a good deal of stress when you remove it from the form.

Soft Forms

There are two types of soft drape forms: pillow drape forms and hammock drape forms. Both forms are easy to make and use.

To make a pillow drape form, you stuff a fabric container with materials such as foam, sawdust, or fabric. The slab will not stick to the soft, absorbent fabric. You can easily modify their shape by propping them up or pushing them down. Because pillow drape forms are irregular in shape, you can use them to make soft, asymmetric, natural-looking pieces.

To make a hammock drape form, you suspend a sheet of fabric in a box (usually a wooden box). Use a strong fabric such as canvas or burlap. The clay slabs will not stick to the fabric. You can modify the shape of the form by tightening or loosening the fabric to make a deeper or more shallow curve. The softly curved, catenary shapes typical of hammock forming are very satisfying.

FIRED-CLAY AND PLASTER DRAPE FORMS

Fired-Clay Drape Forms

Fired-clay drape forms are rigid forms made from bisque-fired clay. One of their many advantages is that they allow a great deal of control over the shape of the piece. Fired clay drape forms are durable and relatively light in weight and encourage work with a variety of shapes. They are easy to use: if you let the drape form dry overnight, its surface is absorbent and the clay piece is easily removed.

Making a fired-clay drape form requires planning. You cannot use these forms right away. First you must form, dry, and fire them.

You will need clay (a strong, grogged clay body is useful), a comb, paddle, rib, and knife.

1. Choose the drape form's shape and size.
2. Begin coiling the form.
3. Using a comb, work the coils together on the inside and outside of the wall.
4. Smooth the coils with a rib.
5. Continue building and smoothing the drape form.
6. Paddle the form to refine its shape.
7. Let the form dry.
8. Fire the drape form to bisque (cone 06). After firing the form is ready to use.

Plaster Drape Forms

Plaster forms are less durable than fired-clay drape forms and they are awkward to handle. Creating a plaster drape form requires planning because you must make the drape form in a mold or turn it on a plaster wheel. You then let it dry for a day or two before using it. Like fired-clay drape forms, plaster drape forms allow the ceramist to create a great variety of shapes.

For plaster work, you must acquire a set of complex skills. If you wish to take a simple approach, you can experiment with a plaster drape form, cast in a flexible plastic bowl. While this process does not let you exploit all of the possibilities of the material, it is effective. The process is simple and straightforward and it can serve as a useful introduction to work in plaster.

To make a simple plaster drape form, you will need two four-liter (five-quart) plastic buckets, petroleum jelly, and two kilograms (five pounds) of fresh plaster of paris.

1. Fill a bucket with fresh plaster of paris.
2. Apply petroleum jelly on the inside surface of the other plastic bucket.
3. Fill that bucket with water.
4. Slowly sift the plaster into the water.
5. At first the water will quickly absorb the plaster. Soon it will begin to form a raised mound. Stir the plaster for a few seconds.
6. Let the plaster in the bucket become firm.
7. After the plaster has set, twist the bowl and the plaster will release.
8. Remove the plaster from the bowl.
9. You may modify the drape form's shape using a rasp.

Do not wash any waste plaster down in the sink because it will block the pipes. Instead, let the plaster set and discard it in the trash.

PLYWOOD DRAPE FORMS

I use a type of plywood drape form in which the drape form supports only the foot of the piece. The result is a simple, quickly made drape form that requires few wood skills. Furthermore, these forms are very durable and easy to handle.

To create a plywood drape form, saw the plywood to obtain the shape you wish. Then refine the shape and bevel the edge with a rasp, plane, and coarse sandpaper. Finally, finish the surface of the drape form with fine sandpaper.

You will need a sheet of plywood, a saw (I use a hand-held electric scroll saw), a rasp, a sanding block, and fine sandpaper.

1. Draw the shape of the drape form on a sheet of plywood. Remember that you will use this form to make the foot of the piece.
2. Cut the plywood drape form using the saw.
3. Use a rasp to bevel the edge of the form so that it is wider at the base than the top.
4. Smooth the edge of the form with fine sandpaper.

MIXED WOOD AND METAL DRAPE FORMS

A form made from plywood and sheet metal will be durable, lightweight, and easy to handle. The materials are easy to obtain: I use common plywood and thin metal sheets made from used zinc offset plates purchased from a local printer. The form is easy to cut from the thin metal sheet with common kitchen shears and the plywood is easy to saw. I use finishing nails to attach the metal sheeting to the plywood.

You will need a sheet of plywood, finishing nails, and sheet metal.

1. Cut two half-circles in the plywood sheet. Make the first half-circle one-third larger than the second. The half-circles will be the top and bottom of the form and will define its shape.
2. Cut the sheet metal in a tapered shape to fit between the two plywood elements.
3. Attach the sheet metal to the plywood elements with finishing nails.

MAKING SHAPES WITH RIGID DRAPE FORMS

Making a Bowl with a Rigid Drape Form

You will need a fired-clay or plaster drape form in the shape of a bowl, a disc-shaped clay slab, and a support ring. (I use support rings made from bisque-fired clay.)

1. Place the drape form on the work table.
2. Lay the slab over the drape form.
3. Press the slab to make it conform to the shape of the drape form.
4. Let the slab become firm for approximately ten minutes.
5. Take the slab (which has now taken its new shape) off the drape form and place it on its lip on the table.
6. Let the clay form become firm for at least an hour (or better, overnight under plastic).
7. Up-end the piece and place it on a support ring.
8. Add a foot and finish the piece (Fig. 4-38).

Building a Spheroid from Two Bowl-like Pieces

You will need a wareboard, two sheets of stout fabric, a bowl-shaped drape form, a support ring, and two disc-shaped slabs.

Fig. 4-38. Joan Mathieu, USA, drape-formed bowls, porcelain, 7, 8, and 9 inches.
Mathieu formed these bowls over a bisque-fired drape form. She kept the form simple. Notice the elegant lips on these pieces. Their simplicity effectively sets off the rich surface of the glaze. Photo by T. C. Eckersley.

Creating and Assembling Two Bowl-like Shapes

1. Lay a slab over a drape mold form (Fig. 4-39A).
2. Cut a section out of the slab so that it will fit over the form (Fig. 4-39B).
3. Press the slab to make it conform to the shape of the drape form. Take the slab (which now has taken on its new shape) off the form and place it on its lip on the table.
4. After it has become firm, up-end the piece and place it on a bisque support ring. Thin the lip of this bottom piece and push it down lightly, pushing *outward* so that it can serve as a flange. This hemisphere will serve as the base of the sphere (Fig. 4-39C).
5. Prepare another bowl shape. Thin its edge by pressing it *inward* (Fig. 4-39D).
6. Apply slip on the inner surface of the lip of the bottom piece. Also apply slip to the outer surface of the top piece. Place the second bowl form on top of the first, making sure that the flanges mate (Fig. 4-39E).

Fig. 4-39A.

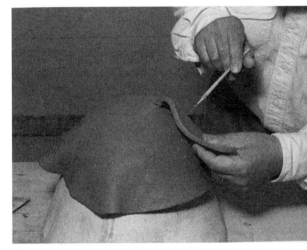

Fig. 4-39B.

Fig. 4-39C.

Fig. 4-39D.

7. Paddle and smooth the outside edges of the flange (Fig. 4-39F).
8. Continue paddling until the outside edges of the flange are smooth (Fig. 4-39G).
9. Create the opening at the top of the piece. Make it large enough so that you can insert either a tool or your hand inside the piece (Fig. 4-39H).
10. Smooth the inside seam using a tool or your fingers.
11. Turn the piece upside down and place it on a cushion.
12. Fill the opening with a slab or strengthen it with a coil of clay.
13. Scrape and smooth the join area.
14. Paddle the join area.
15. Finish the piece.

Fig. 4-39E.

Fig. 4-39F.

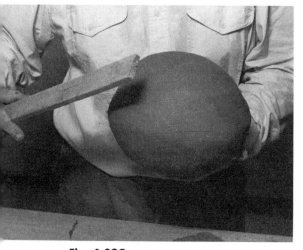

Fig. 4-39G.

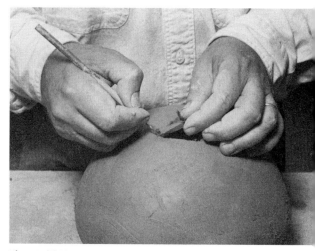

Fig. 4-39H.

Building a Platter Form

To build a platter form, you will use the drape form only to create the platter's base. Form the lip of the platter by pushing down on the overhanging section of the slab. In this way you can use the same drape form to create platters of different sizes and shapes.

You will need a plywood drape form, a clay slab, a workboard, a needle tool, four small wooden blocks, and a sponge.

1. Choose a platter drape form and place a workboard on the table.
2. Place a clay slab on the workboard. The edges of the clay slab should be larger than the drape form.
3. Use the edge of the drape form as a guide to cut out a shape from the clay slab (Fig. 4-40A).
4. Remove the drape form from the slab and place on top of four small wooden blocks. The blocks should raise the drape form an inch above the workboard.

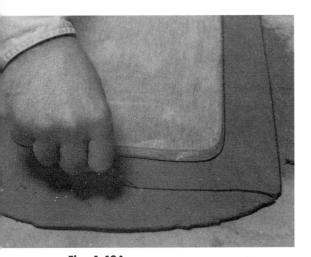
Fig. 4-40A.

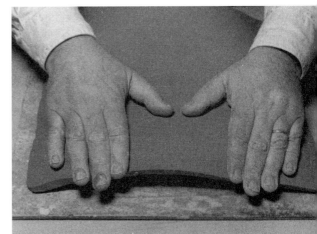
Fig. 4-40B.

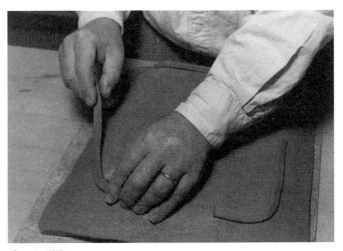
Fig. 4-40C.

5. Press the overlapping edges of the slab downward to form the rim of the platter (Fig.4-40B).
6. Refine the shape so that the angles are even.
7. Let the platter rest on the drape form for a few hours.
8. Place a foot on the platter. Place the foot right at the point where the base meets the beginning of the rim of the platter (Fig.4-40C).
9. Place a small workboard on the foot of the platter to keep the platter rigid as you flip it over. The platter now rests on its foot.
10. Clean and finish the piece.
11. Keep the platter moist for a few days under plastic.
12. Remove the plastic and cover the piece with fabric so that it will dry slowly.

Building an Elliptical Piece

You will need a plywood drape form (Fig.4-41A), a clay slab, a needle tool, small wooden blocks, and a sponge.

1. Use a template to cut out a shape from a clay slab. Cut a tapered shape. This shape will be one of the two walls of the piece.
2. Pinch the edges of the wall along its two long sides.
3. Place the form on the workboard and place the clay wall over the form, pressing it down so that it follows the curve of the form (Fig.4-41B).
4. Cover the piece with newspapers to control the rate of drying. Leave it on the form overnight so that it becomes firm.
5. Remove the wall from the form and wrap it carefully in plastic sheeting.
6. Form the second slab in the same way as the first. Place the slab on the form.
7. After drying overnight, remove the second slab from the drape form.
8. Remove the first slab from its plastic sheeting.
9. Score and slip the pinched edges of the walls.
10. Stand the walls upright—their curved bottoms will ensure that they will stand without toppling over (Fig.4-41C).
11. Join the edges together.
12. Trim and clean the edges.
13. Finish the piece.

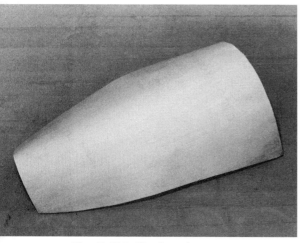

Fig. 4-41A. The drape form.

Fig. 4-41B. Lay a slab over the drape form. When this piece is finished, make another in the same way.

Fig. 4-41C. Stand the slabs upright (their curved bottoms will allow them to stand). Pinch the edges of the slabs and join them together. To finish the piece, trim and clean the edges and attach a slab to serve as the foot.

Making a Drape-Formed Plate

David Gamble makes large platters using drape-forming techniques. The large scale and the smooth, unbroken curve of these pieces are quite striking. Drape forming is an effective way of making large platters.

First Gamble lays the slab over the drape form. He then scores rings as a guide to foot placement (Fig. 4-42A), sprays vinegar on the scored area, and attaches the foot (Fig. 4-42B). He slides the platter off the mold (you must handle a large piece like this with care while it is still wet) and prepares to glaze the piece after bisque firing (Fig. 4-42C).

Fig. 4-42A.

Fig. 4-42B.

Fig. 4-42C.

PORTFOLIO OF DRAPE-FORMED PIECES

Milly D'Angelo formed *Clay Painting with Rabbits* (Fig. 4-44) over a rigid drape form. After taking the piece off the form, she modified its shape by pressing inward at the top to create the recessed area. She then cut the opening at the top. This opening is intended to resemble that of a Kiva (a Hopi religious structure) rather than to serve as a vessel opening. D'Angelo created the animal images using pinch-forming methods. Note the engraved imagery on the sloping sides of these pieces. D'Angelo made this piece to express her admiration for the Indian culture of the American Southwest.

Fig. 4-43. Drape-formed vase, Richard Zakin, USA, cone 03 body and glazes, 15 × 6 inches. "I made this piece from two different bisque-fired drape forms. The form I used to create the base was deeply curved; the form for the top had a shallow curve. I was aiming for a vessel form with a strong, taut contour."

Fig. 4-44. *Clay Painting with Rabbits,* Milly D'Angelo, USA, drape-formed sculptural piece, 8½ × 12½ inches. Photo by Lilly R. Smith.

Guest Artist: Yih-Wen Kuo

Figure 4-45 illustrates a sculpture that has many aspects of a vessel. The piece is similar to a vessel in that it is a hollow, volumetric form. However, the artist has not pierced it at the top as he would if he were making a vessel.

Kuo describes his forming process: *I first develop my forms on paper, using sketches to explore new ideas. If I think an idea has potential, I make a clay maquette to study the form further in three dimensions. At this point I may modify the form. Once I am satisfied with the new form, I make the shape, full size, in Styrofoam. From this I make a two-part plaster mold. I press slabs into each half. When the clay is cheese hard, I join the forms together to create the piece.*

The most obvious aspect of this piece's form is its carefully judged and emphatic contour. The artist paid great attention to the profile of the piece, which is reminiscent of a crystal. Kuo varied the sizes and angles; no two angles and no two lengths are precisely the same; yet all the pieces work harmoniously with one another. As a result, the piece is complex and satisfying. The three small openings break through the broad expanse of the form and open it up without weakening it either visually or structurally.

This carefully designed form shows how the ceramist can benefit from the use of maquettes. The artist has intensively examined and tested every length and proportion before forming the piece. He has also used the press-mold technique to good ef-

Fig. 4-45. *External Home,* **Yih-Wen Kuo, USA, slab-formed elliptical piece, porcelain, 14 × 14 × 6 inches.** The artist uses the elliptical form to create a piece that is poised on the frontier between vessel and sculpture. The smooth ellipse is highly emphasized and defines the character of the piece. This strong arc is broken only by the stepped forms on one shoulder of the piece. By using a slump mold to create the form, the artist could develop and control the curve of the slabs. The large, flat expanse of the slab is relieved by the small window opening. This large expense is a fine "carrier" for the complex and soft glaze imagery. Photo by Barry Stark.

fect, exercising a level of control over the forming process that would have been difficult to establish if he had used other hand-forming methods.

MAKING A PILLOW DRAPE FORM

Pillow drape forms are cloth bags stuffed with sawdust, sand, fabric, or foam rubber. You can make these forms quickly and easily. Use a stout fabric for the pillow drape shell, then modify the shape of a pillow drape form by adding or subtracting filler material.

1. Obtain or make a canvas (or other strong fabric) pillow shell.
2. Stuff the shell with sawdust, foam rubber, or sand.
3. Sew the open end of the shell to seal in the stuffing.

Use pillow forms by placing coils or slabs over them. Pieces made with these soft, compressible forms look softer and more organic than those made over rigid forms. Because the form is soft, the piece can be removed even if it catches on the form.

MAKING A HAMMOCK DRAPE FORM

Make a hammock drape form simply by pinning the edges of a stiff fabric over a sturdy wooden box. The fabric will sag and create a shallow, concave form. Modify the shape of the hammock drape by tightening or loosening the fabric.

You will need a wooden box, a piece of strong fabric, and thumbtacks.

1. Place an open-top wooden box on the work table.
2. Lay the fabric loosely over the box.
3. Use thumbtacks or heavy staples to attach the fabric to the open top of a box (Fig. 4-46A).

Fig. 4-46A.

Fig. 4-46B.

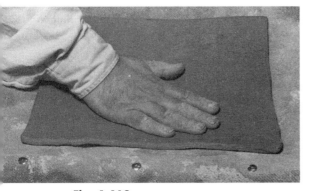

Fig. 4-46C.

Fig. 4-46D.

4. Place the slab in the hammock form (Fig. 4-46B).
5. Press the slab to conform to the shape of the hammock form (Fig. 4-46C).
6. Allow the piece to become firm.
7. Once the piece is firm, remove it form the hammock form. Up-end it and place it on a pillow form. Add the foot (Fig. 4-46D).

To use the hammock drape form, place a clay slab on the fabric. The fabric supports the clay slab but allows the slab to take on the sagging bowl-like form of the fabric. Once the slab becomes firm, it will retain its shape when you remove it from the form.

Making a Bowl Using a Pillow Drape Form

You will need a pillow, a clay slab, and a sharp knife. Make the pillow in a shape that will ensure that the clay piece can be withdrawn from the form at the end of the procedure.

Fig. 4-47A.

Fig. 4-47B.

Fig. 4-47C.

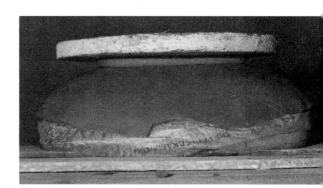

Fig. 4-47D.

Fig. 4-47E.

1. Place the pillow form on the wareboard.
2. Position a slab over the drape form (Fig. 4-47A).
3. Lower the slab over the drape form (Fig. 4-47B).
4. Press the slab to make it conform with the shape of the cushion form (Fig. 4-47C).
5. Place the foot on the form. Use the board to align the foot with the lip of the piece (Fig. 4-47D).
6. Press the clay so that the foot flows smoothly into the form (Fig. 4-47E).

Making a Platter Using a Hammock Drape Form

You will need a hammock form, a clay slab, and a sharp knife.

1. Roll out a clay slab and rest it in the hammock form.
2. Let the form dry in position until it becomes firm.

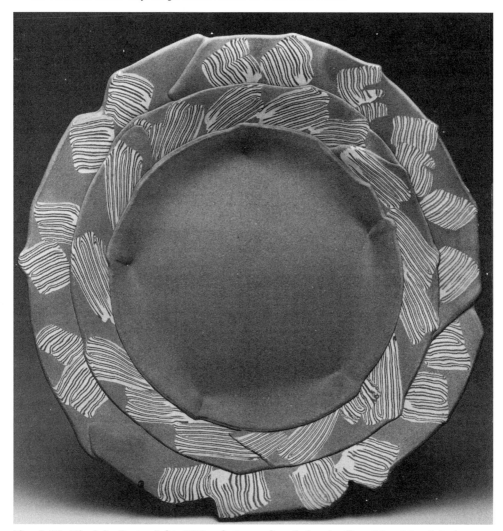

Fig. 4-48. Virginia Cartwright, USA, platter, colored clay bodies, 16 × 16 × 4 inches.
Cartwright used a red stoneware clay body for the base of this piece. She then added striped patches of inlaid, colored clays at the lip. The form was created by folding and joining slabs, which encourages the creation of flowing edges and an irregular silhouette. This forming method and its results have much in common with drape-formed pieces. Both methods rely on the plasticity and compressibility of clay. Photo by Phillip Starrett.

3. Decide where to place the foot. Draw a line at that point on the piece where the base ends and the wall begins.
4. Paint the line with slip.
5. Place the foot coil on the line.
6. Finish the piece.

SOLID FORMING

The solid-forming method is so simple and direct that it no doubt was one of the first methods used by the earliest potters. Solid forming and pinch forming share many similarities. Like pinch forming, solid forming is almost instinctive; you form the piece by moving and manipulating the clay until you obtain the shape you want. Using this method, however, you make the piece as a solid form rather than a hollow one.

Although it has significant advantages, few contemporary ceramists use the solid-forming technique. I find this is surprising because the method is often so pleasing in its consistency and direct character. Solid forming is simple and easy to learn. The simplest and most direct methods are appropriate, and the tools are basic as well. Solid-formed pieces are not only extremely durable, but they can be shaped in ways that are nearly impossible to create in any other way.

Solid forming can be easily misused. The beginner working with a solid form will often rely heavily on carving methods. However, the methods that work so well in wood or stone do not always lend themselves to clay. The surfaces of carved clay pieces often seem fussy and choppy.

Solid-formed work is difficult to fire, to store, and to exhibit. It must be dried very carefully. If any moisture becomes trapped in the clay, the piece will crack or explode. Often part of the wall will explode where the moisture content is at its highest concentration. Most ceramists who work with solid-forming techniques pierce the form with long metal rods during the building process. The channels left by the rods allow moisture and steam to escape.

If they are taller or wider than half a meter, solid-formed pieces are heavy, in fact much heavier than pieces made with other hand-forming methods, such as coil or slab. They range in size from very tiny (three or four centimeters) to very large (see page177 for illustrations of Bruce Taylor's work). Larger pieces than this will be extremely heavy and their weight may make them difficult to handle during the building process. Heavy pieces are difficult to transport and may be difficult to place as well. They may weigh so much that they tax the structure or the furniture they are placed upon.

There is much to recommend the solid-forming method; it can help you create a variety of vigorous and unusual forms.

EXPERIMENTING WITH SOLID-FORMING TECHNIQUES

The methods described will enable you to make solid-formed pieces that will be durable and will resist cracking and exploding during firing. All of the following methods require a coarse, highly grogged clay body. You will also need a cushion made from a large slab of foam rubber or a thickly folded blanket, a paddle, and a sponge.

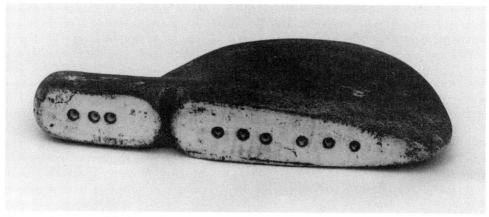

Fig. 4-49. A view of the base of a solid-formed piece showing pierced vents for moisture and steam, William Parry, USA.

Opening Up a Solid Block of Clay Using Rods

In this method you open channels into the interior of the piece to allow moisture and steam to escape during the firing process and encourage even drying. The resulting pieces are heavy because they have not been hollowed out. You can make a great variety of shapes using this method because it is not necessary to create complex hollow forms.

In addition to clay, a cushion, a paddle, and a sponge, you will need a long metal rod with a sharpened point.

1. Wedge a lump of clay.
2. Shape it into the form you wish to use.
3. As the piece begins to take on a defined shape, continue the process of creating and defining the form.
4. Finish the surface with a sponge.
5. Allow the piece to become firm.
6. Place a large slab of foam rubber or a thickly folded blanket on the work table.
7. Place the piece on its side, resting on the cushion.
8. Pierce the piece using a metal rod.
9. Smooth the surface of the piece where the rod has broken through.
10. Dry the piece carefully, examining it periodically inside and out for cracking.

Hollowing a Solid Block of Clay

It seems contradictory to talk of hollowing out a solid form. Hollowing out, however, is a way to maintain the vigor and directness of the solid-formed image while lightening and opening the form. The advantages of solid forming are thus exploited while minimizing the disadvantages.

Hollowing out the interior of a piece will lighten it and ensure that moisture and steam will be able to escape during firing.

In addition to the clay and a cushion, you will need a paddle, a knife, and a loop tool.

1. Wedge a lump of clay.
2. Shape it into the form you wish to use.

3. As the piece begins to take on a defined shape, continue the process of creating and defining the form.
4. Finish the surface with a sponge.
5. Allow the piece to become firm.
6. Place a large slab of foam rubber or a thickly folded blanket on the work table.
7. Place the piece on its side, resting on the cushion.
8. Hollow out the inner cavity with a loop tool; try to follow the outer contour as closely as possible.
9. Save the discarded clay for rewetting and reuse.
10. Dry the piece carefully, examining it periodically inside and out for cracking.

Using a Block of Clay with a Nonclay Core

In this method you build the piece as a hollow shell, building the shell around a bag filled with a granular material. After the clay shell has become firm, you open the bag and remove the granular material. You then remove the bag. This lightens the piece and ensures that moisture and steam will not build up during firing.

In addition to clay, a paddle, and a sponge, you will need a strong paper or plastic bag and an easily removed filler, such as gravel or grog.

1. Wedge a lump of clay into a spheroid form.
2. Thrust your fingers into the lump to create a hollow.
3. Place the bag containing the gravel in the hollow.
4. Place the clay and bag on the workboard and force the lump of clay around the solid core.
5. Begin to give the clay block a shape, turning the workboard as you shape the clay.
6. Continue this process of turning and shaping as the piece begins to take on a defined form.
7. Continue to create and define the form.
8. Finish the surface with a sponge.
9. Allow the piece to become firm.
10. Create a stand for the piece using two bricks and rest the piece on the bricks.
11. Place newspaper under the piece.
12. Pierce the bag and let the gravel fall on the newspaper.
13. Place the piece on its side, resting on the cushion.
14. Using a loop tool, finish the hollowing-out process; try to follow the outer contour as closely as possible.
15. Dry the piece carefully, examining it periodically inside and out for cracking.

If you have used a paper bag, you can reuse the clay (paper fragments will not affect the usefulness of the clay). Remove the larger fragments of the paper bag from the discarded clay and save the clay for rewetting and reuse.

Building a Compound Solid-Formed Piece

Beginning with the materials and techniques described above, do the following:

1. Make several solid-formed elements using either the solid clay or the nonclay-core methods.
2. Hollow out the elements.

3. Cut and deform the elements so that they fit together.
4. You may join the elements with slip or you may fire the pieces separately as a segmented piece.
5. Smooth and finish the forms.
6. Dry the piece carefully, examining it periodically inside and out for cracking.

CUT FORMING

Cut forming is not used a great deal by ceramists because the method allows you only to create a narrow range of forms. However, the imagery it produces can be exciting and unusual. The process also is novel and can be a great deal of fun.

To begin cut forming, you cut into a solid block of clay with a cutting wire. In doing this, you create interesting and unusual imagery that reveals the interior of the clay block. The cutting procedure creates the imagery and simultaneously opens the block, making the piece easy to fire.

To make a cut-formed piece, prepare a solid block of clay. Using a cutting wire, slice into the block to create the images. Then dry the piece slowly and carefully to avoid cracking.

Fig. 4-50. *Composition*, Dong Hee Sung, Korea, sculptural form, cut-formed, 45 × 30 centimeters, cone 10 reduction. This exciting image was created in a simple and swift manner. The method takes a great deal of practice and most results will not be as interesting or satisfying as this one. Photo by Chris Ramsay.

MODULAR FORMING

In modular forming you either divide the piece into segments or assemble the piece from various parts. You may fire the segments together, but usually it is better to fire them separately, joining them only after the firing is complete.

Ceramists value modular forming because it allows them to fire pieces that otherwise would be too unwieldy to load or too large for the kiln. The modular-forming strategy helps control warping and cracking. Warping and cracking are far more easily controlled in a group of small segmented pieces than in one large unsegmented piece. Because each segment is small and lightweight, it is easier to transport than a large unsegmented piece. Finally, firing a group of small forms is easier than firing a large unsegmented form. It may even be difficult to find a kiln large enough to fire a large piece, whereas segments of a modular-formed piece can be fired separately.

The modular-forming procedure has its disadvantages as well: it is difficult to make the segments fit together correctly, and it can be difficult to join the segments securely. You can use various strategies to ensure that the pieces fit together well. The simplest solution is often the best—use building methods that do not require a precision fit.

Segmentation strongly influences the look of the piece and places constraints on the types of form that you may use. The segment lines are hard to ignore. It is often best to ensure that the piece works well as a segmented form by emphasizing the segment divisions rather than trying to disguise them. If you use this strategy, the segment divisions can be a significant asset rather than a problem.

In recent years there has been a great deal of interest among artists in repetitive imagery. They use repetitions of form elements to create a hypnotic imagery. The effect is at once harmonious and intellectually challenging. The use of repetition reflects the influence of music and art from India, Tibet, and Indonesia. On page 192 you will see a wall piece in which the artist used a repeated modular form to create a repetitive image.

Guest Artist: JoAnn Schnabel

Schnabel used a segmented strategy to create the pieces in Figures 4-51 and 4-52. Using this strategy allowed her to create tall pieces with many changes in direction and many appealing puffy forms. The references here are to natural forms, such as the elapsed-time images we see of budding plants. The patterns of growth in nature are images of great power and Schnabel has exploited them well.

In *Offshoot* (Fig. 4-51), JoAnn Schnabel used segmented, slab, and strip-coil techniques to create the form. She started by rolling out the slabs and clay strips and then used strip-coil techniques to create variations in surface texture. To assemble the form, she added one strip upon another. During the construction of the form, she simultaneously constructed a central cylinder for internal support. During the building process, she constantly paddled the clay to compress it and refine the form. She paid special attention to the inner structure, reinforcing and smoothing it as the work progressed. Periodically she created a break between one part and another. In this way she created a segmented form. She used newspaper to keep the segments from sticking together. Using the inner cylinders as a base, she formed a "cup and socket" join at the beginning and end of each segment. These joins served to hold the piece together as the segments were placed one upon the other. She took special care to create a strong structure at the join of the final segment, as the segment is heavy and perched at an angle.

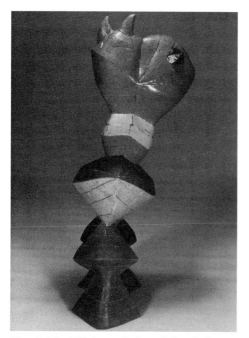

Fig. 4-51. *Offshoot,* JoAnn Schnabel, USA, slab- and strip coil-formed sculpture, terra-cotta clay body, 45 × 22 × 13 inches.

Fig. 4-52. *Rejoinder,* JoAnn Schnabel, USA, slab- and strip coil-formed sculpture, ceramic, 45 × 22 × 13 inches.

In the resulting piece, a soft vegetal silhouette contrasts with the repetition of the lines created between each strip coil and between the segments. Schnabel made no effort to erase the lines between each segment. Instead she emphasized these lines to set up a rich surface pattern and to reveal the construction of the piece.

The segmented character of this piece is of particular interest. This strategy allowed the artist to create a large piece that was easy to glaze and fire.

NOTE: *Offshoot* was built at the Watershed Center for the Ceramic Arts, Edgecomb, Maine, during a two-week "Artists Invite Artists" session.

COMBINING FORMING METHODS

For purposes of study and practice, it is useful to make distinctions between one forming method and another. It is also useful to talk about each method separately. When we go about our work, however, we work with whatever tools and methods seem most promising. Most of us mix our building methods and our work benefits from this flexibility.

Each hand-forming method has its own particular characteristics. Slab forming lends itself to broad, flat surfaces. Coil forming lends itself to curved and undulating pieces. Drape forming lends itself to highly volumetric curved shapes. We often mix these methods in order to come up with a rich and complex image. This work strategy is easy and natural.

For illustrations of pieces made using mixed hand-forming strategies, see the work of Jennifer Lee (Fig. 4-54) and Ruth Dorendo Marcy (Fig 4-57).

By mixing hand forming with other forming methods, you can integrate both thrown and cast forms to create forms with varied shapes and surfaces.

PORTFOLIO OF PIECES CREATED USING COMBINED FORMING METHODS

Fig. 4-53. *As in Life,* **Kenneth Vavrek, USA, segmented sculptural wall piece, stoneware, 34 × 80 × 9½ inches.** In his segmented imagery, Vavrek refers to the processes of nature. He is strongly influenced by the landscape of the desert. These pieces are composed of segments that invoke desert rocks. Vavrek is true to his source here and these pieces stray very little from the character of the subject. Photo by the artist.

Fig. 4-54. Jennifer Lee, England, pinched and coiled vase, colored clay bodies, 16 × 19 × 5 centimeters. Lee used pinch-forming methods to form the base of this coiled cup. Note the simple, pleasing curve of the foot. Photo by Michael Harvey.

Fig. 4-55. Itsue Ito, Japan, hand-formed and hand-modified slipcast elements. Here the artist used slip-cast as well as hand-formed elements. Ito began the piece by making a number of casts of the square bottle form. She also created a number of purely hand-formed elements, then assembled these elements to create a complex sculptural form. During the building process she manipulated the bottle forms by twisting and bending them. The hand-formed elements are different from the bottle forms and contrast strongly in form and mood. Photo by Gert-Jan Van Root.

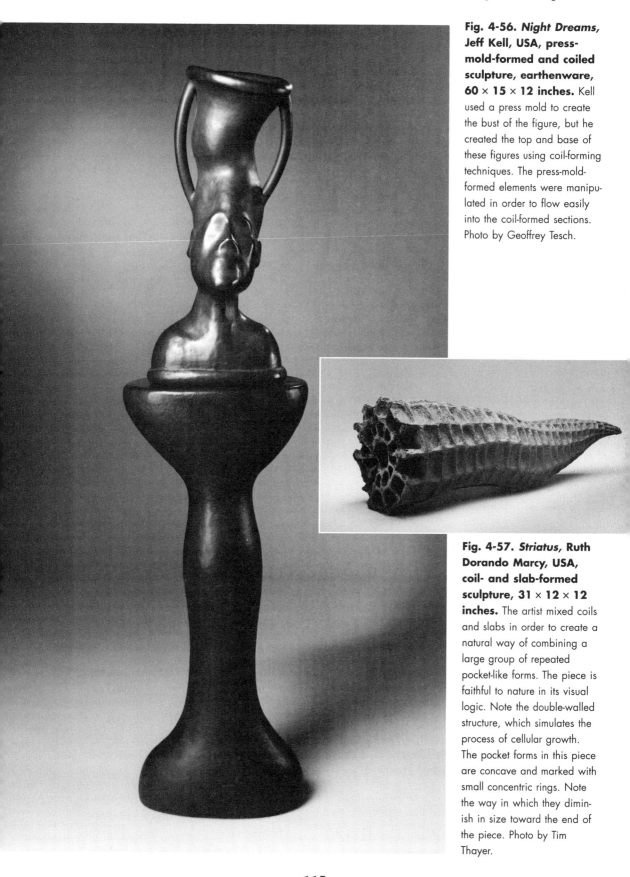

Fig. 4-56. *Night Dreams,* Jeff Kell, USA, press-mold-formed and coiled sculpture, earthenware, 60 × 15 × 12 inches. Kell used a press mold to create the bust of the figure, but he created the top and base of these figures using coil-forming techniques. The press-mold-formed elements were manipulated in order to flow easily into the coil-formed sections. Photo by Geoffrey Tesch.

Fig. 4-57. *Striatus,* Ruth Dorando Marcy, USA, coil- and slab-formed sculpture, 31 × 12 × 12 inches. The artist mixed coils and slabs in order to create a natural way of combining a large group of repeated pocket-like forms. The piece is faithful to nature in its visual logic. Note the double-walled structure, which simulates the process of cellular growth. The pocket forms in this piece are concave and marked with small concentric rings. Note the way in which they diminish in size toward the end of the piece. Photo by Tim Thayer.

MIXED-MEDIA TECHNIQUES

Mixed-media techniques are especially useful to the ceramist who creates sculpture or wall pieces. This strategy allows the ceramist to use forms and surfaces that would not be obtainable in any other way.

Clay works superbly well with some form types but not at all well with others. Mixed-media techniques allow ceramists to build their forms in clay and use other materials when appropriate. Clay lends itself to an organic, volumetric form and to soft edges. The precise and attenuated forms of metal, the transparent forms of glass or plastic, the flexible forms of rope or fabric are not attainable in clay. All these qualities are available to the artist working in mixed media.

Some ceramists rarely venture beyond their chosen medium. This may not be the best strategy for the creation of complex forms. Using a combination of various media of different character may help the artist to produce an imagery of infinite complexity and variety. In fact forms in nature, including the human body often follow this principle. Our bones, rigid and tensile, support the soft parts of our bodies—skin, fat, muscle, and organs. By using mixed-media techniques, we can retain the fluency of the ceramic medium and its volumetric character while we exploit the special advantages of other media.

Some surfaces too are difficult or impossible to create in the ceramic medium. By combining clay with other media, you will be able to create them easily. You can apply many materials to the surface of your pieces and they will provide excellent contrast with those elements made from clay.

Ceramists often employ materials in mixed-media strategies that cannot withstand the rigors of the fire. You must combine them with ceramic forms after firing. Some materials, however, can be fired (at least in the low fire) and can be integrated with clay during the building process. Fired clay and temperature-resistant glass and wire fall in this category.

MIXED-MEDIA MATERIALS

Metal

Thin and attenuated metal forms such as rod-shaped forms and paper-thin sheets are particularly useful when combined with clay because these forms are not natural to clay. Metal has the flexibility and resiliency required to make these forms possible. You can integrate shapes made from heat-resistant metal alloys with wet clay during the building of the piece. You can use kiln-element wire to create attenuated visual elements that contrast with the volumetric clay shapes.

Glass

The transparency of glass can make glass a useful partner to clay. Its characteristic forms also differ, tending to be sharper and more angular. In some ways, however, glass is similar to clay. Both are rigid and brittle and neither encourages the creation of attenuated or flexible forms. Because most glass will melt in the fire, you must apply it after firing. During the building process, however, you can use glass designed to resist high temperatures.

Fired Clay

You can integrate fired-clay elements with wet clay elements to create interesting and unusual forms. The most common use of this strategy is the surface inlay technique. Push the fired-clay elements into the surface of the wet clay. They will often be chosen to contrast in color and form with the rest of the piece. You can also apply

116

fired-clay elements to the piece after firing. In recent years, for example, a few ceramists have begun to apply mosaic tesserae to the surface of ceramic sculpture. (See Roy Cartwright's pieces in Figures 4-60 and 4-61.)

Wood

Even though wood is solid and dense, it has flexibility and resiliency, two characteristics that clay lacks. Wood lends itself to attenuated forms that will not work in clay, such as sheets and rods. Wood can have an organic or highly mechanical character, either of which makes it a useful partner to clay.

Plastic

Plastic is difficult to characterize because it takes so many forms. Many plastics have the flexibility that clay bodies lack. Many are transparent or translucent. These characteristics can enlarge the form vocabulary of a mixed-media sculptural piece and make plastics particularly interesting to use with clay.

Fabric and Leather

Fabric, like plastic, varies so much in character that it is hard to characterize. Because it is easy to work with and is highly flexible, fabric can be another useful partner for clay forms. Fabrics can be strong and flexible and thus useful to the ceramist. Leather is similar to fabric in its working qualities and its flexibility and strength.

Rope

Rope is very different in character from clay. Rope is extremely tensile and can hold segments together, but it is also flexible and bendable. These characteristics make it a suitable partner with clay. It is very easily used with ceramic forms: holes may be placed in the wet clay forms and the rope passed through them after the firing is complete.

Paper

Paper, especially handmade paper, has a clay-like look and can work well with clay. Because paper tears under stress, the ceramist should design unstressed paper forms when using it with clay. On the other hand, paper is easily worked and this flexibility makes it a useful, interesting partner with clay.

PORTFOLIO OF MIXED-MEDIA AND SCULPTURAL PIECES

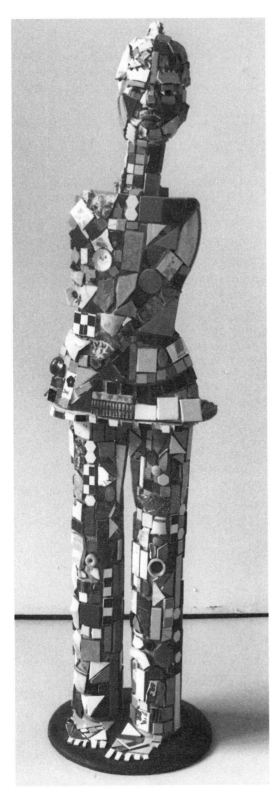

Fig. 4-58. *Donna,* Sally Michener, Canada, ceramic shards, tile, mirror, sculptural figure with mosaic surface, **5 feet 3 inches × 18 inches.** Michener combines her sculptural forms with her recent explorations in working with mosaics and tiles. She has been able to establish a strong connection between the form and the mosaic/tile elements. Note the strong value contrasts that she sets up on the tiled surface of the piece. Photo credit by the artist.

Fig. 4-59. *See No Evil, Hear No Evil, Speak No Evil,* Rimas Visgirda, USA, sculptural vase, coil formed with sheet-lead elements (this is a mixed-media strategy), **46 × 11 × 11 inches.** Although the ceramic form predominates, the sheet-lead elements in this piece are significant. They enrich the surface and enhance the emotional power of the piece. Their dull sheen has a strongly menacing character. The painted and mixed-media imagery contrasts strongly with the rhythmic and elegant coil-built vessel form.

Roy Cartwright has constructed the forms in Figures 4-60 and 4-61 using pinch and coil methods. In these pieces the mosaic elements take second place to the form. Note the way he used light- and dark-colored tiles as a way of differentiating one form from another. Cartwright has painted the surfaces of his sculpture for many years. In these pieces he uses a mosaic surface as an alternative to paint.

Fig. 4-60. Roy Cartwright, USA, sculptural piece with mosaic surfaces, red earthenware, 27 × 30 × 34 inches, fired to cone 1. Photo by Jay Bachemin.

Fig. 4-61. Roy Cartwright, USA, sculptural piece with mosaic surfaces, red earthenware, 27 × 36 × 27 inches, fired to cone 1. Photo by Jay Bachemin.

Combining Ceramic and Nonceramic Elements

The possibilities for materials suitable for use in mixed-media ceramics are so great that it is difficult to cover them all. The basic process is easy to describe. Start with clay and a nonceramic material, such as plastic, glass, wood, metal, or twine. Design a piece in which a nonceramic element is either a support for the clay elements or an important part of the form. It is a good idea to make a maquette of the piece. Next, using the drawing as a guide, make the ceramic elements. Finish and fire them. Using adhesives, openings, and lugs in the clay form, create ways for the nonceramic elements to work with the ceramic elements. Install the nonceramic elements and finish the piece.

Here are two suggestions for specific mixed-media pieces. Feel free to try your own variations.

Combining Clay and Flexible Plastic Elements

My first suggestion is for a piece made from clay combined with a soft, flexible plastic tubing. The tubing passes through holes in the clay form. The clay is rigid and volumetric and lends itself to compact forms, while the plastic hose is flexible and elongated.

You will need clay, plastic tubing, scissors, a knife, and a needle tool.

1. Create a group of drawings of the piece.
2. Make a small maquette of the piece, using wire as a substitute for the plastic tubing.
3. Create the form.
4. Place the openings for the plastic tubing.
5. Finish the piece and fire it.
6. Cut and install the tubing.

Combining Clay, Wood, and Metal Wire

My second suggestion is for a piece made from clay combined with a wooden superstructure and tied together with metal wire. The nonceramic elements pass through holes cut in the clay form. The holes must work well with the wire elements and the wooden superstructure. This combination of materials is exciting. The clay is rigid, volumetric, and compact in shape, while the wood is rigid in shape but elongated in a way that would not be possible with clay. The wire is elongated and tensile and has limited flexibility, but its main contribution to the character of the piece is its usefulness as a connecting element.

You will need clay, wood, a wood saw, metal wire, metal cutters, a knife, and a needle tool.

1. Make a group of drawings of the piece.
2. Make a small maquette of the piece, using thin wire and foil sheeting to substitute for the wood and wire elements of the finished piece.
3. Create the form.
4. Place the openings for the wires.
5. Finish the piece and fire it.
6. Saw the wood elements.
7. Cut the wires.
8. Place the wires in the openings in the clay.
9. Attach the wires to the wooden elements.

PART TWO

USING FORMING METHODS TO CREATE FINISHED PIECES

CHAPTER FIVE

VESSELS

In ceramics the technology of the method used has a strong influence on the form the piece eventually takes. This is particularly true of the technology of hand forming. Each hand-forming method exerts a particular influence upon the form and character of the vessel. Because there are many hand-forming methods, hand-formed vessels vary a great deal in the character. Pinch-formed vessels look pieced together, whereas coil-formed pieces take on rich full forms with surfaces often marked with coil-derived textures. We recognize slab-formed vessels from their joins and drape-formed vessels from their characteristic platter or bowl forms.

In the following section I will discuss the various methods used for forming vessels and will illustrate examples of vessels made with each forming method. I will also discuss the way the forming method influences the form and character of the piece.

FORMING METHODS FOR VESSELS

A vessel is a hollow container. The vessel form did not originate in any particular place or in any particular culture. It appeared in many places independently. The origins of the vessel form predate antiquity and perhaps reach back at least twelve thousand years or more, thus predating even the written word by many millennia. The vessel form has often been an engine driving the development of culture. I have seen wonderful pieces from 8000 B.C. in Japan and 4500 B.C. in northern Iran, at a time when these cultures were developing. These early vessels are among the most exciting pieces in the history of our medium. They are of particular interest to hand-builders because all of them were hand formed.

As ceramists, we often forget just how many materials are appropriate for making vessels. In most cultures, however, clay has been the premier material for creating vessel forms. This is no accident: clay and the vessel form suit each other very well. The enclosed vessel form with its base and enveloping walls exploits the strengths of clay (strength in compression) and minimizes its weakness (weakness in tension). The vessels we use should be comfortable to handle and easy to clean, and they should also have pleasing forms and surfaces. Over time ceramists have developed many ways to accomplish these features.

When we think of the vessel form, we often think of it only in a utilitarian context. Vessels naturally, it seems, were made to be used. Contemporary ceramists make utilitarian pieces as containers for holding all sorts of objects and for many different purposes. We use vessels in the kitchen for cooking food or containing or serving food. We use vessels to hold plants or flowers or small objects such as tools or desk implements (for example, scissors, pens, and pencils). These forms have been used throughout history all over the world and over time they have evolved into highly efficient and sophisticated objects.

Although they can be satisfying as utilitarian pieces, vessels can be much more as well. The vessel form over time has taken on a powerful role as a universally recognized and admired form. Many striking and beautiful vessel pieces of the past, though influenced by utilitarian antecedents, were ceremonial or decorative rather than utilitarian. At present we use the vessel form for both utilitarian work and for pieces that are strictly decorative or are works of art.

Many ceramists who work in the vessel form inhabit a frontier that is neither purely utilitarian nor purely decorative. They borrow utilitarian forms in order to create work that is essentially decorative; they do not really intend that their pieces be used. The ceramist who uses utilitarian forms for a decorative purpose often will experiment with traditional forms and exaggerate their characteristics. The transformation of these forms, from the useful to the decorative, is often inventive and surprising.

HOW USE INFLUENCES FORM

Of the many types of vessel forms, all have a strong family relationship. The form is composed of a base and side walls and sizes of each may vary. In terms of pure form, the difference between them is a matter only of varying proportions.

Vessel forms evolved in response to different aspects of use. Cups have a wide base to give them stability so that they will not tip over easily. Pitchers are taller than they are wide because these proportions make pouring liquids easier. A plate is the best shape for serving food that must be cut before eating. Bowls with steep sides obviously are most appropriate for serving liquids such as soup that must be eaten with a spoon.

The ceramist who wishes to create truly useful utilitarian pieces must design durable objects that function well and are pleasurable to use. The objects also must function well as hand-formed pieces. Every hand-forming ceramist must face the fact that many of the accepted forms of utilitarian pieces are not compatible with hand-forming imagery. We can see this as a problem or an opportunity. Some ceramists may feel daunted by the requirement to justify a new way of looking at traditional forms. For the hand-forming ceramist who enjoys a challenge, this may serve as a spur, forcing a reexamination of forms that we have accepted for many years.

COIL-FORMED VESSELS

Although coil forming is not as fast as other hand-building methods, many ceramists like some of the advantages it offers. Coil forming lends itself to the creation of full, swelling forms that have a natural quality. The ceramist can use a great variety of surfaces, from completely smooth to highly textured. Furthermore, the textured surfaces that result from coiling have a natural and appealing quality. Coil-forming methods are useful to the ceramist who wants to create large vessels. Since even the largest pieces are built up from small, easily handled coils, the building process is facilitated. The coil-forming method lends itself to the creation of cups and bowls, but vases are the most common coil-formed vessels.

Many artists adapt the coil method in order to create pieces that have complex, irregular shapes. Mary Barringer's piece in Figure 5-3 is an examples of this. The coil-forming method is the most appropriate choice for a piece of this shape. Barringer's piece is also a fine example of the way in which the artist can exploit the textural possibilities of the coil process. We also see examples of the opposite approach, in which the surface of the piece is smooth. Fiona Salazar's and Robin Levanthal's pieces are examples of this strategy. In Salazar's piece (Fig. 5-2), the vessel surface serves as a background for a complex painted imagery. In Levanthal's piece (Fig. 5-1), the smooth surface sets off the organic patterns of the sculpted imagery.

PORTFOLIO OF COIL-FORMED VESSELS

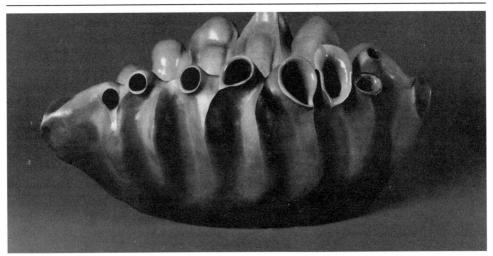

Fig. 5-1. *Continuum,* **Robin Levanthal, USA, coil-formed sculptural vase, 18 × 33 × 14 inches.** Levanthal uses the repetition of these emphatic but softly curved forms to create a strong image reminiscent of plant forms.

Fig. 5-2. *Limpets Pot,* **Fiona Salazar, England, coil-formed vase, low-fire earthenware, painted and burnished slip decoration, wax finished, 31 centimeters high.** Salazar uses coils to create pots with taut contours. She smooths and burnishes the surface of her pieces to create a smooth ground for painted imagery. This form is narrow at its foot, full at the shoulder, and strongly banded at the neck. The contour is full yet tightly controlled, which imparts a classical character to the piece. These pieces are made in the tradition of the painted pots of the ancient Mediterranean.

Guest Artist: Mary Barringer

While not a functional piece, Mary Barringer's covered jar (Fig. 5-3) derives some of its identity from the vessel form. The jar is full and strongly volumetric. Barringer made this piece using a pinch and coil strategy. The jar is fairly small and compact and its surface is marked with highly visible scratches. Subtle dips and raised areas run along the surface of the piece in a rhythmically repeated pattern. The artist created these in a natural way during the building process.

Mary Barringer has said of her work:

> *Craft or technique functions for me as a groove along which my ideas flow. A certain mastery is important so that I don't get bogged down in problem solving. It sometimes seems that "creativity" doesn't begin to operate until I have figured out* how *to work.*

For many years Barringer began her pieces at the base and built the piece up until she finished it at the top, the normal manner for coil work. In recent years, however, she has begun to build in a different, more "allover" way that allows her to develop the form at many points simultaneously. She now begins by pinch forming a rough shape; then she adds coils or pieces and paddles and scrapes until she achieves the form she wants. She no longer feels that she has to begin the piece at the base. This free approach allows her as she works to concentrate on the relationship of all the parts to one another.

Both pinching and coiling are incremental processes by nature. As such, they have much in common with the natural growth processes of many forms in nature, such as shells and coral. As a result, Barringer's piece seems to be the product of a natural growth process. The piece is natural—direct and unforced—rather than naturalistic. The naturalistic imitates nature, while the natural is *part* of nature.

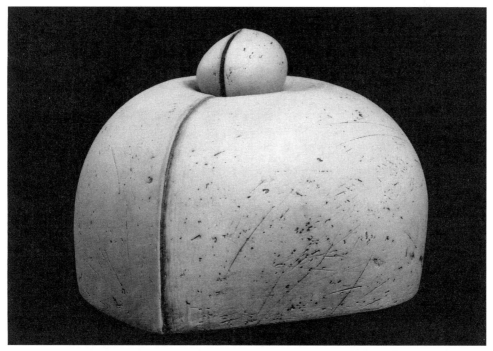

Fig. 5-3. Mary Barringer, USA, coil-formed covered jar, 9 × 10½ × 11½ inches. Photo by Wayne Fleming.

PINCH-FORMED VESSELS

Pinch forming lends itself best to small pieces marked with strong visual textures. Although pieces made with this technique are limited in size, their highly worked surfaces can have a strong personal character. Pinch forming lends itself most easily to vases, but you may use it for nonutilitarian cups, pitchers, and teapots as well.

Kirk Mangus exploited the pinch-forming method to create a vase in which he combined a strong surface texture and an expressive painting style (Fig. 5-4).

SLAB-FORMED VESSELS

Many ceramists use slab-construction methods to create vessels. Most vessel forms lend themselves easily to slab-forming methods. The Portfolio of Slab-Formed Pieces illustrates some highly creative vases and bowls. The method allows for the efficient construction of complex forms of all sizes and shapes. Many ceramists exploit the angular character that results from assembling straight-sided slabs. Others prefer to bend and curve their slabs to create softly curved pieces.

In this section you will see pieces that are loose and freely made, such as those by Deborah Black (Fig. 5-9). In Richard Devore's piece (Fig. 5-8), we see a sinuous form, while in William Brouillard's (Fig. 5-6) we see a form that is emphatically angular. Donna Nicholas's piece (Fig. 5-7) is controlled and austere, while Deborah Groover's (Fig. 5-10) is loose and exuberant and Judith Salomon's (Fig. 5-5) is crisp.

Fig. 5-4. *Femme Vase,* **Kirk Mangus, USA, pinch-formed vase, earthenware, 5 × 3 × 3 inches.** The extended, emphatic foot conveys a sense of strength and assurance. The form seems to grow naturally out of the foot. The handles are simple and direct but have great energy. The contour of the piece is soft and speaks of the plasticity of wet clay. The energetic painted imagery complements and highlights the form.

PORTFOLIO OF SLAB-FORMED VESSELS

Fig. 5-5. Judith Salomon, USA, three slab-formed vases. The tallest is 22 × 5½ × 6 inches.
Salomon makes her slabs by pouring casting slip onto a flat plaster slab. She emphasizes the angular
character of her slab forms in these four-sided pieces. Note that all horizontal surfaces at the feet, shoul-
ders, and top are flat rather than softly domed. Note as well that the slabs are flat rather than curved.
Of particular interest are the sharply stepped feet and the geometric circle of the openings at the top of
the pieces. The silhouettes are strong, straight, and uncompromising. This precision is relieved by carefully judged and slightly surprising proportions and by the witty painted shapes on the sides. Photo by
Nesnadny & Schwartz.

**Fig. 5-6. *Bowl for the Machine Age*,
William Brouillard, USA, segmented,
slab-formed bowl, 16 × 23 × 14 inches.**
The title of this piece is telling, for there are
many conscious mechanical details here, including the repetition of the slab segment forms and
the parallel, repetitive relief lines impressed on
the insides of the slabs. The edges of the slabs
are emphasized, as is the strong lip. All this is
contrasted with the soft curves of the slabs. The
result is a piece in which the artist pays homage
to the machine age while allowing the clay to
remain plastic. Photo by the artist.

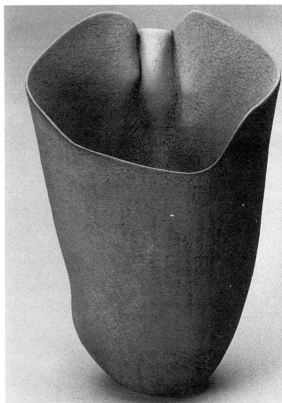

Fig. 5-7. *Black Vessel,* **Donna Nicholas, USA, cylindrical slab-formed vase, low-fire clay and glazes, 26 × 7 × 7 inches.** The sides of this simple and austere form taper softly and the curves are subtle and highly controlled—for example, in the slight bulge in the contour of the sides. Note the parallel, diagonal ridges, which give the form strength and break the line in an interesting way. These careful touches are very effective in this piece. Photo by Howard Goldsmith.

Fig. 5-8. Richard Devore, USA, slab-formed vessel, 16¼ × 11¼ inches. Devore has made the most of his resources and has created a simple but lively form. The slab-forming method can result in a piece with little spatial character, but Devore has avoided this by creating subtle changes in the contour of the lip. The curve of the form, from the foot to the lip, is well thought out. Devore created a dip in the contour toward the bottom left side of the piece; below this, the form fills out again, making a rich volumetric image. Photo by John Buffington and Eve Vanderwent.

Fig. 5-9. *Flowerholder #2 with Flowers,* **Deborah Black, Canada, slab-formed vessel, earthenware with slips, glazes, and terra sigillata, 13 × 8 × 3 inches.** This piece is meant to be used and is complete when it contains flowers. Basically a four-sided slab, the piece derives its soft, organic character from the segmented nature of the forming and the irregular silhouette. Its blocky segments contrast nicely with the more linear and delicate shapes of the stems and flowers it is meant to hold. Photo by Ed Gatner.

Fig. 5-10. *Bessie Lived in Cooperville,* **Deborah Groover, USA, carved and slab-formed vase, painted and layered with majolica glazes and Mason's stains, fired to cone 04 in an electric kiln.** This oval piece is loose and relaxed. Note the softly curved dips and rises at the lip and the simple handling of the foot. The broad expanses of the long walls of the piece are made for imagery. Groover's imagery has the same relaxed attitude as the form. The two complement each other well.

DRAPE-FORMED VESSELS

Drape-forming methods can be used to create highly effective vessels. You can use this method to create vases, plates, platters, cups, saucers, casseroles, pitchers, and teapots. This forming method is useful for creating sets of vessels of a uniform size and shape. You may also want to try combining drape-formed bowl shapes to create highly volumetric closed forms.

In the illustrations in this section, we see three pieces that vary greatly in character. In the platters of David Gamble and Matthias Ostermann (Figs. 5-11 and 5-12), we see how simple and direct shapes can serve as a background for complex imagery; William Parry's sculptural bowl form exhibits complex contours (Fig. 5-13).

Guest Artist: William Parry

William Parry used a highly grogged whiteware body to create the piece in Figure 5-13. He made the piece over a drape form, then pierced the bowl wall in several places. Finally, he added the three slab forms that act as feet.

Fig. 5-11. David Gamble, USA, large drape-formed platter, multifired and finished with velvet glazes, 23 inches in diameter. Gamble exploited the drape-forming method to create a series of large, robust platters. The form is simple and direct. The curve of the platter's surface is smooth and unbroken by a rim. The artist has paid great attention to the edges of the form, which are textured and rough. The platter is made from a thick slab that enhances the robust character of the piece. The direct, emphatically drawn imagery and strongly textured painted surface complement the form. Photo by Jeffrey P. Sandoe.

Fig. 5-12. *Fish Platter,* Matthais Ostermann, Canada, drape-formed slab plate, low-fire, cone 05–06 oxidation, majolica glazes, 42 centimeters wide. Ostermann used a combination of controlled curves and rounded corners to create an appealing shape. While the imagery is the focal point of this piece, its shape plays an important role. With such powerful imagery, it is especially important to find the right shape. Photo by Jan-Thijs, © Jan-Thijs.

Fig. 5-13. William Parry, USA, drape-formed sculptural vessel form with pinch-formed additions, whiteware clay.

The feet play an important part in defining the character of this piece. If you block them off with your hand, you will see a very different piece. The feet elevate the bowl, heightening it visually and emotionally. Because clay will warp in subtle ways during the firing, the tripod foot is far better suited to ceramics than four feet. A three-footed piece will remain stable even if one foot warps during the firing. Parry carefully integrated the feet with the bowl form, using similar contours and the same textured surfaces that he used on the bowl.

Parry added several shapes to the lip area of the bowl. These shapes break the regularity of the silhouette and make the most of the negative volume of the bowl form.

Parry has used simple textures very successfully. He created most of the textures during the slab-forming process. He made some by placing one slab over another, some by paddling the clay, and others by making the slab on a coarse fabric. These textures enrich the surface, creating a soft and natural imagery. During the glazing process, Parry emphasized these textures by using an intaglio glaze strategy.

In this piece Parry took a simple form and transformed it into one that is quite complex. He did this by adding elements, cutting out shapes, and manipulating the surface.

MIXED-MEDIA VESSELS

We rarely associate a mixed-media strategy with vessels. Many teapots, however, technically can be considered mixed media because they have straw or wood handles.

Mixed-media methods are probably more appropriately used by ceramists who create nonutilitarian vessels. It is surprising that there are not more ceramists who make nonutilitarian mixed-media vessels. Aurore Chabot's footed vessel (Fig. 5-14) is a fine example of a mixed-media vessel piece. Chabot has treated the vessel form in a highly sculptural manner. She has combined the clay vessel form with a complex and arresting welded metal foot. Both vessel and foot are angular with sharp corners. That, however, is the extent of the similarity; the metal support structure is slim and flexible, while the clay vessel is dense and massive.

COMBINING FORMING METHODS TO CREATE VESSELS

For the sake of clarity, I will discuss each ceramic forming method separately. In the studio, however, there is no need to separate these methods. In fact it is a good idea to use more than one building method on a piece. The resulting forms can have a great deal of variety and vitality.

The piece by Jolyon Hofsted will illustrate this (Fig. 5-15). He has combined the slab formed body of the piece with pinch-formed additions, creating the ceramic equivalent of a collage. He makes the smooth surfaces of the slab forms contrast with the restless, highly modeled surfaces of the pinched forms. The seemingly unrelated surfaces and images work together to create a thought-provoking piece.

Fig. 5-14. *Genesis: Spawning Disorder,* **Aurore Chabot, USA, vessel form with metal pedestal, 35 × 36 × 40 inches (sculpture alone), mixed media.** This sculptural interpretation of the vessel form is not intended to hold or contain anything. Chabot combined a vessel form with a metal pedestal structure. Both forms are sharply angular with a triangular form predominating. The strong texture of inlaid clay on the ceramic vessel is matched by the texture painted on the metal. In this piece we see how an alternative view of the vessel form can be quite effective. Photo by Brad Hansel.

TYPES OF VESSEL FORMS

To make vessels using hand-forming methods, the ceramist must understand the properties of the various forms because each form has its distinct character and its particular forming requirements. Vessel forms can be usefully divided into the following categories:

- Open forms with low walls—platters, plates, and saucers
- Open forms with high walls—vases, cups, and bowls
- Covered forms—covered jars and casseroles
- Pouring vessels—pitchers, bottles, and teapots
- Openwork pieces—baskets and colanders

135

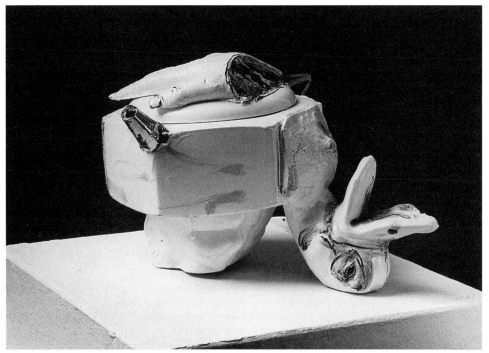

Fig. 5-15. *Duck Teapot*, Jolyon Hofsted, USA, slab-formed, ceramic with low-tempera-ture lusters, 12 × 14 × 9 inches. Hofsted mixed disparate elements (mostly slab formed) to create this piece. The result looks like a three-dimensional collage. Photo by Katherine Drabkin.

Platters, Plates, and Saucers

Plates have low side walls to allow easy access to food. Their bases are wide for stability. Usually a rim surrounds the side walls. The rim is both useful (it contains the food on the plate) and decorative. Usually the rim is set at a slight angle so that stray food tips back onto the plate. This angle also helps the form resist warping and sagging in the fire. The base of the plate is usually lower in the center than at the edge; this too keeps food on the plate and helps resist warping in the fire.

Utilitarian plates, platters, and serving pieces should heighten the pleasure of eating and should be easy to clean. Surfaces should be simple and smooth and finished with durable glazes.

Many ceramists make nonutilitarian pieces in which they "borrow" the plate form in order to make wall pieces. The ceramist usually uses such pieces as the background for clay or glaze imagery. These pieces serve as a bridge between the vessel form and the wall-piece form.

Plates and platters lend themselves particularly well to drape forming. The ceramist can use this method to produce an excellent plate form quickly and efficiently. Simple slab forming will work as well. Other methods are not so appropriate; a coil-built platter, for example, most likely will open and crack in the fire.

Vases

Vases can be made in many sizes and shapes and can be strongly utilitarian in form, although many ceramists today make nonutilitarian vases as well. Because its purpose, shape, and size can vary so much, the vase is a hard form to define. This lack of definition contributes to the popularity of vases because the form is not limiting in any way. The vessel form lends itself to utility, and most utilitarian potters employ several variations of the vessel form. Ornament works well with vessel forms, as do inventive handle and foot treatments. The form is especially popular among those inventive and imaginative ceramists who want even more freedom to create. All hand-forming methods are appropriate for vase forms.

The two most common types of utilitarian vases are flower containers and planters. Flower containers must be watertight and stable. They should not be so heavy as to be difficult to carry when filled with water. Planters should have a wide base and be very stable. Unlike flower containers, they should *not* be watertight because plants need good drainage. Leave the interior of a planter unglazed.

Hanging Vases

The hanging vase is an interesting variation of the vase form and many contemporary ceramists take advantage of the form and use it as a background for imagery. Ornament works well with hanging vessel forms, as do inventive handles and lugs. All hand-forming methods are appropriate for hanging vases.

Cups

Cups are utilitarian in origin, but many ceramists today make nonutilitarian cups as well. All aspects of the cup form are dictated by its function. The base must be wide enough to prevent tipping. Cup shapes are almost invariably cylindrical because square, oval, and triangular cups are difficult to drink from. The rim must be comfortable to drink from and the interior of the cup must be smooth and easy to clean. In nonutilitarian cups, aesthetics or artistic expression are more important than utility or comfort. Nonutilitarian cups can be complex in form and ornament.

The handle on the thin-walled utilitarian cup that we are used to using must not only be comfortable to hold but also must be durable in order to resist the rigors of use. Often the handle on nonutilitarian cups serve only to enhance the design; comfort and utility are not important.

The ceramist can use any hand-forming method to make cups. Drape-forming strategies are especially appropriate. They produce results that are highly effective and the method is quite efficient. Other forming methods, while less efficient, allow the creation of unusual or even surprising forms or textures. Many forming methods are appropriate for forming handles on hand-formed cups; braided or coil- and strap-formed handles are especially interesting (see page 146–7 for making handles).

Not all cups need saucers, but if you want to make saucers, drape-forming strategies are appropriate. Usually a saucer will have a shallow inset in which the cup is set.

Bowls

Bowls are open vessels usually wider than they are deep. Although ceramists developed the bowl form for serving food, now many make bowls for decorative purposes. Bowls often have a wide rim or handles for easy handling; in nonutilitarian pieces, they function as decorative elements.

Utilitarian bowl forms are usually round or oval (angular forms are not as useful for serving food). Though bowls may have straight sides, the walls of utilitarian bowls often flare outward. Here, as in the cup form, the bowl's foot must be wide enough to ensure stability. Utilitarian bowls should have thin or moderate wall thicknesses so that they can be handled easily. The nonutilitarian ceramist will not worry about shape or weight limitations and may concentrate instead on a complexity or ornament that would not appropriate on an utilitarian piece.

Drape-forming and coil or slab methods are all suitable for making hand-formed bowls.

Covered Jars and Casseroles

Covered forms are containers with lids that enclose the form. They can be very useful. In the past, ceramists made covered pieces strictly for utilitarian purposes and they remain a popular format for the utilitarian ceramist. Covered forms may be used to store food, such as tea, flour, or beans, or personal items such as souvenirs and jewelry.

The form is no longer considered appropriate only for utilitarian forms. Contemporary ceramists often make covered containers with little thought to their eventual use. The classic example is the large covered jar with a very small lid. It would be difficult to put anything inside the container. While based upon a utilitarian form, such a piece is purely decorative.

Casseroles are practical and useful for baking, warming, and serving food. They usually have thick walls to retain heat and handles or ridges to make handling easy. Almost all casseroles are utilitarian.

Pitchers, Bottles, and Teapots

Pouring vessels to hold and serve liquids have pouring spouts and usually handles as well. The spout may be merely an angled extension of the container wall or it may be an attached form. Handles on the top or sides of the piece help the user control the flow of liquid. Slab and drape methods are appropriate for creating these forms.

Pitchers are useful for holding and serving liquids. Most pitchers are taller than they are wide, often much taller. They must be lightweight because they will hold heavy liquids; a pitcher that weighs too much empty will not be comfortable to use when filled. The interiors of a pitcher must be smooth and easy to clean. Most pitchers fall, at least nominally, into the utilitarian category.

Bottles can be simply defined as narrow-necked containers. The long neck makes handling and pouring easy. This form was originally highly utilitarian; ceramic bottles were everyday objects that saw a great deal of use, just as we use glass bottles today. For ceramists the form has changed in character. No longer utilitarian, it has become decorative or nonutilitarian.

Teapots enjoy great prestige. Many ceramists consider teapots to be one of the most interesting and challenging vessel forms to create. Because many parts must meld together perfectly, teapots challenge the ceramist's skill. The teapot is a difficult but highly rewarding format.

Utilitarian teapots should be durable yet light and easy to hold and use. The lid should fit securely and the handle should be easy to hold. Finally, they should be easy to clean.

Nonutilitarian teapots are an interesting variation on the standard teapot form. The ceramist need not worry about practical matters and can freely explore exciting forms and images. The nonutilitarian teapot form is popular among contemporary ceramists: many teapots are highly experimental and imaginative and have overtones of fantasy and humor.

Openwork Vessels: Baskets and Colanders

To create clay baskets, the ceramist pierces the wall of the piece or uses openwork techniques. While the form can be decorative, there are definite utilitarian reasons for employing openwork techniques: clay baskets are excellent for containing foods such as fruits that need exposure to light and air. They are also useful if you wish to contain and display objects simultaneously, such as dried flowers.

Colanders are useful in the kitchen for cleaning and draining foods. The openings are small enough to allow liquids to drain. Colanders should be durable and easy to clean. While the form can be pleasing, colanders are usually utilitarian rather than decorative.

A HAND-FORMED TEAPOT—BARBARA FREY

In recent years Barbara Frey has been working on a group of hand-formed teapots. She uses simple shapes but ornaments them with varied surface imagery. While they look as if she intended them only to be decorative, Frey designed these pieces so that they function very well as teapots.

1. Frey rolls a fossil (called a crinoid) over a soft porcelain slab to create a band of texture (5-16A). To her the texture represents rock strata.
2. She thins the edge of the porcelain slab to prepare a lap join. Then she lifts the slab from the table and creates the body form of the teapot while the slab is still soft (Fig. 5-16B).
3. Using a rubber ball as a drape form (Fig. 5-16C), she forms the domed top of the teapot.
4. Frey lets the top and the base become leather hard and then attaches them (Fig. 5-16D).

Fig. 5-16A.

Fig. 5-16B.

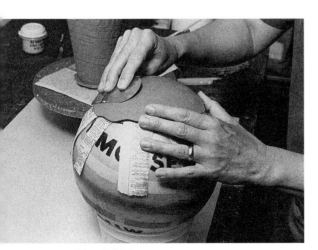

Fig. 5-16C.

Fig. 5-16D.

5. She applies a coat of colored slip to the top of the pot (Fig. 5-16E).
6. Here she has attached rock-like forms to the top and has carved into the colored slip (Fig. 5-16F). She now carves an opening in the top for the lid (Fig. 5-16G).

The finished teapot is shown in Figure 5-16H.

Guest Artist: Sandi Pierantozzi

Sandi Pierantozzi is concerned with the way utilitarian ideas can be expressed in clay. In this way she feels a connection with "honored ceramic traditions and forms."

Pierantozzi formed the teapot in Figure 5-17 using slab- and pinch-forming methods. She starts a piece by forming a slab with a rolling pin, then applies texture by pressing objects into the clay. She has used many textures on this piece and the patterns are complex. No area of the piece is without texture.

She then cuts the slab to the desired size and shape and wraps it around a cardboard tube. Next she forms the foot area by cutting and pinching. She lets this area become firm before proceeding. She then pushes the walls out and cuts darts into

Fig. 5-16E.

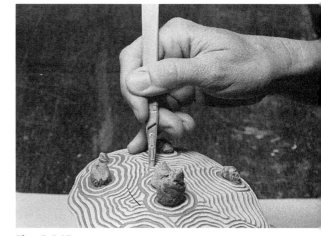

Fig. 5-16F.

Fig. 5-16G.

Fig. 5-16H.

Fig. 5-17. *Alligator Teapot,* **Sandi Pierantozzi, USA. Slab-formed, cone 04, terra-cotta clay body, burnished terra sigillata, 12 × 10 × 6 inches.** Photo by John Carlano.

the upper and lower edges of the form to create a full, round silhouette. This is difficult to do because she has to be careful not to destroy any of the elaborate textures on the surface of the piece.

The basic shape of this piece is cylindrical. Pierantozzi has modified it using her technique of cutting and pinching. The result is a piece with a block-like contour whose edges are softly curved. This shape is strong and appealing.

The feet in this piece are very interesting. Pierantozzi's method of cutting and pinching enables her to create a foot that seems to grow naturally out of the basic form. The feet raise the piece up and lighten and heighten the form. The arched curve that moves from foot to foot has great appeal.

The surface of the piece, which is quite strong, is an excellent example of the way in which the hand-builder can produce rich bas-relief surfaces. In stamped surfaces of this sort, the artist can create an imagery integrated with the form rather than applied over it. The simple monochromatic clay surface unifies the complex relief imagery.

PORTFOLIO OF SLAB-FORMED TEAPOTS

Fig. 5-18. *VooDoo Jazz,* **Deborah Groover, USA, slab-formed teapot, painted and layered with majolica glazes and mason stains, fired to cone 04 in an electric kiln.** This piece is highly painted and at first seems to be purely decorative, the form merely a vehicle for the complex, exciting imagery. A second look. however, reveals that Groover carefully designed the form to be strong and useful as well as aesthetically appealing. Note the broad base; this teapot will not tip over. The spout, while exciting in its seemingly arbitrary form, appears to be durable and useful and will pour well. Also note in the pot handle an appealingly relaxed look, but the handle will function well, as will the smaller lid handle. While the imagery is the prime factor in this piece, concepts of utility play an important part in its character.

Fig. 5-19. *Square Grey Teapot,* **John Neely, USA, slab-formed teapot and stand, white stoneware clay body, saggar fired to cone 11.** This four-sided teapot and stand is utilitarian in mood. It is well thought out for use: Neely has designed the spout for pouring and the lid handle for picking up. The piece is compact and the ceramist has paid attention to proportions and how one part relates to another. Photo by the artist.

Fig. 5-20. Lana Wilson, USA, slab-formed teapot, 6 × 9 × 3 inches. Wilson played with the teapot form to create a piece with strong ceremonial associations. She enlarged the lid handle to the point where it plays the major part in the formal scheme of the piece. She strongly textured all surfaces with stamped imagery. In this way she united the various parts into a convincing whole. Photo by Martin Trailer.

Fig. 5-21. Barbara Frey, USA, slab-formed teapot. The form of this piece is simple and understated. Frey uses the form itself to carry a complex surface imagery. Note the pattern of parallel lines carved into the body of the teapot, the contrasting oval insets carved into this field, and the painted imagery on the handle and spout. Photo by T. C. Eckersley.

Fig. 5-22. *Folded Teapot*, Virginia Cartwright, USA, slab-formed, colored clay bodies, 8 × 6 × 6 inches. Cartwright folded and tucked the clay slabs to create this piece. This technique allowed her to create an organic form from slabs. Using a colored clay inlay technique, which works well with slab forming, she built the form from slab strips. As a result, the striped inlaid pattern is complex and appealing. Photo by Phillip Starrett.

TECHNICAL ASPECTS OF VESSEL FORMING

In working clay, the technology has a strong influence on the form of the piece. The hand-forming ceramist must develop a group of techniques that work well for each vessel form.

Vases

There are few rules that you must follow if you wish to create nonutilitarian vases. The vase must be strong enough to withstand the fire and stable enough to be placed with assurance on a flat spot. If you are making utilitarian vases, you must be concerned about their use. Pieces that will be filled with water must be watertight. Pieces that will be used to hold flowers or plants must stand securely when filled. Vessels that will be handled often require a strong lip and a stable foot. Design the interior of utilitarian vessels so that the user can clean them easily. If they have handles, they must be useful and durable (see the section on handles on page 146–7).

Hanging Vases

Be sure to create strong lugs with good-sized holes for cord. Flatten the back of wall-hanging pieces.

Plates

Make the piece strong enough to resist warping and cracking. You can ensure this by making your plates and platters with strong lips and bases. If the plate or platter will be used to hold food, make sure that its base curves downward at the center. For sets of plates, you may want to use a template to create the outline of the platter. In this way you will be able to create a group of plates of the same size. Decorative platters require two holes in the foot ring for hanging.

Cups

Great care should be taken when creating the lip on a utilitarian cup. It should be strong and durable. It should be smooth and well-formed so that the cup is pleasant to drink from. The foot should be stable to ensure against tipping. Ideally, the interior of the cup should be seamless so that the piece is easily cleaned. Handles are also very important. Design them so that they will not break in use. Also make sure that the user can grasp them easily. If you are making a set of cups, use a template to control form variations.

Bowls

There are few rules that you must follow if you want to create nonutilitarian bowls. The bowls must be strong enough to withstand the fire and must be stable. If you ornament the sides of the bowl, the ornament should be placed toward the top of the bowl, where it is easy to see. Ornament placed under a heavy lip or near the foot of the bowl will be less visible. Utilitarian bowls must hold liquid without leaking and must have strong lips to ensure durability. The feet should be sturdy and wide set to ensure stability. In addition, the bowls must be easy to clean. If you are making a set of bowls, use a template to create the outline of the piece.

Casseroles

By definition, casseroles are utilitarian and must withstand a good deal of stress during use. Because they have large lids, be sure to dome the lids well to ensure durability. Be sure to make strong lips as well. Give the lid a deep and thick flange so that it will be strong and will not accidentally tip or fall off.

Covered Jars

Nonutilitarian covered jars need only a cover that works well and a stable foot. Utilitarian covered jars should have lids that fit well and are easy to place and remove. The lid should be secure and not fall out easily even when tipped. Give the lid a good-size flange to ensure this.

Teapots

The teapot format presents the artist with difficult aesthetic problems. A teapot is a collection of unrelated forms. It is the ceramist's job to bring these forms together. Nonutilitarian teapots (or teapots with limited utility) need only to be identifiable as teapots; this usually means that they have a spout and a lid.

Utilitarian teapots require careful design. Many exposed parts of a teapot face stress. Reinforce handles, lugs, lids, and spouts. The lid should have a deep flange so that it cannot fall out accidentally. The various parts must work together in terms of form. It is extremely difficult to make a utilitarian teapot that is both useful and aesthetically pleasing.

Openwork Vessels

The form of openwork vessels must be strong enough to withstand the rigors of the fire and of use. Because lips can be quite weak in openwork vessels, it is a good idea always to reinforce the lip.

VESSEL FORM DETAILS

The familiar saying "God is in the details" is often true in ceramics. The details mean a great deal to the character of the vessel. Specific parts of the vessel, such as lips, handles, and feet, will strongly influence the character of the finished piece.

THE FOOT

The foot that is placed on a piece strongly influences its look and structure. Feet raise the piece above the surface of the table and enhance its aesthetic qualities. They also enhance its durability and stability. Most vessel forms need additional clay at the foot. The addition of a coiled foot will enhance the stability of the piece and greatly strengthen it.

Think of the foot as the foundation of the piece. A stable foot on a vessel is as important as a stable foundation for a building. If the foot is placed at a point where it makes the form stable, it will also contribute to the structure of the vessel. The two, stability and structure, go hand in hand. A wide foot will be more stable than a narrow foot. It is a mistake to make small feet because the piece will be unstable and easy to knock over. When a piece contains liquid, its center of gravity is higher. If you place that foot badly, the liquid will spill and the piece may break.

Making feet using coils of clay takes little time and can enhance the piece.

1. Roll a coil of the same clay as the body of the piece.
2. Place the coil near the edge of the base of the piece. If the piece has a rounded bottom, place the foot at a point where it contributes to the stability of the piece while not breaking the line of the form.

3. Blend the foot into the form. This will improve the look of the piece and strengthen the bond between the foot and the form.

THE LIP

All vessels have lips. Many, however, seem to happen by default, while others are persuasive and look as though they were well thought out. Lips finish the piece, enhance its aesthetics, and make it more durable. On pieces without a handle, a lip is often where the piece will be picked up. For this purpose they should be easy to grasp and should be smooth and pleasant to hold.

A good lip will go well with the rest of the form and will be durable. In a utilitarian vessel, the durability of the lip is particularly important. We have all seen plates with chipped lips. A stronger, thicker lip makes the piece much more durable.

To make a lip stronger, you must often add more clay to the lip area. Add a coil of clay to the lip and blend it in. The lip should be rounded rather than sharp-edged. A sharp edge will chip.

Creating a Lip by Adding a Coil of Clay

1. Finish the piece.
2. Clean the lip.
3. Sponge the lip.
4. Apply slip.
5. Roll a coil of clay twice as thick as the vessel wall.
6. Paint one side of the coil with slip.
7. Join the coil of clay to the top of the lip.
8. Lightly paddle the lip to strengthen the join between it and the body of the piece.
9. Cover the lip with a wet sponge and draw it along the length of the lip. This will shape and finish the lip.

HANDLES

Handles must be wide enough to allow the user to hold it without discomfort or slipping. They must be burly enough to be durable after constant use. They also must support the weight of the vessel and of anything inside the vessel.

Handles also serve an important aesthetic purpose: they add interest to the form and give the piece character. Often the ceramist will make a simple form and use handles to dramatize the form. Many contemporary ceramists who make purely decorative pieces use handles for their aesthetic impact. Often they exaggerate their size and shape.

Handles made from straps or coils of clay work best with hand-built vessels. Ornament the handles if you wish. There are many methods for doing this. Using two or three twined thin coils, you can make a braided handle. With wet fingers or a sponge, you can draw ridges down the length of a strap or coil handle. Similarly, you can make an interesting handle by using the edge of a length of wood to stamp lines in a strap or coil of clay.

Making a Strap Handle

1. Roll a thick coil.
2. Flatten the coil. It should be as thick as the wall of the piece.
3. Place the edge of a stick along the length of the handle a few times. Make a group of parallel lines on the surface of the handle.

Fig. 5-23. Tim McHenry, USA, slab- and drape-formed bowl, 10 × 14½ inches. The basic form of this piece is taut and highly controlled. The mood is cool and precise. The mouth is simply and carefully formed, as is the gently curved base. The handles are the most dramatic elements in the form. They are strong in contour and precisely lined up. McHenry repeats them and lines them up in parallel to enhance their power. The holes at the top of the handles are carefully formed and elegantly placed. Photo by Laurie Smith.

4. Score each end of the handle. Paint the ends with slip.
5. Curve the handle and apply it to the piece.
6. Smooth the ends of the handle into the wall of the piece.

Making a Handle from a Thick Coil

1. Roll a thick coil.
2. Thin the coil *in the middle* of the handle. The handle should taper from thick to thin and back again.
3. Score each end of the handle and paint it with slip.
4. Attach the ends of the handle to the wall of the piece.
5. Smooth the join between handle and piece.

COVERS AND LIDS

Covers and lids protect the contents of the vessel or keep them warm or dry or clean. They are also important in defining the look of the form and often are used to make the form visually complete. Covers are usually dome-shaped. A flat cover is under great stress and is likely to crack in drying or in the fire. By adding a flange on the inside of the cover, you can be sure the cover will stay in place. You also need a convenient way to remove the cover. You can make a handle or shape the cover for easy handling or add a broad lip to the cover to act as a handle.

Making covers and lids is one of the most complex problems the hand-builder faces. All hand-forming methods encourage small variations and asymmetries and these make it difficult to create a lid that fits well. With a little work, however, you can make a fine lidded jar using hand-forming methods. Two methods will allow you to make covers that fit: you can cut into a closed form or you can use drape-forming methods. In the first method you create a completely closed form. You then cut through the wall of the piece to make a cover. The cover and the body of the piece will match because you make them from one form. If you use this method, add a flange to hold the cover in place during use.

Making a Lid from a Closed Form

You will need six fairly firm clay slabs, a sharp knife (a scalpel is a useful tool because it is sharp and very thin), a wareboard, a banding wheel, and two pieces of stiff fabric.

1. Build a rectangular form using four slabs (follow the directions on page 80).
2. Fillet the corners to strengthen them.
3. Close the form by adding top and bottom slabs.
4. Trim and clean the closed form.
5. Place the piece on a banding wheel and make a smooth circle on the top of the piece.
6. Make a cut along this line; this will be the basis for the cover.
7. Score and slip the underside of the cover near its edge.
8. Make a small cylinder to act as a collar. It should be three centimeters deep or more. Score and slip it and firmly attach it on the inside of the cover. This will secure the top so that it cannot fall out when the piece is tipped.
9. Finish the collar and the lid.

If use drape-forming methods, you can make special drape forms for the body of the piece and for the cover. While the process of making the drape form is exacting, you can use the form again and again, thus paying for your investment of time.

Making a Cover Template

1. Make a cylinder seven centimeters wide and four centimeters deep.
2. Clean and trim the *inside* of the cylinder.
3. Fire the cylinder to bisque.

Using the Cover Template to Make a Lid

1. Make a closed-form piece.
2. Place the cylinder against the top of the piece. Run a needle tool along the *inside* of the cylinder to cut out an opening.
3. Clean and smooth the opening.
4. Make a slab of clay to fit along the inside wall of the cylinder.
5. Press the slab against the inside wall of the cylinder. You have made another cylinder.
6. Let the wet clay cylinder become firm.
7. Remove the cylinder you have just made from the template. Try not to change its shape or size.
8. Cap the cylinder. Make sure there is an overlap of half a centimeter or more. This is the lid.
9. Fit the lid into the opening on the top of the pot. Make sure the fit is good. Finish the opening and lid.

CHAPTER SIX

CERAMIC SCULPTURE

AESTHETIC ASPECTS OF CERAMIC SCULPTURE

Hand forming has always been the primary method for creating ceramic sculpture. The most useful hand-building methods for sculpture are slab forming, coil forming, and solid forming.

Sculptures are three-dimensional art objects. The ceramist defines a ceramic piece as a sculpture if it is three-dimensional but is not in the vessel or wall-piece format. This simple definition has worked well for us in the past. While many definitions can be limiting, this one liberates in that it places few restraints on the artist's creativity. As a result, many contemporary ceramists feel that ceramic sculpture is the least constrained of all the ceramic formats. Whether or not this is true, the power of this belief is such that many ceramists feel freer to experiment in ceramic sculpture than in any other ceramic idiom. The explosion of creativity in this area has been of great value to the field of ceramics.

Clay is an excellent medium for creating sculpture. Ceramic sculpture offers many aesthetic opportunities not only for appealing and exciting forms but also for rich surface treatments. Ceramic sculpture has its own identity; it has its own clearly defined sense of form and its unique group of surface finishes. To exploit these elements, ceramic sculpture requires its own building and finishing processes. The characteristics are the very attributes that give ceramic sculpture its unique character.

Compared to other materials used for sculpture, clay is easy to form. As a result, creating ceramic sculpture is not as time-consuming as making other types of sculpture. In addition, the medium encourages forms that are full and volumetric. Ceramic sculptors naturally work from the inside out, pushing the clay wall outward from the inside. This strategy promotes these appealing full forms. It also encourages the implementation of additional strategies. The ceramist creates a group of forms and then combines those forms to construct the piece.

As well as being easy to form, clay lends itself readily to relief imagery. The process is direct and easy. During the construction process the ceramist can either add clay elements to the surface or cut or stamp into the surface of the piece. This relief imagery enriches the surface and adds to the complexity of the image.

The ceramic sculptor can finish the piece in a variety of rich surfaces. The surface can be finished with thick glass-like glazes or with the drier, more revealing surfaces of stains and engobes. The ceramist can use these surfaces as an overall texture that becomes a patina on the surface of the piece. The ceramist can also use surfaces to color individual areas of the piece in a painterly manner.

Contemporary ceramic sculptors use clay to create a great variety of imagery. Pieces can range in character from the precise and elegant to the direct, natural, and organic and from realistic to abstract. The subjects also can vary a great deal. Sculptors have always made human and animal figures and many contemporary ceramists continue to work in this tradition, often in nontraditional ways. Others use images that traditionally were not considered sculptural. These include landscapes, mechanical objects, architectural forms, and abstract formal compositions.

Ceramic sculpture has disadvantages as well: Clay is a dense, heavy material. Large ceramic sculptures thus can be extremely heavy Clay is also brittle, so ceramic sculpture is not as durable as other types of sculpture. Although it is superb for creating volumetric forms, clay has form limitations and is not suitable for creating many other form types, such as thin, attenuated shapes. These shapes are useful for the sculptor and ceramists often lament that they cannot accomplish them in sculptural pieces. Finally, there is a perception problem: many people think marble or bronze is more appropriate than clay for sculpture. While this perception is no longer as prevalent as it once was, there are still many who continue to think of clay as an inappropriate medium for sculpture.

Contemporary ceramists have become adept at creating sculpture in which they stress the advantages of the medium and minimize the disadvantages. Ceramic sculpture has come to dominate the area of small-scale work. Typically this work is slab formed and finished with brilliantly colored, low-fired glazes. The heavy weight of large ceramic pieces and forming and firing problems have tended to limit the popularity of larger ceramic sculpture. In recent years, however, contemporary ceramists have created some wonderful large-scale pieces.

TECHNICAL ASPECTS OF CERAMIC SCULPTURE

Like other kinds of sculpture, ceramic sculpture begins with an aesthetic idea that the artist will develop in order to define the central character of the piece. The material, however, also plays a big part in defining the character of the work. Thus the medium has a great influence on the ceramic sculptor's choices in terms of the clay body, the size, and the formal and spatial imagery of a piece.

The choice of a clay body is an important one for the ceramic sculptor. The sculptor who makes small pieces will not have to worry so much about what kind of clay body to choose. Even such intractable clay bodies as porcelain are appropriate for small sculptural pieces. However, the sculptor who wishes to make mid-sized and large pieces must select a clay body appropriate for the special demands of large work. Most sculpture clay bodies contain coarse clay with grog additions. They are durable and they shrink very little. This is important because it is shrinkage that causes warping and cracking. These clay bodies enable the sculptor to work in the large scale.

Scale is an important matter to the ceramic sculptor. Small and medium-sized pieces are easy to make and fire, while large pieces are not only difficult to make but are prone to warping and cracking in the fire. Furthermore, most ceramic sculptors must work with kilns that are three cubic meters or less, which places a strong size limit on their work. The weight and bulk of large pieces make them difficult to place and some might be appropriate only for installation in public spaces. Therefore, the tradition of small-scale ceramic sculpture has remained vital to the ceramist.

There is a strong connection between scale and form in ceramic sculpture. The elegant forms created by ceramists working with small sculpture are not durable enough for larger work. In the mid-size and large scale, thin, elongated, unsupported forms will be prone to breakage. The ceramist must avoid weak forms and instead choose forms that ensure durability, such as compact forms, which are strong and durable. As a result, ceramic sculptors deal with form differently than sculptors in other media. For example, we often see in other sculptural media a thin shape serving as a bridge between two massive forms. We see airy pieces with eloquent spaces. Mid-size and large pieces with forms of this sort are subject to stress and may sag or crack in the fire. If these pieces did survive the fire, they would be very fragile and likely would break afterward.

Many ceramists do work with large-scale pieces that require a large-scale presentation. With experience, they have developed and perfected the techniques they need to deal with the creation, drying, and firing of large pieces. Now we often see ceramic sculpture that is more than a meter in size.

Ceramic sculptors have created small, mid-size, and large-scale pieces in the past. The genres are different enough that each has developed its own tradition. These distinctions continue to this day. We can divide ceramic sculpture into three size classifications: table sculpture (up to ten inches), mid-size (eleven to thirty inches), and large (more than thirty inches). Different clay bodies and forms are appropriate for each size.

SMALL-SCALE SCULPTURE (TABLE SCULPTURE)

In the small scale, clay lends itself to forms that would be impractical in larger work. Sculptors making small pieces can use thin, elegant forms with an ease and freedom unknown to those who make larger work. Because the sculptor of small pieces can use forms unavailable to other ceramic sculptors, table sculpture has its own repertoire of forms and its own unique character. The sculptor can use delicate and elegant clay bodies such as porcelain for work in this scale, whereas these would not be appropriate for work on a larger scale. In the past many ceramists used porcelain to make small sculpture. These pieces were part of a great tradition of elegant table sculpture. Historical representatives of this group include Te Hua figures from southeastern China, Edo figures from Japan, and Meissen figurines from Germany. A good deal of the work from contemporary ceramists is low-fire, brightly colored, and has a highly developed surface imagery. Much of this work is sculptural and small in scale.

MID-SIZE SCULPTURE

We do not need to associate mid-size sculptural pieces with reserved, compact forms. With mid-size pieces the sculptor has a good deal of freedom and can use extended forms. In the past, ceramic sculptors made mid-size pieces in China during the Tang dynasty, in Renaissance Italy, and in the eighteenth century in Dresden, Germany. Today a good deal of work is done in this size. Their makers use low-fire bodies to make these pieces and then finish them with complex surfaces. Many sculpture pieces illustrated in this book fall in the mid-size category.

LARGE-SCALE SCULPTURE

The problems of size in ceramic sculpture are compounded in large pieces. The sculptor must design them with an understanding of the character of clay to give them some promise of survival in the fire and permanence afterward. Large sculptural pieces are associated with massive, compact forms. In the past, large-scale work was not common. However, ceramists made interesting pieces in the large size in China during the Han dynasty, in eighteenth-century Japan, and in nineteenth-century France. Large-scale sculpture has many proponents today. The late Robert Arneson, for example, produced a strong group of large ceramic sculptures (see Fig. 6-33).

Sculptors have been grappling with problems of large-scale ceramic sculpture for a long time. If you want to deal with these problems, you will have to experiment and lose some pieces in the fire until you come up with forms and work strategies that are successful. You will probably have to modify your forms to acknowledge the character of the medium. You should build your pieces carefully and modify your building methods. Your pieces will have to be segmented or buttressed and you will need to pay great attention to the way you dry them. Finally, you will need to modify your firing methods.

The proof that all of this can be done is illustrated here. Notice how the artists in this chapter have made the most of the ceramic medium. Doug Baldwin builds his pieces from tiny modules to create small, complete worlds. Mary Barringer makes her mysterious, oblique objects using coil-forming techniques. Aurore Chabot uses angular forms and rich inlay surfaces. Many of these pieces are stacked forms, including the coil pieces of Ric Hirsch (Fig. 6-1). Ann Roberts makes her nearly life-size figural sculptures using stacking modules; Nancy Jurs makes her large pieces in segments (Fig. 6-2). Angelica Pozo combines tile and volumetric forms. We see pieces from Mitch Messina in which he combines clay with wood and metal to make large-scale work. Virginia Scotchie uses groups of geometric forms to cover large spaces. Graham Marks builds his pieces coil by coil until he has created a massive and complex form.

BRACED FORMS

Bracing, which strengthens the piece and helps it to resist warping and cracking, is especially useful for the ceramic sculptor. Many ceramic sculptors construct a web-work of braces hidden inside the piece. Braced pieces will withstand the rigors of the fire far better than unbraced work. Bracing may take a number of forms, including a series of horizontal braces or box- or honeycomb-shaped interior structures.

The ceramist may also create a double-walled piece and place bracing structures between the walls. In this way the ceramist can construct what is in effect a thick wall. This kind of wall will be as strong or stronger than a solid wall of the same thickness, but it will be much lighter in weight.

The ceramist will sometimes want to reveal the bracing structures and use them as part of the imagery of the piece. Since a complex bracing structure can have great aesthetic appeal, incorporating that structure can be a useful strategy.

Fig. 6-1. *Pedestal Bowl with Weapon Artifact #5*, Richard Hirsch, USA, coiled and slab-formed sculpture, copper-bronze raku glaze, sandblasted, 64 × 36 inches. This piece with its strong silhouette and rich surface gains monumentality and impact from its scale.

Fig. 6-2. *Goddess,* **Nancy Jurs, USA, large segmented sculptural form, 9 feet high.** Jurs made this large piece in sections and then assembled it. Note the strong, irregular silhouette with its references to a rocky cliff. Photo by John Kage.

METAL ARMATURES—JACQUIE GERMANOW

In college Jacquie Germanow studied sculpture and ceramics and learned to work in clay, metal, cement, and stone. Clay is the primary medium for her current work and she uses metal armatures to support her pieces.

To create her pieces, Germanow first creates the ceramic forms. She then constructs an armature from metal rods. The ceramic forms slip over the armature. When using a steel armature, she spray-paints it to seal it from rusting. This step is not necessary for copper, brass, or aluminum. For larger pieces, however, she uses steel because she values its great strength. She designs the armature so that part of it extends below the ceramic forms. She sets this part into a heavy anhydrous cement (*ciment fondu*) base. The weight of the base stabilizes the piece.

Using an armature allows Germanow to create thin, gravity-defying forms, forms she could not use with clay alone (Fig. 6-3).

SCULPTURE FORMING

Ceramic sculpture and hand forming are closely tied together. Most ceramic sculptors use hand-forming methods. All of the hand-forming methods are appropriate for the creation of sculptural work. The nature of the ceramist's choice is very im-

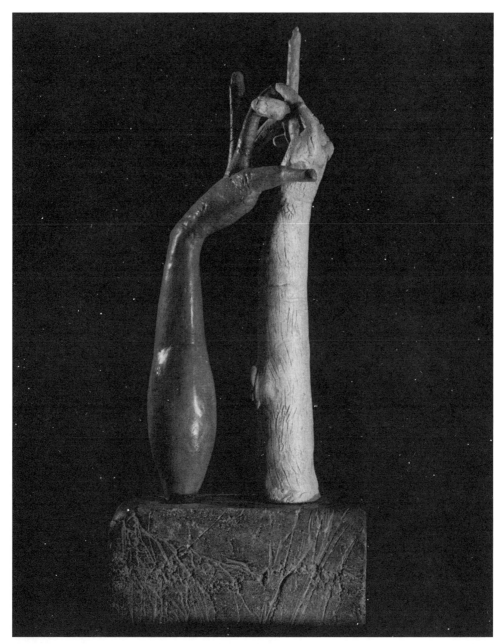

Fig. 6-3. *Ancient Voice*, Jacqui Germanow, USA, ceramic and stone elements and steel inner supports, 38 × 26 × 7 inches. By using a steel armature to help support these pieces, the artist can use extended forms. These forms could not support their own weight if they were only in clay. Through these forms Germanow captures the sinewy character of the human body in her work. Photo by Walter Chase.

portant. Each method puts its own mark on the character of the piece and as such is an important source of variety in the character of ceramic sculpture.

The next section illustrates a portfolio of sculptural work made by many different forming methods: pinch forming, coil forming, slab forming, drape forming, solid forming, mixed forming strategies, and mixed-media techniques.

PINCH-FORMED SCULPTURE

The earliest ceramic sculpture was pinch formed and ceramists still find pinch forming useful today. Pinch forming is generally used for small sculptural pieces. You can use it to create either solid or hollow forms. We associate pinch-formed pieces with rough, highly textured surfaces. These highly worked surfaces can express a sense of energy, a feeling for the clay, and a strong personal character.

Ceramic sculptors often combine pinch forming with other forming methods, using it as a bridge between one form and another (perhaps one slab-built form and another, for example) or to create additions to the piece.

In Figure 6-4, the Bulgarian ceramist Ruska Valkova used slab-built forms to serve as a background for a complex pinch-formed imagery.

COIL-FORMED SCULPTURE

Coil forming is perhaps the premier method for producing ceramic sculpture. It is especially appropriate for constructing large pieces and pieces with complex forms. Since even the largest pieces can be built from small, easily handled coils, the method lends itself to the creation of large-scale ceramic sculpture. Coil-formed sculptures can be quite complex and rich in spatial variation because coil forming has so few form limitations.

Many pieces in the Portfolio of Coil-Formed Pieces are large. Their makers adopted the coil method in part to be able to work in the large scale. Virginia Scotchie's piece illustrated in this section is an example (Fig. 6-5). Ric Hirsch's coil- and slab-formed pieces (Figs. 6-1 and 6-37) are also fine examples of this type of work.

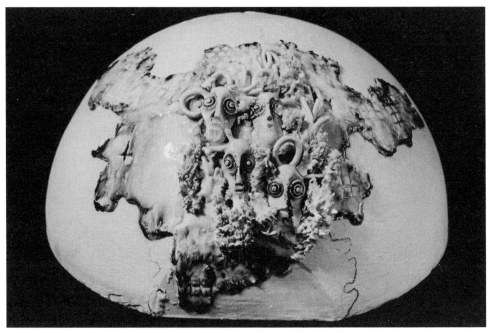

Fig. 6-4. *World,* **Ruska Valkova, Bulgaria, sculptural form with figural elements, porcelain, 30 × 30 × 14 centimeters.** When porcelain was first developed in Europe in the early 1700s, many artists began to make porcelain sculpture for table placement. This work is known for its inventiveness, energy, and vitality. The tradition remains strong in Europe today. Valkova's piece is very much in that tradition. The artist emphasized the whiteness and special character of the porcelain clay body. The figural elements in the piece were created with a precision and delicacy we associate with porcelain.

Other pieces illustrated here have complex, irregular shapes, such as Mary Barringer's (Fig. 6-10. Coil-forming methods are particularly appropriate for shapes of this type. In some of these pieces the ceramist exploited the textural possibilities of the coil process. This is particularly true of the work of Martha Holt (Fig. 6-6). In other cases, such as the work of Eva Kwong (Fig. 6-9), the surface is quite smooth. Here the form and the painted surface are the important issues for the artist.

HAND-FORMING A LARGE-SCALE CERAMIC SCULPTURE—VIRGINIA SCOTCHIE

Virginia Scotchie makes large-scale sculptures using geometric forms. She relieves the starkness of the imagery by working with softly textured surfaces. Her surfaces greatly enhance and emphasize the character of the clay. In this photo series, Scotchie makes a sphere.

1. Scotchie begins by pressing a slab of clay into a bisque-fired form (Fig. 6-5A).
2. She rolls a coil of clay and flattens it with a mallet until it is an inch and a half thick (Fig. 6-5B).
3. She adds this coil to the base of the piece (Fig. 6-5C). To ensure a strong join, she scores the edges and applies slip on both surfaces.

Fig. 6-5A.

Fig. 6-5B.

Fig. 6-5C.

Fig. 6-5D.

Fig. 6-5E.

Fig. 6-5F.

Fig. 6-5G.

Fig. 6-5H.

4. She continues to add the strip coils (Fig. 6-5D).
5. She paddles the form periodically to control the contour and strengthen the piece (Fig. 6-5E).
6. She beings moving the contour inward at this point to create the top part of the sphere (Fig. 6-5F). She paddles on the outside of the wall while supporting it with her left hand on the inside (Fig. 6-5G).
7. She turns the piece on a revolving stand to facilitate the building and paddling processes (Fig. 6-5H).

Scotchie's finished spheres with their various surface textures are shown in Figures 6-5I and J.

Fig. 6-5I.

Fig. 6-5J.

Guest Artist: Martha Holt

Martha Holt has worked with coil-forming methods to make highly stylized tree forms for a number of years (Fig. 6-6). Of her coiling methods, Holt writes:

> *Coiling is throwing in slow motion. I use the oriental coil technique. I use long thick coils. I place the front part of the coil on the lip of the form and attach it to the form by using my left thumb to move some clay from the coil to the base. Meanwhile my right hand holds and guides the coil around the top of the piece. I do not need armatures but control drying and work with the clay when it is at an appropriate drying stage. The base of the piece is always stiffer than the part I am working on. When the form is complete, I cover it in plastic for a week*

This method allows Holt to work quickly and fluently. Forming, coil-welding, and smoothing are done simultaneously.

Although the base is heavy, the tall, thin trunk-like form and the outspread element at the top create a graceful, airy effect. The spiral ramp-like form on the trunk gives the piece energy and makes the form complex and more interesting. The open foot and the openings in the top piece lighten the form and give it more lift. As a consequence of the building process, the surface has a highly textured and rugged quality, reminiscent of the bark of a tree. In this piece, Holt has expressed her strong feelings for nature.

Guest Artist: William Stewart

William Stewart's pieces in Figures 6-7 and 6-8 are a departure for the artist. Usually he works with large coil-formed figural sculptures. He obviously enjoys making these pieces a great deal.

He says of these ebullient and striking pieces:

> *Last November I decided to purchase a lamp for a Christmas gift. What I assumed would be a simple task turned into an afternoon of frustration. I discovered quickly that there are thousands of generic lamps out there, devoid of personality, poorly designed, and incredibly expensive. Most craft shops featured thrown ceramic forms with shades, but these were only slightly better than the mass-produced lamps I found in the mall stores. With this frustration as an incentive, I decided to break away from my usual studio work and try to produce some tables and lamps that would be unique, humorous, well designed, and affordable. So far, they have been very well received.*

Fig. 6-7. William Stewart, USA, ceramic table, earthenware, coil formed, low-fire.

Fig. 6-6. *Woman Tree with Vine,* Martha Holt, USA, coil formed, low-fire. Photo by Mark Perrott.

Fig. 6-8. William Stewart, USA, ceramic lamp, earthenware, coil formed, low-fire.

PORTFOLIO OF COIL-FORMED PIECES

Fig. 6-9. *From Blue to Blue,* Eva Kwong, USA, coil-formed sculpture, stoneware, painted slips, salt glazed, 34 × 30 × 14 inches. This piece is symmetrical, which is unusual in sculpture. It is composed of a base and two identical projections. Furthermore, the height of the base is similar to the height of the projections. Kwong varies the symmetry by covering one of the elements in a dark glaze and the other in a light glaze with dark rings. She has taken a difficult problem (symmetry) and used it to create an unusual piece. Photo by Kevin Olds.

Fig. 6-10. Mary Barringer, USA, coil- and pinch-formed sculptural form, stoneware, 7½ × 16 × 12 inches. Although Barringer's former work was solely in the vessel form, in recent years she has been developing a group of sculptural pieces. This piece is reminiscent of her previous work in its scale and volumetric quality. In this new work, the imagery takes on a mysterious quality as we try to guess the origins of this complex and poetic form. Photo by Wayne Fleming.

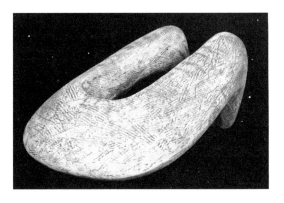

Fig. 6-11. *Hydnocerus Series IV–#1,* Paul Sherman, USA, coil-formed sculptural form, earthenware, 4 feet × 24 inches. Photo by T. C. Eckersley. In this large, double-walled piece, the artist used the symmetric vessel-like form to create a sculptural identity. Note the complex, rich surfaces. Sherman created the surfaces by combining carved clay with slips, glazes, and aggregate containing gritty slips. He says of the structure: "Working with the double-walled structure gives me more surfaces to texture while giving the viewer a more involving visual experience."

Figs. 6-12 and 6-13. Graham Marks, USA, sculptural form, earthenware, coil formed, low fire. These two pieces are on the border between vessel and sculpture forms. The forms, monumental and compact, sit in place in a most natural way, slightly tipped because of their conical form. Marks used sandblasting to create these rich and highly textured surfaces. Although they are contemporary, their surfaces seem to bear witness to processes of erosion and abrasion that have taken place over a long time. Photo courtesy Habitat/Shaw Gallery.

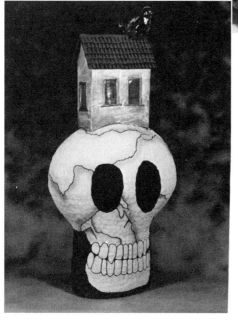

Fig. 6-14. *House with Bird*, Rimas VisGirda, USA, coil-, slab-, and pinch-formed sculpture, 40 × 24 × 13 inches. VisGirda uses the different forming methods in this piece to create a strongly contrasting imagery. He formed the skull imagery with coils, the house with slabs, and the bird form with pinch techniques. The vessel form at the base is an elegant and classical form, the house form is blocky and awkward, and the bird is stylized and child-like. The piece is covered with VisGirda's foreboding and threatening painted imagery.

SLAB-FORMED SCULPTURE

Many ceramic sculptures use slab construction methods either alone or with another method such as coil or pinch forming. Slab construction allows for the quick construction of complex and large forms. It also allows the ceramist to create a great variety of both open and closed forms. Many ceramists enjoy exploiting the slab and join pattern of the slab-forming technique.

In this section on slab-formed sculpture, you will see pieces that are open and planar, such as the work by Ann Tubbs (page 170). You will also see many pieces in which the artist has used slabs to create a volumetric form—for example, the sculptures by Jeff Irwin and Nina Höle. You will see highly abstract forms by Aurore Chabot and Liliana Malta as well as pieces with recognizable imagery, such as those by Roberta Laidman and Sally Michener. We even see an example of functional sculpture in the William Parry's ceramic table, which is a highly abstract treatment of a common form.

CREATING A SLAB-FORMED SCULPTURE—AURORE CHABOT

Aurore Chabot creates ceramic sculptures with complex inlaid clay imagery. She worked on this piece at the Archie Bray Foundation in Helena, Montana, in the summer of 1993.

1. Chabot begins the piece by breaking up a slab of colored clay. She gathers colored clay fragments along with some fossil-shaped clay forms and "buries" them in the surface of a slab made from a plastic clay containing grog and sawdust. She calls this process "reverse inlay." At this point, the fragments are invisible. Chabot derived the shape from an eclectic group of sources, including window shapes, dividing amoebas, and Siamese twins.
2. The double-walled construction begins (Fig. 6-15A). Chabot builds up a wall a few inches at a time in order to control the form. Each time she leaves the piece to stiffen in the air, she keeps the exposed layer (to which more layers will be added) moist by wetting it with slip and covering it with a thin strip of plastic. Chabot repeats this process until she achieves the desired height. As the piece grows in height, Chabot uses her fingers and wooden, metal, and rubber ribs to define the edges of the sculpture. The inside form begins to develop into a shape different from the outside form (Fig. 6-15B).
3. Chabot has completed the construction of the piece and it is now in a leather-hard state. She carves the outside surface of the piece with a variety of carving and trimming tools. She has first carved a spiral form and is now partially covering that image. At the end, only vestiges of the spiral will remain (Fig. 6-15C).
4. Chabot scores and textures the surface of the piece to create a bark-like texture that contrasts with the smoother interior of the piece. Contrasts of surface and color are important to the final appearance of this sculpture (Fig. 6-15D).
5. Chabot places the sculpture on its side on a piece of foam rubber to check the underside and determine if any more carving or smoothing needs to be done inside. One can now see the hidden, reverse inlaid layer. The piece will ultimately be displayed in a position that reveals the inlay (Fig. 6-15E).

Fig. 6-15A.

Fig. 6-15B.

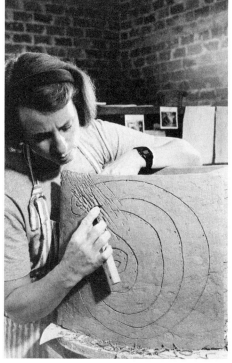

Fig. 6-15C.

Fig. 6-15D.

6. Before she bisque-fires the piece, Chabot paints layers of black and yellow iron oxide and terra-sigillata slips on the outside to enhance the rough texture. After the bisque firing, she paints various colored underglazes on the inside and outside surfaces. She fires the piece to cone 06–04. She paints black copper oxide stain on and sponges it off to add depth to the surface (Fig. 6-15F).

7. A third firing at cone 06–04 completes the piece. The inlaid layer is now visible.

Fig. 6-15E.

Fig. 6-15F.

PORTFOLIO OF SCULPTURAL, SLAB-FORMED, AND MIXED-MEDIA PIECES

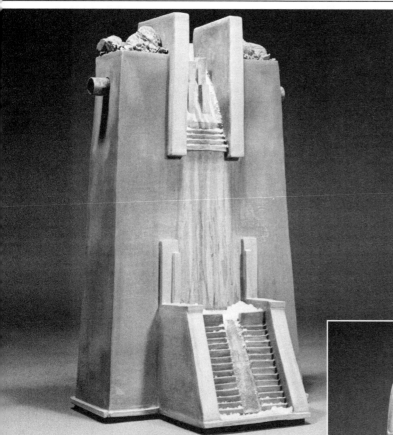

Fig. 6-16. *Aqueduct,* **Joanne Hayakawa, USA, sculptural form, terracotta, 22 × 16 × 31 inches.** This piece is strongly architectural in both its imagery and mood. The slabs are smooth and flat and the edges are crisp. The imagery is monumental with references to Egyptian and Mayan ceremonial and tomb structures. The step forms running in a band up the front contrast with the broad, flat areas and dominate the piece. The piece feels like a maquette for a life-size brick structure.

Fig. 6-17. William Parry, USA, ceramic table form. This piece is on the frontier between sculpture and furniture. It is highly sculptural and yet functions well as a table. Ceramic furniture is strong and durable, but its main advantage is that it offers the artist a wide choice of forms and surfaces. Since few artists have worked with ceramic furniture, we do not have many set ideas of what it ought to look like. This area of exploration is free and open. Parry's piece has simple, emphatic forms and rich, contrasting textures. Note the strong handling of the transition areas between the legs and the top of the table. Photo by Richard Zakin.

Fig. 6-18. *Mutable Passage,* **Joanne Hayakawa, USA, sculptural form, terracotta with copper and gold luster, gold leaf, and cement, 27 × 14 × 30 inches.** In this piece Hayakawa contrasted a broad, flat volumetric element with a linear structure. The linear elements have a strong scaffold-like identity and are closely tied to the volumetric form. The base is heavy and plinth-like with a rocky texture. It is pierced by three symmetric openings that have the look of drainage pipes.

Fig. 6-19. *Warriors*, Jeff Irwin, USA, slab-formed sculpture, earthenware, with vitreous engobes, 23 × 29 × 6 inches. Irwin plays with imagery in this piece. The form suggests a torso. The central image on this torso-like form is a careful drawing of a fragmented classical Greek pot. A landscape is drawn over the form and its space is deep and three-dimensional. The drawn sgraffito imagery is carefully executed and highly developed. This piece is hard to define. It is a sculpture, but its sculptural elements are not highly defined; it is a highly defined sgraffito drawing placed on a sculptural form. The subject is a pot in a landscape. Photo by the artist.

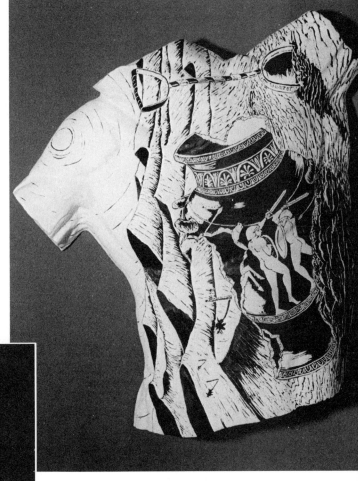

Fig. 6-20. *Rox*, Nancy Jurs, USA, large segmented sculptural form, 47 inches high. Jurs often works in the large scale because she enjoys the freedom and impact that large work offers. She uses a paddle to create strong textures on the surface of the raw clay. These marks give the piece a rock-like quality. In this piece Jurs combined a softly curved and folded top element with a triangular bottom section and a square plinth. Photo by Marty Czamanske.

Fig. 6-21. Mary Roettger, USA, ceramic sculpture, 9 × 36 × 20 inches. Roettger uses repetitive elements to create her forms and simple, natural shapes to offset these complex images. Note the way she enlivened these slabs by ruffling them.

Fig. 6-22. *Beverly*, Roberta Laidman, USA, animal figure, 20½ × 12½ × 22 inches. Laidman uses hand-building techniques to create strongly volumetric animal figures. Note the highly textured, unglazed surfaces. Laidman has tackled a difficult problem: in a culture where animals are often pictured as "cute," it is difficult to make pieces that are lively and unsentimental. Laidman clearly wants to present an image that mirrors the vitality of her subjects. Photo by Philip Cohen.

Fig. 6-23. *Boxed Snake*, Elyse Saperstein, USA, figural sculpture, earthenware, slab- and solid-formed, with glazes, slips, and terra sigillata, 30 × 10½ × 6½ inches. Some of the earliest ceramic pieces are among the most powerful and evocative. Saperstein has seen these pieces and fallen under their power. In this piece, she placed one figure on top of the other to create a kind of totemic tower. The figures, mostly of animals, are stiff, schematic, and dramatic in pose. They do not relate to each other; each one is a symbol-laden form unto itself. The animals are powerful and mysterious symbols. Photo by John Carlano.

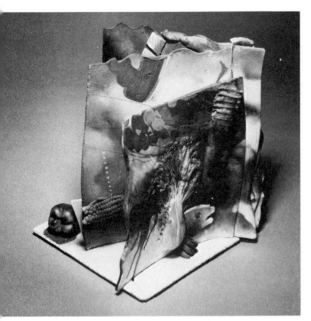

Fig. 6-24. *Garden Notebook,* **Ann Tubbs, USA, mixed-media sculpture, 18 inches high.** Tubbs has created a three-dimensional piece that is composed mostly of flat slab forms rather than volumetric forms. These slabs take the form of juxtaposed panels. The panels suggest the pages of a book. The artist placed imagery on the pages and plays with it by combining two- and three-dimensional images. She moves from one to the other in a restless manner. Each slab or page was fired separately in a smoke fire and assembled after firing. Photo by Stephen Johnston.

Fig. 6-25. *Archaic Trophy,* **Liliana Malta, Italy, sculptural form, reduction fired to 1150 °C, 90 centimeters high.** The artist used thick, flat slabs to create this piece. She uses opposing masses and forms, mostly diagonals and verticals. The joins are emphasized and kept quite sharp, which gives the impression of strength and conflicting energy. Angular forms predominate, but these are softened by some of the curved edges. The surface is a coarse-grained highly grogged clay. Photo by Massimiliano Ruta.

Fig. 6-26. *Power,* **Nina Höle, Denmark, sculptural form, raku, 30 × 22 × 8 centimeters.** In this piece Höle has created a dense, heavy image of a house form. She lightened the image by placing elements on the upper part of the structure. The surface is a highly grogged clay. Photo by Kristian Krogh.

Fig. 6-27. *Autumn,* **Yih-Wen Kuo, USA, sculptural form, press formed, 14 × 14 × 6 inches.** This sculpture has many aspects of a vessel in that it is hollow and volumetric. However, the artist has not pierced it at the top as he would if he were making a vessel. Photo by Barry Stark.

In Figures 6-28 and 6-29 Cimatti uses a strategy that is more common in vessel making: he forms a hollow volume from two shaped slabs. There are no added or subtracted elements. The sculptural impact of these pieces is derived from simple, strong volumes and exciting and well-thought-out silhouettes. Their position on the frontier between the vessel and sculptural formats is strengthened by the rich and inventive surface imagery.

Fig. 6-28. *Scoglio*, Giovanni Cimatti, Italy, slab-formed sculptural piece, 90 × 35 × 13 centimeters.

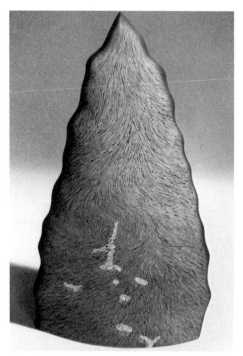

Fig. 6-29. *Scoglio*, Giovanni Cimatti, Italy, slab-formed sculptural piece, 85 × 40 × 12 centimeters.

SEGMENTED AND ASSEMBLED SCULPTURE

Many ceramic sculptors build their pieces using construction techniques that rely on segmented forms. The simplest modular procedures are some of the best: the sculptor places elements next to each other or stacks one element on top of the other. The segmented pieces may merely rest on or by each other or the sculptor may fashion connecting elements to bind one segment to another. Ned Krouse (Fig. 6-30) and William Parry (Fig. 6-31) have both made highly successful segmented work.

Segmented pieces are easy to work with and are much less prone to cracking during building, drying, and firing than large monolithic work. Each individual segment is light and easy to handle. You can make each piece as a separate segment and fire it separately. With this method it is easy to make pieces that are larger than the kiln. When the segments are complete and fired, you can assemble them at the site. In this section I include a series of illustrations of the Canadian sculptor Ann Roberts building a segmented piece.

Fig. 6-30. *Reconstructed Form,* **Ned Krouse, USA, earthenware, 16 × 10 × 10 inches.** This slab-formed piece is compact and volumetric. It is made from slab elements, all of about the same size. The piece is highly angular and the edges where each slab is joined are strongly emphasized. The result is a repetitive and strongly rhythmic image. At its best, the repetition of elements can produce powerful imagery. Photo by the artist.

Fig. 6-31. William Parry, USA, segmented, solid-formed sculpture. This piece mirrors Parry's love for the energy and rhythms of nature. Although his forms do not necessarily mirror the shape of rocks, they have a strong rock-like character. Note that each segment is made up of smaller segments with a spiral form serving as an axis. This is a garden piece meant to be placed outdoors. Its segmented and solid forms make it particularly well suited to withstand the rigors of the climate of Upstate New York. Photo by Richard Zakin.

Ceramists also assemble a large sculpture from smaller parts because they find the imagery exciting, or they might assemble related forms to create a piece with a strongly repetitive character. A good example of this approach is the work of Doug Baldwin (see Fig. 6-34), who uses repeated imagery to create a kind of miniature world.

A SEGMENTED SCULPTURE—ANN ROBERTS

Ann Roberts constructs her large clay sculptures as hollow forms made of coils, strips, or slabs. She sometimes emphasizes the joins and incorporates them into the imagery. At other times she eliminates the joins to create the illusion of volumes that move through, over, or against one another. Notice the ring of toothpicks set into the wall of the piece in a narrow band (Fig. 6-32A). Roberts uses these to indicate the place where she will segment the piece. She uses toothpicks because they allow her more opportunity to work the surface freely. She places a thick coil of clay on the inside wall of the piece where she will make the segment cut. This coil will strengthen the wall and discourage warping.

Fig. 6-32A.

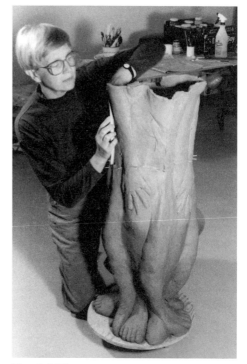

Fig. 6-32B.

Fig. 6-32C.

With her right hand on the outer surface of the piece, she pushes inward with a tool. She uses her left hand inside the piece to push outward and create full volumes (Fig. 6-32B). She says of this method: "I very much enjoy the rhythmic interplay of my hands 'speaking to each other' through the thin wall of the clay."

Roberts cuts the piece apart when the clay is at the leather-hard stage. She does this right before she finally uncovers the piece for drying. Even after she has uncovered most of the piece, she places a thin strip of plastic over the cut to prevent the two sections from warping unevenly. When the piece is dry, she disassembles it and prepares it for firing (Fig. 6-32C).

Roberts glues the piece together when she completes it. The wide join area at each segment helps ensure a strong glue join.

Guest Artist: Robert Arneson

The late Robert Arneson constructed *Mountain and Lake* (Fig. 6-33) in two parts: the section that rests on the floor is made from tiles and the freestanding sculpture is made from blocks. He used the tiles to create the image of a lake and the block composition to create the image of a mountain. The piece is large and imposing.

Arneson used segmented tiles for the floor piece with its image of a lake. These tiles are flat, thick, and irregularly shaped. He used relief and painted imagery to create the images of water and of the reflection of the mountain on the lake. To create this relief imagery, he ran a rounded tool (perhaps a spatula) across the surface of the wet clay. The segmentation lines follow the contours of the imagery.

To create the mountain form, Arneson used segmented blocks. These are similarly irregular in shape in their vertical axis and follow the imagery. On their horizontal axis, however, they go straight across the piece and cut through the imagery. Arneson made the mountain form from modular block segments. Each block is four-sided with a top and a bottom. The blocks can be pulled apart for easy disassembly and reassembly. The blocks taper on their horizontal axes at the top of the mountain.

Arneson textured and grooved the surfaces of the segments. To create this rock-like relief imagery, he folded and gathered the surface of the blocks (in a manner similar to the folding and gathering of cloth). The folds continue across the horizontal cuts, making it evident that Arneson made the front surfaces of the blocks as a single large unit using a large clay slab. Once this unit became firm, he cut it into segments. Each segment then became the front surface of a block. The blocks were then fitted together and finished and glazed. Next, he took them apart for firing.

Fig. 6-33. *Mountain and Lake,* **Robert Arneson, USA, slab-formed floor tile and free-standing segmented sculpture. Floor tiles: 2.5 × 320.6 × 230 centimeters. Sculpture: 83³⁄4 × 175¹⁄2 × 38¹⁄8 inches.** Photo by T. C. Eckersley.

The modular strategy allows the creation of a massive piece of this sort without running the risks of cracking. Furthermore, it allows for easy firing and easy and convenient handling of the finished piece. Arneson's intelligent use of hand-forming methods enabled him to create rich textures and monumental form.

Although many of Arneson's pieces dealt with ironical treatments of popular culture and imagery, this was not his approach here. In this piece he deals almost reverently with the glories of nature. He seems to have wanted to create a beautiful object, one that is monumental in feeling, conveying an affection for the subject.

Guest Artist: Douglas Baldwin

The artist Doug Baldwin made the base of the piece in Figure 6-34 from a thick slab. He made the bricks that make up the walls of the piece from a slab that he cut into tiny rectangles. The duck figures and furniture were made with pinch-forming methods.

Subject matter is very important here: the sculpture re-creates the various activities that go on in the ceramics department of a university. Baldwin uses extensive repetition to create this imagery. It is almost as if he is allowing us to examine the studio under a microscope. He ornamented the floor of the studio with a pattern of square tiles and used almost a thousand small brick forms to construct the walls. A series of identical columns runs along the side of the walls. Baldwin placed a series of small cubicles, all of the same size, in the front of the studio. In the back area are three identical beehive kilns covered with a tiled imagery. Baldwin

Fig. 6-34. *The Great Duck Ceramic School*, Douglas Baldwin, USA, low-fire, terra-cotta clay body, slab- and pinch-formed. Photo by Robert Noonan.

places tiny stylized figures in each cubicle; they are also placed in an even pattern at the back of the studio. He has treated these figures with a great deal of irony. The denizens of this potting studio are ducks; however, they are doing all the things that ceramists do in a potting studio.

Baldwin works here with assembled forms. He has made each individual part simply and deftly. Then he combined these forms to create a complex image. The result is a complete world in miniature.

SOLID-FORMED SCULPTURE

Solid-formed pieces are unusual because during their creation the ceramist works on solid masses of clay. The ceramist using solid-forming strategies must dry and fire the work carefully. Any moisture that the interior of the solid clay piece retains will convert to steam during the early stages of the firing. Steam pressure is powerful and can easily shatter the work. For directions on drying procedures, see Chapter 3.

Solid-formed pieces by nature can be heavy. Those ceramists who use this method, however, often intentionally exploit the weight of the piece. The weight gives a piece a monumental and primal character. We see an example of this approach in the work of Bruce Taylor (see Figs. 6-35 and 6-36). Because the ceramist does not form them from complex hollow structures, solid-formed pieces often have a natural rock-like look. William Parry takes this approach in his solid-formed work (see Fig. 6-41).

Guest Artist: Bruce Taylor

Bruce Taylor uses press forming to create solid clay sculptural pieces. He uses a red burning brick clay that he purchases from a local brick manufacturer. He obtains the clay in its dry state and during the mixing process adds aggregates that burn out in the fire, such as Perlite, Vermiculite, coffee grounds, or sawdust. In this way he "opens up" the body so that it dries and fires evenly. This is important if the artist is to fire these thick pieces of solid clay successfully.

Taylor's work is sectional; he makes each section separately. He uses press forms to shape the clay and various materials to create these press forms—Masonite, plywood, plaster, and gypsum cement. To deal with the weight of the solid clay, he often has to reinforce the press forms with fiberglass or metal rods.

The artist presses this aggregate-filled clay body into the press forms using mallets. He lets the pieces dry for a few weeks. Right before the firing, he places them in a warm area for a few days to complete the drying process. Long and careful drying is essential for solid pieces. If any pockets of moisture remain, the steam produced by the moisture will cause fissures or explosions during the firing. After the firing, Taylor assembles the pieces and completes the form.

Solid-formed pieces such as this one are extremely heavy, Taylor exploits this weightiness: his pieces are heavy and they *look* heavy. Their weight gives them a monumental, primitive, and brooding character. The soft stony, abraded surfaces of the clay contrast with the geometric and mechanical forms. I think this is the way an artist in a neolithic culture would interpret the sophisticated machines of our industrial culture.

Fig. 6-35. *Cone,* Bruce Taylor, Canada, ceramic and lead, solid-formed clay with lead elements, brick clay, 45 × 30 × 30 inches.

Fig. 6-36. *Three Wheeler,* Bruce Taylor, Canada, solid-formed clay with lead and wood elements, brick clay, 48 × 24 × 40 inches.

USING MORE THAN ONE FORMING METHOD ON A SINGLE PIECE

Ceramists often use several techniques to build a single sculptural piece. Blending various building methods can be an effective way to create sculptural forms. When employing several different form types in a single piece, the ceramist can employ several forming methods as well. An example would be a piece in which the ceramist combines drape-formed spheres with coil-formed pylons and slab-formed ellipses.

The ceramist may also combine two or more forming methods to create a single complex form. For example, the ceramist can join slab forms with heavy coils to create a complex combination of flat surfaces and massive, curved joins. To illustrate this strategy, I chose pieces by Ric Hirsch (Fig. 6-37) and Angelica Pozo (see Fig. 6-38) as examples. Both mix coil and slab techniques in their sculptural work.

Guest Artist: Angelica Pozo

Angelica Pozo made the sculptural piece in Figure 6-38 in three parts: a large leaf-like form that serves as the backdrop for the piece, a sculptural leaf form in the center foreground, and a mosaic-tiled base.

Fig. 6-37. Pedestal Bowl with Weapon Artifact #4, Richard Hirsch, USA, sculpture, coiled and slab-formed, low-fire glazes, sandblasted, 53 × 33 inches. In this piece Hirsch placed a vessel-like form on top of a simple and forceful base. A good deal of the energy here comes from the strong silhouette of the vessel form. The surfaces, too, are rich and enhance this piece.

Fig. 6-38. Oak Leaf Icon, Angelica Pozo, USA, sculpture, slab- and coil-formed, cone 04 terra-cotta clay body, 44 × 26 × 8 inches. Pozo combined slab- and coil-building and mosaic methods and two different clays to create this piece. Photo © The *Plain Dealer*, Cleveland, Ohio, September 1993.

Pozo started by making the leaf form at the back of the piece. She rolled out a large slab made from a coarse, terra-cotta tile body. Then she cut the slab into thirty-two tiles. After she fired the tiles, she mounted them on a plywood board for support. Pozo used colored grout to hold the tiles in place and to create the contrasting vein imagery. She used more of the tile clay to create the mosaic pieces at the foot of the sculpture, which she also mounted on a wooden board.

In making the foreground piece, Pozo mirrored the background shape in that both are leaf-shaped. This leaf shape, however, is sculptural, coil-built, and hollow. Pozo used a plastic terra-cotta hand-building body to make this part of the piece.

Pozo has successfully combined two- and three-dimensional space, different materials, and coil- and slab-forming strategies. The character of images varies a great deal, from soft and cloud-like to crisp and angular. These combinations work well together in this strong piece with rich and varied imagery.

MIXED-MEDIA SCULPTURE

Clay can be combined with other materials to create effects that the ceramist cannot obtain by using clay by itself. These nonclay materials are at their best when they serve as a strong contrast to the clay elements. For example, fired-clay forms will work well with a flexible material such as plastic hose. The clay is rigid and volumetric and lends itself to compact forms, while the plastic hose is flexible and elongated. You may also create a piece made with clay forms supported by a wooden superstructure. Lattice-like wooden elements support the volumetric clay elements.

A mixed-media strategy is a wonderful way to work because it allows the ceramist to create images that are otherwise impossible or are fraught with difficulty. Mixed-media work can be novel and very striking. One such example is by Mitch Messina (Fig. 6-39). The sculptor combined clay with metal and wood elements,

Fig. 6-39. *World Scribe,* **Mitch Messina, USA, mixed-media sculptural form, 56 × 40 × 48 inches.** In this piece Messina used wood, metal, and clay—materials and forms that are very different in character. The wooden and clay forms are joined closely together. Messina designed the clay and metal forms to look as if they are passing through the wood—a very dramatic image. The artist exploits the grain of the wooden forms and creates strong textures on the surface of the clay forms. A metal basket, made from thin wire, surrounds but does not conceal one of the clay spheres. Photo by Walter Colley.

contrasting the thin, attenuated form of the wire elements with massive clay and wood elements. Thomas Seawell contrasts clear plastic with opaque clay, and William Parry contrasts the ninety-degree angles of a wooden document holder with irregularly shaped clay elements (Figs. 6-40 and 6-41).

A MIXED-MEDIA PIECE—THOMAS SEAWELL

Thomas Seawell is a printmaker who occasionally creates mixed-media pieces. He constructs these pieces using a central clay structure with applied clay imagery. He then fires the piece and attaches nonclay elements to it. Seawell plays the transparency of the plastic against the opacity of the low-fire clay. The subject in Figure 6-40 is an abstract treatment of the architecture typical of an American small town. The completed piece is shown in Color Plate 33.

1. Seawell places an opening in the surface of a slab wall that he will use to form the piece (Fig. 6-40A).
2. He presses a cardboard form into the surface of another slab to give it texture (Fig. 6-40B). These are the same cardboard forms he uses as stencils in his prints. He also carves textures into a slab.

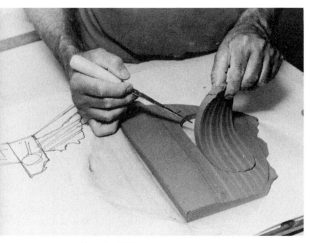

Fig. 6-40A.

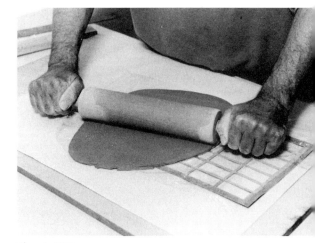

Fig. 6-40B.

Fig. 6-40C.

Fig. 6-40D.

3. Here he has begun to assemble the piece (Fig. 6-40C). We see him drilling holes in the clay wall (Fig. 6-40D). He will use these holes to attach elements to the basic form after he has fired the piece.
4. He applies a colored slip to the form (Fig. 6-40E).
5. He applies glaze to the form (Fig. 6-40F).
6. After the firing, he attaches plexiglass elements to the form (Fig. 6-40G).
7. He weaves mesh fabric through openings in the form (Fig. 6-40H).

Guest Artist: William Parry

In Figure 6-41, William Parry combined modular clay elements with two found objects: a wooden document holder and a cast-metal footstand. The document holder is made from oak. It is a mass-produced wooden box with evenly spaced dividers made for office use in the early or mid part of the century. The simple, serviceable footstand is made from cast iron.

Parry first cleaned the letter holder and mounted it on the cast-metal foot. He then made the clay elements. He used a roller to make flattened slabs and coils. Parry cut textures into the roller to produce the raised linear patterns on the sur-

Fig. 6-40E.

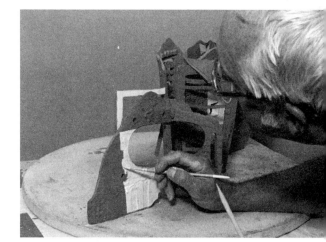

Fig. 6-40F.

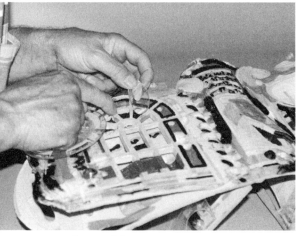

Fig. 6-40G.

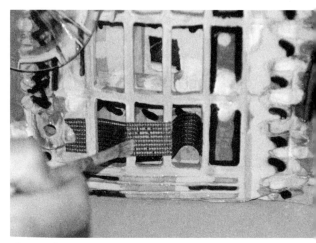

Fig. 6-40H.

Fig. 6-41. William Parry, USA, mixed-media piece, wood and clay, slab formed, cone 9 reduction stoneware.

face of the clay. He fired these pieces in a high-fire reduction kiln. After firing, he attached them to the letter holder, gluing them to the wooden dividers inside the holder.

Parry has used rhythm and repetition here to great effect. The clay elements are asymmetric and dynamically balanced and contrast with the symmetric, static elements of the wooden dividers in the document holder.

Incorporating found objects in this sculpture enabled Parry to create a piece with a great deal of warmth and elegance. The contrast between the wooden, metal, and clay elements is pleasing. The highly textured surface of the unglazed clay is rich and natural. The color and grain of the wood (scarred from use in its previous life) is warm. The dark color and pebble finish of the metal footstand is also pleasing and contributes yet another texture.

Pieces in which clay is combined with found objects are unusual. After examining this piece, it is hard to understand why. As we see here, the results can be highly original and thought-provoking.

CHAPTER SEVEN

INSTALLATION ART AND WALL PIECES

INSTALLATION ART

In the last twenty-five years, artists in all fields have become interested in installation art. Responding to this movement, ceramic artists as well have begun creating installation pieces. These artists have come to feel that this way of making art is highly liberating. For the ceramic artist who is interested in the play of ideas, this is an excellent way to work. They can use their work to deal with any issues they like in any manner they wish. They like the ability to try anything, to work in a scale as large or small as they please, to use as much or as little craft as they want, and to mix media in any way they wish.

Most installation art pieces have a strongly spatial character. They are akin to sculpture but with an expanded scope. I include the work of three artists in this discussion: Paul Astbury, Roberta Griffith, and Katherine Ross. Many pieces illustrated in this chapter include vessel, sculpture, and wall-piece forms. The artists have combined various clay bodies, surface finishes, and firing types. In all these pieces the artists have employed mixed media strategies. The artists have included other nonform aspects of art as well, incorporating, for example, such phenomena as time, sound, and movement.

Held Under Wraps (Fig. 7-1) by Paul Astbury is a large installation piece composed of a three-dimensional form—a mannequin covered with ceramic elements. A layer of transparent plastic sheeting shrouds the mannequin. A tile piece with related imagery rests on the floor. The mannequin is a turn-of-the-century dressmaker's dummy that Astbury found in a trash can on the street. He covered the surface of the mannequin with ceramic tiles with attached cup handles.

Fig. 7-1. *Garden 2* (foreground) and *Held Under Wraps* (background). **Paul Astbury, England,** *Garden 2* **is 10 × 10 feet by 3 inches.** Photo by Michael Harvey.

Emmanuel Cooper, in the catalog written by him for the exhibition *On the Edge: Art Meets Craft* (which toured England and Wales in 1993), says of this piece: "These works are about the way men and women are socially and psychologically constructed, about male and female sexuality and the part clothing plays in signifying and defining attitudes as well as proclaiming gender."

Homage to Suizenji (Fig. 7-2) by Roberta Griffith consists of a group of slab-formed elements. Griffith has tethered the ceramic elements in a pond with nylon line and lead weights. This is a site-specific installation. The clay elements cannot be appreciated outside their context. They function only in the way Griffith wants them to when we see them in the context of the water and reeds and the reflections in this pond.

The artist made this piece to fit into the natural environment rather than dominating it. The environment, therefore, strongly influences the way this piece looks to us. It is always changing as the light, the atmosphere, and the season changes. This is part of the energy of the piece. We see the piece as Griffith wants us to see it. The wiry grasses at the edge of the water serve as a strong contrast to the slab discs. The soft masses of leaves of the bushes above the discs also contrast strongly with the discs. More subtle is the contrast with the soft clouds we see reflected in the water. We often disregard reflections like this: we "look through" them. If there is a breeze it ripples the water around the discs and moves them to and fro. Finally, the rocks on the bottom of the pond, partly concealed by the cloudy water, also contrast with the discs. All these forms and events together conspire to make a strong, evocative image.

Fig. 7-2. *Homage to Suizenji,* Robert Griffith, USA, installation piece, each clay element is 6 × ¼ inches. The ceramic, slab-formed elements are tethered in the pond with nylon line and lead weights. This is a site-specific installation. The clay elements cannot be appreciated by themselves and function only in the way Griffith wants them to when they are seen in the context of the water, the reeds, and the reflections in this pond. Photo by the artist.

Katherine Ross's *Water Cure: Contamination and Cleansing* (Fig. 7-3) is part of a larger installation in which the artist uses a wooden table, sandblasted wall-mounted water glasses, cups, and saucers, and photographic images. Ross says of her work: "Water is the subject of my current work." *Water Cure* shows two life-size, hand-formed ceramic tubs, one filled with used bars of soap, the other with animal hair. Soap is the symbol of cleansing and animal hair is the symbol of contamination. The names of the most polluted bodies of water on earth are sandblasted on thirty water glasses displayed in another part of the installation.

Fig. 7-3. *Water Cure: Contamination and Cleansing,* Katherine Ross, USA. These two objects are part of a larger installation with a wooden table, sandblasted wall-mounted water glasses, cups, and saucers, and photographic images.

WALL PIECES

Wall pieces have been important in the history of our craft for a long time. Now the format is taking on new significance as contemporary ceramists begin to see it as equal in potential power and importance to the vessel and sculpture formats. Wall pieces can offer the ceramist a variety of creative options. Since most wall pieces are made by hand-forming methods, this format can significantly enlarge the scope of the hand-building ceramist. In the next section I will discuss many types of wall pieces and how hand-forming ceramists make them.

Because of the durability of the ceramic medium, many wall pieces made long ago still survive. The wall pieces that adorned palaces in the Middle East are especially noteworthy. The large glazed brick wall murals of the Achaemenids are colorful and impressive. This impulse led to the much later tile walls of Persian mosques from the tenth to the seventeenth century. These are perhaps the finest examples of ceramic wall-piece work ever made.

In Europe and North America, wall pieces became especially popular in the late nineteenth and early twentieth centuries. They often added life and vitality to urban architecture. Much of the splendid decorative "stonework" of the late nineteenth and early twentieth century city is really clay that has been molded and carved to create decorative facades. Louis Henri Sullivan, the great turn-of-the-century Chicago architect, designed a wonderful series of buildings with terra-cotta ornament. This was also the era that saw the beginning of many great train and subway projects. Many of these prominently feature ceramic tile, often of great beauty. By the 1920s interest in ceramic wall pieces faded but now, after a lapse of many years, there is renewed interest in these projects. Many contemporary ceramists spend a good deal of their time creating wall pieces for public spaces.

Another facet of ceramic wall work has begun to attract great interest—the use of ceramic wall pieces in domestic interiors. This format has a different orientation: it is private and personal. In this approach the ceramic wall piece becomes an art object not so different in its intent from a painting. Although this aspect of wall-piece work has little grounding in tradition, it seems to be promising and many ceramists have begun to work in this genre. Whatever the approach, ceramists working in the wall-piece format have many advantages. They can employ complex and rich imagistic strategies and have great freedom in the way in which they handle the clay and finish their pieces.

Once you choose to work in the wall-piece format, you must make a whole series of further choices. Wall pieces do not fall into one format but into many. You can work with segmented or unsegmented wall pieces. If you want to work with a segmented format, you must choose between tiles and mosaics. You must also choose between pieces that are freely movable or fixed to the wall, and you must select your backing method and material. All these significant choices will strongly influence the character of the work.

UNSEGMENTED TILE PIECES

Perhaps your most important choice will be whether to use segmented or unsegmented clay elements. Unsegmented tile pieces are simple to make and exhibit. However, there is a size limit for unsegmented tiles because large tiles are difficult to make and fire. If you want to make large wall pieces, you will have to cut the piece into separate sections. Although the boundaries between sections can be intrusive, they encourage great flexibility as compensation. If you want to section the piece, you must also choose the size of the sections. They may be tiny (mosaic tesserae) or large (tiles). Mosaic tesserae range in size from one or two millimeters to two centimeters, while tiles range in size from three centimeters to forty centimeters.

In nonsegmented compositions, a single tile or panel makes up the image. You can make such a tile simply and directly. Make a slab and create imagery on it. Because of this simplicity, making this kind of piece is the easiest, most natural introduction to the wall-piece format. This format has few problems, but one significant problem is tile size. It is difficult to create ceramic tiles that are larger in any dimension than fifty centimeters; large pieces will crack and warp.

Unsegmented tiles may have a fixed mounting in the wall or you may mount them using the freely movable format. Many ceramists use a panel backing, but you can design them to hang without a backing panel. You can also place mounting holes or lugs on the back of the tile for picture-hanging wire.

Guest Artist: Neil Forrest

Neil Forrest combined stoneware with Egyptian paste in his piece (Fig. 7-4). Thus his work has the strength of stoneware and the color and surface response of Egyptian paste. He begins with a stoneware form, which he dries slowly and fires to stoneware temperatures in a reduction kiln. Parts of this stoneware form will be left to show in the final piece while he covers other parts with Egyptian paste tiles. He makes these tiles separately and at a different time. Forrest lays the tiles over parts of the stoneware armature and cuts them to fit with tungsten cutters. He then fires the composition to cone 010 in an electric kiln. During this firing the Egyptian paste tiles become soft and weld themselves to the stoneware armature. Egyptian paste is self-glazing (it contains ingredients that create a glaze on the surface of the piece) and the tile sections take on a glazed finish as well.

Forrest has made the stoneware section in high relief (something that stoneware does very well). He finished this section with a simple and monochromatic glaze. The Egyptian paste tile is thin and flat (Egyptian paste does not lend itself to relief imagery) and the tile surface is very smooth. Color is strong. In the colored clay surfaces, clay and glaze are one; thus they look very different from the glazed surfaces. The contrast between these two elements defines the character of this piece. The stoneware imagery has a piled-up and irregular character. The colored clay imagery is smooth, flat, and glass-like. Forrest carefully exploited the possibilities of the ceramic medium in this wall piece.

SEGMENTED TILE PIECES

Segmented ceramic tile compositions are groupings of clay elements meant to be placed on the wall or floor. We see tile compositions all the time in our everyday lives. Most of them are strictly utilitarian and made in industrial settings. The surfaces of industrial tiles are generally smooth and covered with monochrome glazes. Ceramic artists, however, conceive of tiles as vehicles for personal expression and their tiles are usually highly individual.

The segmented tile format encourages great flexibility and allows the ceramist to create large compositions. Once ceramists developed this strategy, they could cover walls or even whole structures with tile images. Segmentation, however, has its price: segmented imagery is always "broken up." If you use segmented imagery, you must choose between compositions in which the segment boundaries reflect the design of the imagery and those in which the segment boundaries follow their

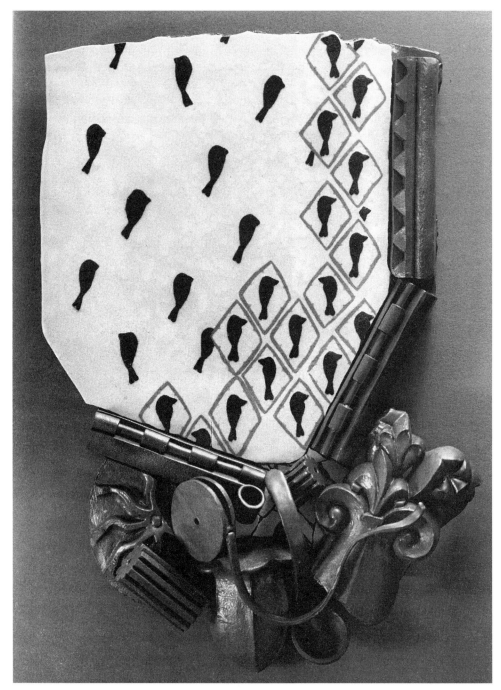

Fig. 7-4. *Ornament with Bird Tile*, Neil Forrest, Canada, wall piece, slab-formed, made from stoneware and Egyptian paste. This tile wall piece is unsegmented and movable. It hangs on the wall in the same way as a painting, drawing, or print.

own logic. When faced with this choice, many ceramists decide to use tile forms that do not follow the logic of the imagery. They ask the viewer to "look beyond" the lines created by the segment boundaries and concentrate on the imagery itself. It might seem that the strategy in which the artist exploits the segment lines as part of the design of the piece would be inherently superior. Both approaches, however, have resulted in wonderful pieces.

Tile shape strongly influences the character of the work. The most common tile shapes are simple squares, rectangles, ovals, and circles. These shapes work well and are familiar. Complex tile shapes, which are more unusual, are harder to make but give you a chance to express your individuality. Both approaches have advantages. Complex tile shapes will work well when they serve as the main drama of the piece. Simple forms will work well when they serve as a background for the imagery.

You may want to make a tile composition in which all the tiles are of the same shape or you may choose to create a composition in which each tile has a unique shape. We are all familiar with tiles whose shape is absolutely uniform; the most obvious are the tiles on our bathroom walls. Although it seems that uniform tiles might be dull, tiles of uniform size and shape can work well. They do not draw attention to themselves; they let the imagery take first place. In those tile compositions whose tiles are unique in shape, the tile shapes dominate the composition. These pieces can be strongly compelling.

Tile size is also an important factor. Tiles vary in size from about three to forty centimeters. The choice is mostly personal preference. Large tiles can look quite dramatic, whereas smaller tiles are less prone to warping. Warping can be a real problem for the ceramist working with the wall-piece format.

Most tiles are sheet-like and flat. Flat tiles are especially useful if you intend to ornament the surface of the tiles themselves. They are easy to make, but it is difficult to dry them so that they are warp free.

There are good reasons for making tiles whose surfaces are curved or angled. The complex forms of shaped tiles can be pleasing to look at and they resist warping. The forming process is more demanding than that for making flat tiles, but drying and firing are easier.

You may want to leave your tile composition with an unadorned clay surface or you may want to add a surface finish. Slips, engobes, terra sigillatas, and glazes all are useful for this purpose. You may make your choice based on aesthetics or durability. Wall pieces intended to be placed in the home do not need to have a durable surface finish. Wall pieces intended for placement in a public space will need to have a durable surface finish. Use a shiny, highly durable glaze coating so that the tiles will be easy to clean and will resist grime and graffiti.

TWO- AND THREE-DIMENSIONAL IMAGERY

You can use two-dimensional painted imagery or you can choose to work with relief imagery. If you limit yourself to two-dimensional imagery, your work may look like an imitation of a painting in the ceramic medium. If the artist respects the character of the ceramic medium, however, the results can be good. Artists have made many fine painted tile wall pieces that do retain their ceramic identity.

The advantage in using relief imagery is that the work almost automatically will have a strong ceramic identity. Its character is unique and obviously different from a painting. Furthermore, most ceramists enjoy the wide variety of options available to them when they combine two- and three-dimensional imagery.

Fixed Wall Pieces

You must choose between movable wall pieces and wall pieces that are permanently fixed to the wall. In the past, most wall pieces were fixed in place. The building wall was their backdrop and support. This is still the best way to make a strong, permanent wall piece.

Ceramists have used the fixed mounting format for millennia and that format is still used more often then any other. The wall piece is fixed and anchored in the wall with mortar and grout. The artist cleans the surface of the piece, leaving the grout only in the spaces between the ceramic elements. (See the series on pages 199–203 of George Mason's work: Mounting a Large Tile Wall Piece.")

The construction requirements for fixed mounting are formidable, and the fate of the permanently mounted wall piece is dependent on the fate of the building. Recently, however, we have become all too aware of the ephemeral character of many contemporary building projects. We are not so comfortable linking the fate of the wall piece to the fate of the building.

Panel Wall Pieces

Ceramic artists developed the mounted panel format to deal with the problems of fixed mounting. In this variation on direct mounting, the artist glues the ceramic elements to a panel, then bolts the panel to a docking structure set in the wall. Only the docking structure is permanent. In this way the piece can be moved to another site with a minimum of expense.

Movable Wall Pieces

Much of the artwork that we look at in homes, galleries, and museums follows a common pattern. Artists create and mount these pieces in a way that makes them easy to exhibit. When the exhibit is over, the pieces can be moved easily to another location. If purchased, their owners can hang them easily where they wish. If the artist uses paint to create one of these pieces we call the piece a "painting." In other examples of this genre the artist uses other media and we call them by the names of their media, using such terms as "drawings" and "collages." We think of freely movable artwork as entirely unremarkable.

Because the technology has changed, ceramic artists can now use this format as well. They can rely on improved mastics to hold the ceramic elements in place on freely movable panels. Ceramic artists have responded to the flexibility of the movable piece format. They want their work to be as portable and easy to exhibit as any other hanging artwork (including paintings). The audience for the fine arts has also responded positively to the moveable wall piece format. This audience wants access to ceramic wall pieces they can treat in the same way as other artworks for the wall. This combination of technical and aesthetic innovation has lead to a good deal of interest in freely movable ceramic wall pieces.

To exhibit a freely movable wall piece you mount the ceramic elements on a board or panel and equip it with hardware for hanging. Pieces treated in this way must be light enough to hang without straining the wall structure.

Rigid and Nonrigid Backing

The ceramist can also choose between rigid and nonrigid backing strategies. In the past rigid backing was the only type used for wall pieces. However, you can support the wall piece using flexible materials such as string, twine, and cable. Their arrangement of wires or cords and clay elements can be very pleasing. They have an unusual characteristic for pieces made in clay; their elements have movement. Ceramic wall hangings are light in weight and they are easy to move and to hang. This format is practical and aesthetically pleasing.

PORTFOLIO OF INSTALLATION ART AND WALL PIECES

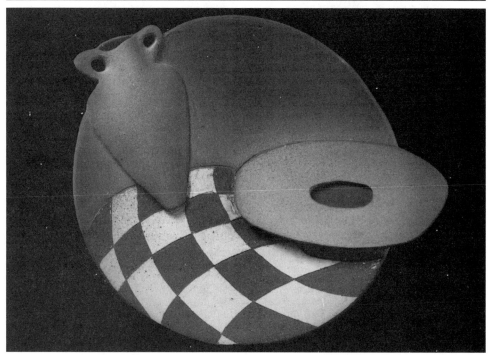

Fig. 7-5. *Tondo XVI,* **Anna Calluori Holcombe, USA, two wall pieces, earthenware clay and terra sigillata, 18 inches in diameter.** In these wall pieces the artist uses vessel forms in high relief. One characteristic of relief imagery is that it creates the illusion of deep space with the use of shallow modeling. Holcombe exploits these possibilities to create a complex spatial character. She further complicates the imagery by applying sprayed shading on the surface. Photo by Jim Dusen.

Fig. 7-6. *Cup #2,* **Nancy Selvin, USA, sculptural wall relief, mixed-media, 12 × 12 inches.** Selvin set a cup in a shelf setting and then uses the setting to de-emphasize the functional aspect of the cup and to concentrate on its formal aspect and its connotations as a container. The shelf element is made from wood covered with gesso and painted. Photo by Charles Frizzell.

Fig. 7-7. *Forest Shrine: Penumbra,* Angelica Pozo, USA, 93½ × 68¾ × 13½ inches. The artist has combined a coiled vessel form on a pedestal with a large tile piece made from slab-formed tiles. The structure is oriented to the wall and is a wall piece with some sculptural characteristics. It is reminiscent of an altarpiece and has strong ceremonial associations. Photo by the artist.

Fig. 7-8. Elizabeth MacDonald, sculptural tile piece, press-mold-formed tiles. The wall is 40 feet high with a 4 × 8 × 8 foot pyramid. The artist used the repetition of simple tile forms to create a powerful and hypnotic imagery.

Fig. 7-9. *Garden Series I,* Susan Kowalczyk, USA, wall tile, earthenware, 24 × 19 × 6 inches. The artist shows that she understands the difference between a wall piece and a painting. Complex, three-dimensional painterly space does not work well in the tile medium. Tile pieces demand an imagery that has few spatial qualities. It should have broad, flat areas bordered by strong outlines. Patterned imagery works well. We see all of these elements in this piece. The juxtaposition of low and high relief is surprising and effective. Note the way the artist used the grouted lines to create a linear imagery and made them an integral part of the design.

TWO WALL PIECES FOR PUBLIC SPACES—DALE ZHEUTLIN

(Parts of this description were excerpted from "Site-Specific Wall Sculpture" by Dale Zheutlin with Eilene Howe, Ceramics Monthly *41 [June/July/August 1993.])*

Creating art for a large corporation or a public agency requires collaboration with architects, interior designers, art consultants, and the client. It takes considerable preparation to accomplish this kind of work and to make it enhance but not compete with its environment.

I first question the clients about the purpose of a projected sculpture. Then I examine the site, appraising dimensions, colors, lighting, architectural detail, and even geographical setting. With this information, I design the piece. To communicate my ideas, I build a scale model of the work and make sample porcelain tiles depicting color and texture.

Images

Images, my ceramic wall construction for Wang Laboratories, Inc., began when the company hired an art consultant to find an appropriate sculpture to complete its new executive briefing center. The company invited me to view the site, a raw space on 47th Street in New York City. Raw space, in this instance, meant no walls, hanging wires, plasterboard piled on concrete floors, and open ducts—in short, a construction site. I had to envision the finished space only from blueprints, paint chips, and fabric swatches.

After several visits to the site, I realized that Wang wanted to locate the sculpture on a wall that could be seen from four perspectives: when the viewer got off

Fig. 7-10. *Images,* **Dale Zheutlin, USA, 13 feet long with an accompanying statement.**
Photo by Paul Warchol.

the elevator and entered the reception area; when the viewer descended a spiral staircase that connected the third floor with the fourth floor; from the computer demonstration center; and while sitting in the relaxation area twenty feet away. The sculpture had to be interesting from all four perspectives. Last, it had to express Wang's six technologies: data, text, voice, image, networking, and human factors.

The proposal selected consisted of a model for *Images* that I would make from six adjacent wedges. I embossed the surface of each slab with symbols of the six technologies.

After I had a signed contract, the real work began. To get a sense of the proportions of the piece at the site, I measured off the space on my studio wall and hung a full-scale cardboard model of the work. From this model I determined the size of the slabs based on a 5 percent clay shrinkage. Next, I began the many stain and glaze tests, which resulted in a thirty-two color palette.

My assistant and I rolled out slabs, letting them stiffen before placing them on the floor. We were now ready to carve the slabs and apply stains and glazes to them and cut them into manageable sizes. Then we covered and weighted them so that they would dry flat. After firing, I attached the clay sections to an armature. I assembled the sections for a trial hanging in my studio.

Installation is an exciting and exhilarating process. Wang had an inflexible schedule because of a press conference it had called the morning after I was to install. To avoid damage from movers bringing in furniture and other people working around the sculpture, I had asked that it be the last object to be put in place. On arrival, I discovered fifty frantic people carrying and installing everything from chairs to computers. Amid the confusion, I managed to barricade a small area with ropes and chairs to begin my own installation.

I started immediately with tape measure and chalk to guarantee correct placement. Every time I made a mark, the painter (who had finished the walls in a deep purple he called "eggplant") rushed up behind me and removed it! I explained what I was trying to do and asked for his patience. When the installation was finished, both the painter and I felt an element of relief and satisfaction.

Twin Span

My project for the Delaware River and Bay Authority in Wilmington, Delaware, began with a stressful interview. I had to appear before a group consisting of the engineers and architect who had built the Delaware Memorial Bridge. They wanted a complete explanation not only of the aesthetics of the sculpture but of every technical aspect of construction as well. I knew the project was mine when the chief engineer stood up from the conference table and said, "I think it's time to show Dale the bridge from the top down." We put on hard hats and protective clothing (perfect with my high heels), then crowded into a small elevator. We ascended 440 feet to the top of the southeast tower. Its gently swaying motion was in rhythmic harmony with my shaking knees and feeling of euphoria.

Working for a public agency was unlike any prior experience. It required a lengthy contract, $1 million in liability insurance, and month-by-month documentation of my progress (including how many pounds of clay I was using and the firing schedules).

My proposal had been complicated because I was offering to work with clay in a clearly unclaylike fashion. The committee had chosen the most difficult and most sculptural model. I wanted to position myself in the middle of the twin spans; therefore, I needed a new perspective. I used archival photographs, then a computer to draw the image in perspective. Ultimately it required five sculptural elements fit-

Fig. 7-11. *Twin Span,* **Dale Zheutlin, USA, 15 feet long.** Photo by Andrew Bordwin.

ted together to create the dynamic tension of the bridge. Upon entering Authority Headquarters, people would have to "read" my sculpture from a distance of 100 feet, and yet up close it had to be as precise and accurate as the bridge itself.

On hand to observe my progress were the architect and engineers, who were justifiably proud of the elegant span they had created. To complement their achievement I wanted to capture the blue light, the wind, the reflection off the water, the strength and beauty of the span, and my own unforgettable experience at the top of the tower. To judge by everyone's reactions at the installation, the bridge and sculpture worked well together and fulfilled their expectations.

The creation of hand-crafted art is a private endeavor. Yet my pleasure is much enhanced by being a part of a group dynamic that increases the art's accessibility to its intended audience.

MAKING TILES

The hand-forming ceramist makes tiles from clay slabs. Any of the slab-forming methods is appropriate for making tiles. Thickness may be uniform or it may vary, but you must control these size variations so that the piece does not warp or crack. Tile shapes can be uniform or not. If you want to make uniform tiles, use a template to cut them (see page 36). Tiles that are not uniform in shape and size can be cut freehand. You will probably want to cut them to conform with the imagery of the piece.

FLAT TILES

While the tile form is simple and seems to present no technical problems, the tile maker must deal with warping. A slightly warped and cupped surface that would not be noticeable on a three-dimensional form can ruin a tile. To deter warping, the clay body should be low in shrinkage (see page 23). Workability need not be exceptional because the format offers little challenge in this area. Clay bodies for tiles need only be plastic enough to hold together without cracking during the forming process.

Grog additions (up to 10 percent) and chopped nylon (up to 1 percent) will deter warping. Avoid the use of high-shrinkage, fine-particle clays such as ball clay. Wollastonite, a calcium silicate, is a useful flux because its fibrous makeup discourages warping.

You will find that the drying process is critical here. Dry the tiles slowly so that they resist warping and cracking. I dry tiles on raised racks covered with plastic sheeting. This allows air as much access to the back of the tile as the front. Both sides of the tile now have a chance to dry at the same rate.

The firing is also important. Long and even firings also discourage warping and cracking. There must be special emphasis on slow firing at the beginning and end of the firing (see page 39).

Making Flat Tiles

1. Form a slab.
2. Cut the tiles.
3. Trim and clean the tiles.
4. Cover the tiles with plastic sheeting.
5. After a few days, take off the plastic sheeting and clean the tiles.
6. Move the tiles to a rack and place the rack on blocks to raise it.
7. Cover the tiles with plastic again, letting the plastic drape onto the work table.
8. Place a rolled cloth partly inside and partly outside the plastic. This will allow a small amount of dry air to enter and moisture to exit.
9. Let the tiles dry slowly for a week or two.
10. Remove the plastic and cover the tiles with a light cloth.
11. After a few days, remove the cloth and let the tiles air-dry.

The tiles are now ready to be fired.

SHAPED TILES

Shaped tiles are curved or angled. The curved surfaces of these tiles can be pleasing to look at and they resist warping. If you wish to create curved surfaces that are uniform in shape form the tiles on a plaster or bisque drape form. Tiles that are not uniform in shape do not lend themselves to the use of drape forms. You can, however, shape them by hand by pressing each tile upward at its center.

Shaped tiles require a clay body that is quite different from flat tiles. You will need a workable clay body to shape the tile successfully. The clay body should contain from 10 to 15 percent ball clay to help make it plastic and bendable.

Warping is not a problem with shaped tiles. Thus the drying procedure is less critical for shaped tiles than for flat ones. Leave shaped tiles under plastic for a day or two. Then cover them with a layer of cloth. I prefer to dry shaped tiles under a layer of cloth because the cloth allows drying but controls its rate.

MAKING SHAPED TILES

1. Form a slab.
2. Cut the tiles.
3. Trim and clean the tiles.
4. Shape the tiles.
5. Cover the tiles with plastic sheeting.
6. After a few days, take off the plastic sheeting and clean the tiles.
7. Move the tiles to a rack and place the rack on blocks to raise it.
8. Place plastic sheeting over the tiles again for a few days.
9. Remove the plastic and cover the tiles with a cloth.
10. After a week, remove the cloth and let the tiles air-dry.

The tiles are now ready to be fired.

1. The slabs for the tiles have been cut and shaped and the first thin slab relief imagery has been placed (Fig. 7-12A).

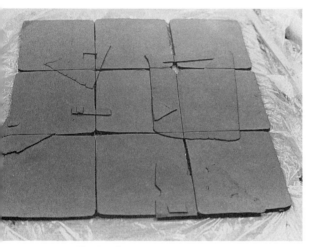

Fig 7-12A.

Fig 7-12B.

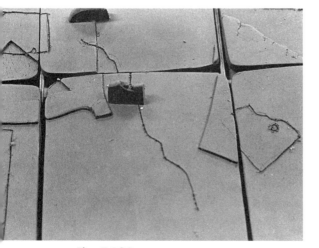

Fig. 7-12C.

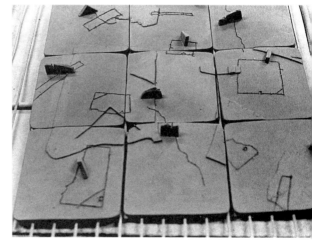

Fig. 7-12D.

2. More relief imagery is placed (Fig. 7-12B).
3. Lines are engraved in the tiles (Fig. 7-12C).
4. The complete tiles (Fig. 7-12D).
5. Supports are added at the back of the piece (Fig. 7-12E).
6. The supports are placed on the back of each tile. The corners of the tiles are pressed downward to create a curved contour (note the curved edges of the back of the tile in Figure 7-12F). The completed piece is shown in Figure 7-13.

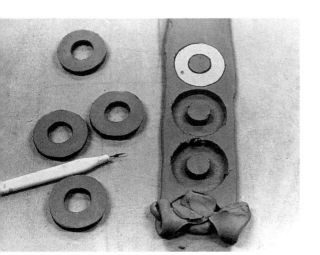

Fig. 7-12E.

Fig. 7-12F.

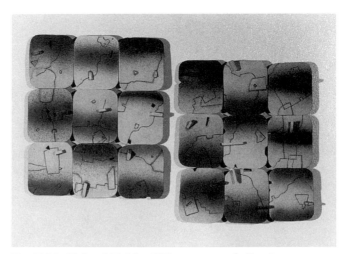

Fig. 7-13. Richard Zakin, USA, two-panel tile piece mounted on plywood, 13¾ × 12¼ inches. Each tile is slightly rounded to resist warping and produce an interesting undulating surface.

INSTALLING WALL PIECES

MASTIC, MORTAR CEMENT, AND GROUT

Mastic is a paste-like cement used to attach ceramic elements to a base such as a panel or a wall. Modern mastic adhesives are strong and reliable. Their manufacturers have developed them for use with brick and tile and they are suitable for interior or exterior use.

Mortar cement is a traditional mixture of sand and water with lime or cement that creates paste-like mixtures in which tiles can be set. With new technology, mortar-like mixtures now combine the superior bonding qualities of modern adhesives with the look and feel of a traditional mortar.

Grout is a thin, fine-grained mortar that can be used to fill the spaces between tiles or tesserae. It supplements the action of the mastic and holds the tiles or tesserae in place. It also enriches the surface of the piece. The natural color of grout is an off-white, which sets off well the color of most mosaic compositions. However, some compositions will benefit from the use of a colored grout and you can color the grout if you wish.

Mount tiles on a base surface of plaster, cement, precast cement panels, cement blocks, brick, or plywood. The surface should be clean, sound, and dry. Sand smooth surfaces to roughen them.

A WORD OF CAUTION: Artists who create large wall piece installations must deal with problems of legal liability in case of injury to passersby. If a fragment from a tile piece injures a passerby, the installer is liable to suit. If the artist also acted as the installer, there might be an assumption that the artist did not carry out the installation in a fully professional manner. Therefore, it is wise to require that the patron (individual or governmental) make provision for professional installation of wall pieces in public places.

MOUNTING A LARGE TILE WALL PIECE—GEORGE MASON

George Mason produced many architectural wall pieces in the 1980s and he continues to work in this format. These pieces are large and permanently mounted. Mason uses a highly stylized imagery that is often abstracted from nature. He likes to create pieces without spatial imagery. This kind of composition works well with the tile medium.

In this series we see Mason and an assistant mount a tile wall. He uses buckets, mixing tools, trowels, a flexible tile mortar, and a thin-set mortar.

1. Mason and his assistant have laid out the piece on the ground, leaving room for the grout (Fig. 7-14A). Mason carefully checks to see that the piece will fit in its niche. This is his last chance to make sure that all the elements fit.
2. The assistant pours the flexible mortar into a bucket (Fig. 7-14B). She will then add a thin-set mortar to the mix.
3. Mason stirs the mixture vigorously and lets it set for five minutes (Fig. 7-14C). Then he stirs again and begins. The consistency of the mortar should be thick and full but not too dry and stiff. The hand-mixing procedure is effective for small batches.

4. Mason and his assistant apply a skim coat to the wall to prepare the area for the mortar (Fig. 7-14D). They apply this one row at a time and try not to get too far ahead of themselves.

5. The assistant applies mortar to the back of the tile (Fig. 7-14E).

6. She carves furrows into the mortar with a trowel (Fig. 7-14F). These furrows create suction when the tile is pressed to wall and help ensure a strong bond. She returns excess mortar to the bucket.

7. They check the level of the tiles as they go (Fig. 7-14G). Mason feels that it is important to make small adjustments as needed. He warns against waiting until you are ready to install the last two rows to adjust the piece to fit the niche. At this point they make small adjustments until the piece "feels" even. This is necessary because tiles are not uniform in size. Making constant small adjustments results in the irregularities being less obvious.

8. The assistant presses the tile into place (Fig. 7-14H). She uses several up and down motions, then raps the tile with a rubber mallet several times

Fig. 7-14A.

to get a secure bite. She uses spacers to ensure a proper distance between the tiles. Mason usually uses two one-quarter-inch spacers instead of a single half-inch spacer. Once the mortar has dried, it is easier to remove two thin spacers than one thick one.

9. Mason and his assistant are now almost half finished (Fig. 7-14I). They have used one batch of mortar and the two have been able to move along quickly.
10. The installation process is almost finished (Fig. 7-14J).
11. When the installation is complete (Fig. 7-14K), Mason lets the thin-set mortar dry overnight.
12. The spacers are removed with pliers (Fig. 7-14L).
13. Now they apply duct tape to the tile surfaces to protect the tiles from the grout (Fig. 7-14M). Mason says of this procedure: "While it is not absolutely necessary to mask the tiles, inevitably some grout will get on

Fig. 7-14B.

Fig. 7-14C.

Fig. 7-14D.

Fig. 7-14E.

the mural surface as well. This is difficult to clean up. If I use a solution of muriatic acid and scrub the tiles, I may leach the color from the grout. I've found it is easier simply to cover the tiles. This step is time-consuming, but there is almost no cleanup."

When Mason finishes applying the grout, he removes the duct tape before the grout gets too dry. Then he goes back and finishes and shapes the joints to make the grout surface smooth and consistent. At this point, a heavy-duty vacuum cleaner is useful for cleaning up the shavings that fall on the edge of the relief. After a week, Mason returns to give a light muriatic acid wash for any areas where scumming has occurred. Finally, he rinses the whole piece with a hose or a few buckets of water.

Fig. 7-14F.

Fig. 7-14G.

Fig. 7-14H.

Fig. 7-14I.

Fig. 7-14J.

Fig. 7-14K.

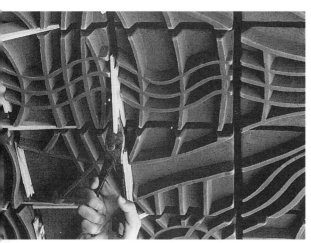

Fig. 7-14L.

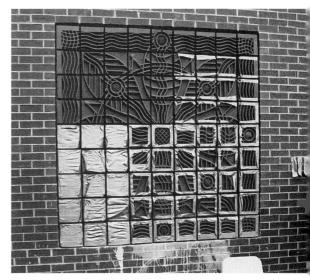

Fig. 7-14M.

CREATING A WALL-HANGING TILE PIECE—RICHARD ZAKIN

Over the last decade I have worked with a group of pieces that I call "wall-hanging tiles." These have some of the character of wall-hanging pieces made by fabric artists (this is probably where I got the idea). In these pieces I suspend clay forms using a network of cords.

I have come to believe that this format has many advantages. Modern technology has contributed spun fiberglass cording, which is inexpensive, strong, and long lasting. The combination of clay and fiber is pleasing and the resulting structure composed of knotted cords and tiles has its own logic. Furthermore, the piece as a whole has a flexible, fabric-like character that is a refreshing change from the rigid mounting of most ceramic wall pieces. Finally, considering their size, these pieces are lightweight. They are easy to hang and do not require elaborate installation strategies.

In these pieces I combine knotted cords with clay elements. This structure strongly influences the character of the finished piece. I have found that hanging wall pieces require a good deal of planning and preparation. Even seemingly insignificant details have a great influence over the look of the completed piece. For example, the positioning of the holes in the tile through which the cords will pass is extremely important; these holes dictate the way in which the piece will hang (even a difference of a centimeter will have a strong effect). When I understand the structure and logic of the piece, it becomes physically stronger and aesthetically more persuasive. Therefore, to create a piece of this sort, I find it helpful to make several preliminary sketches and trial pieces before I begin to work.

After I plan the piece, I make and shape the tiles and create the holes through which the string will pass. I glaze and fire the tiles. I create an armature for hanging the tiles and string them together.

If you wish to try this format, you will need clay, lightweight metal sheeting for templates, engobes or glazes for finishing the tiles, a wooden strut to make the understructure, and spun fiberglass cord 70 to 200 lb. (30 to 90 kilos) test.

Making the Piece

1. Create a template, choose a pleasing shape. Place guides for cord holes through the surface of the template. Place the guides with care because they will influence the way the tiles hang and also strongly influence the look of the assembled piece.
2. Roll a large slab on the work table.
3. Place the metal template on the slab.
4. Make the first tile.
5. Place the cord holes in the tile.
6. Make the rest of the tiles in the same manner.
7. Give the tiles their curved shape.
8. Allow the tiles to become firm overnight under plastic.
9. Cut a groove to hold the wooden strut in the top row of tiles (make the groove 10 percent larger than the understructure to allow for shrinkage).
10. Trim and clean the tiles.
11. Place the tiles on a rack and allow them to dry.
12. Apply an engobe or a glaze to the tiles.
13. Place the wooden strut in the top row of tiles.
14. Fire the tiles.
15. Assemble the tiles.
16. Glue the top row of tiles to the wooden understructure.
17. String together the rest of the tiles.
18. Hang the completed piece using screw eyes and picture-hanging wire.

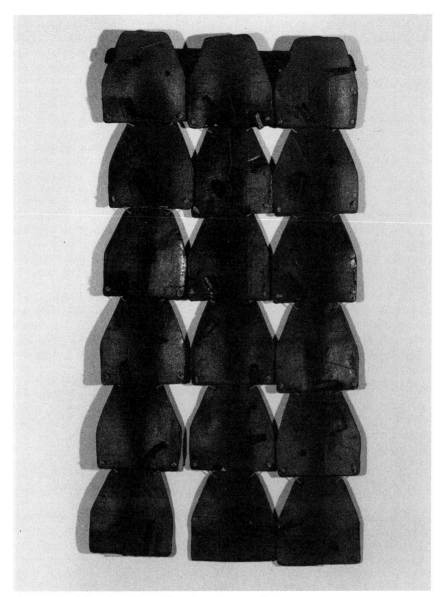

Fig. 7-15. Richard Zakin, a free-hanging wall piece.

PORTFOLIO OF WALL PIECES

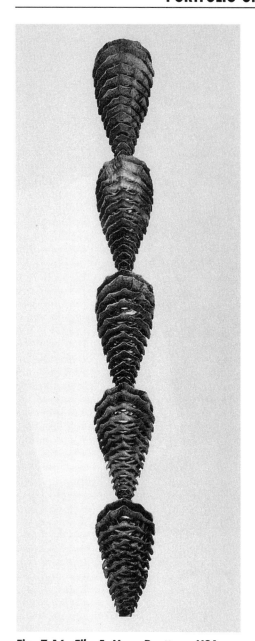

Fig. 7-16. *Fib. 5,* **Mary Roettger, USA, wall sculpture, 9 feet × 7 × 12 inches.** Mary Roettger makes her pieces from slabs. In the building process she pinches and shapes the slabs to simulate the processes of growth in nature. To do this, she uses repetition and variation based on natural, organic forms and mathematical progressions.

Fig. 7-17. Richard Zakin, USA, hanging tile piece, ceramic and twined fiberglass, 73 inches long. Recently I have begun to work a great deal with pieces in this format. At one time I emphasized the ceramic elements and allowed as little string to show as possible. Now I often use the string as an important visual element. I see these pieces as moving in the direction of a mixed-media strategy. Photo by T. C. Eckersley.

MOSAICS

The artist creates mosaics by assembling many small elements called *tesserae*. The artist sets the tesserae in a matrix of grout, a cement-like material that fills the spaces between the tesserae. Although there is no specific size limitation, the tesserae must be small enough to blend optically when the observer steps away from the piece. You can make tesserae from many materials; stone, glass, and clay are the classic materials used for making tesserae. The Iranians were the greatest historical exponents of the ceramic mosaic. They covered both the interior and exterior surfaces of their mosques with rich, highly stylized imagery.

Some artists may see mosaics as nothing more than a way of making a painting permanent and weather-resistant. This approach never seems satisfactory—the results are always a pale imitation of a painting and do not exploit the strengths of the mosaic medium. Mosaic imagery is at its best when its space is shallow and it is free of such painterly effects as shading and modeling. The result is a decorative, patterned abstract or highly stylized imagery that exploits the richness of the medium. Mosaic surfaces are perhaps as appealing as any in the arts and crafts. They contrast smooth, raised tesserae with the grainy, recessed grout. Furthermore, the tesserae are not uniform in height, nor do they lie absolutely flat. Although height and angle change very little, they create a composition of shifting planes in which the light seems to move and play as the viewer moves. The result can be truly magical.

MAKING TESSERAE

The mosaic format makes few demands on the technical skills of the ceramist. Because tesserae are small, there is no problem with warping or cracking. If you intend to shape the tesserae after firing (as do many artists), the clay body should be a bit soft and underfired.

Many ceramists finish their tesserae with slips or glazes. Slips can be quite effective (be sure to pick slips with a durable surface). Slip-painted tesserae will have a mat, clay-like surface. The surfaces of tesserae finished with glazes are more durable than those finished with slips. They are often richer in color as well. Depending on the character of the recipe, glazed tesserae will be mat, stain, or shiny.

Rather than using an applied surface, you can make tesserae out of colored clays. Unfortunately, clay bodies require much more colorant than slips or glazes. Therefore, ceramists rarely use expensive colorants in clay bodies but rely instead on the inexpensive, naturally colored clays. While color will be limited (no greens, blues, true reds, or oranges), you still have many color choices. These include white, ocher yellow, burnt orange, tan, earth red, brown, and umber. Naturally colored clays are rich in color and produce an interesting surface.

Making Glazed Tesserae

1. Make a thin slab.
2. Score the surface of the slab.
3. Let the slab dry.
4. Apply a glaze to the slab.
5. Fire the tesserae.
6. Break the slab along the scored lines to create the tesserae.

Making Tesserae from a Colored Clay

1. Use a colored clay body to make a thin slab.
2. Score the surface of the slab.
3. Let the slab dry.
4. Fire the slab.
5. Break the slab along the scored lines to create the tesserae.

Loading and Firing

Kiln loading is especially easy if you use colored clays; you can pile the tesserae randomly in a bisque-fired container; the colored clays will not stick together in the fire. This method saves a great deal of room in the kiln. Glazed tesserae are less convenient to fire because they stick together when their glazed surfaces touch. If you glaze the tesserae, fire them in sheets (and break them along the scored lines after firing). Because you cannot stack one over the other, you must lay each sheet on its own shelf.

Firing is a simple process. Ceramic tesserae need not be bisque-fired; after forming and drying the slab, coat it with a layer of slip or glaze and put it in the final fire.

Creating the Image

Once you have fired the tesserae, you are ready to create the piece. It is at this point that you must make your image, form, and color decisions. You must also decide whether to mount the tesserae directly on the wall or on a mounting board. If you decide to use a mounting board, you can place the tesserae directly on it. It is more effective, however, to plan the piece on an identically sized workboard. In this way you can glue a group of tesserae all at once. This is much faster and more efficient than gluing each tessera individually. Try to vary the color, height, and angle of the tesserae to create an effective imagery.

To create the imagery:

1. Prepare the mounting board or the mounting area.
2. Prepare an identical workboard (or identical workboards if the mosaic piece is large).
3. Sketch the outline of the imagery.
4. Assemble the tesserae to form the image.

MOUNTING THE PIECE

Use a mastic adhesive to attach the tesserae securely to the mounting board or mounting area. Fill the spaces between the tesserae with grout. If you wish, you can color the grout, which will considerably enhance the decorative quality of the piece. Mastic, grout, and grout colorants are available from tile dealers.

1. Prepare a plywood board or wall mounting space for mounting the tesserae.
2. Cover a section of the area with a thin layer of mastic cement.
3. Transfer the image, tessera by tessera, from the workboard to the mounting board or the wall.
4. Press the tesserae into the mastic. Be sure to anchor them securely.
5. Continue the process until the image is complete.
6. Fill the area between the tesserae with grout. Leave as little as possible on the surface of the tesserae.
7. Clean the surfaces of the tesserae with a rag.

8. Allow the grout to dry.
9. Bits of grout will be left on the tesserae. Clean off as much as you can while the grout is still moist.
10. Clean off the film of grout that remains on the surface of the tesserae with muriatic acid.

NOTE: When using muriatic acid wear rubber gloves, protective glasses, and a safety mask with filters for fumes.

There is a way to transfer the tesserae from the workboard all at once to the mounting board or mounting area. If you are creating a large-scale mosaic piece, you may want to try this method. It requires two people.

1. Glue a large sheet of paper to the front of the tesserae. Use a water-soluble glue.
2. Cover the mounting area with a layer of mastic.
3. Hold the paper with the tesserae facing away from you.
4. Place this against the mastic-coated mounting area.
5. Your helper should now press and smooth the paper. The tesserae are pressed into the mastic layer. Be sure that you have securely attached all of the tesserae to the mastic.
6. Let this set overnight.
7. Soak the paper over the tesserae to loosen the glue.
8. Peel off the paper.
9. Carry out the grouting procedure (see directions above).

MOSAIC NOTES—SALLY MICHENER

Sally Michener creates ceramic sculptures and tile pieces. She uses a great deal of figural imagery in both formats. Her pieces are large-scale and highly stylized. Michener likes to express ideas in her work. Her tile pieces work especially well for this.

For mosaic work, Michener recommends the following tools and materials.

- Large work table
- Buckets
- Rubber gloves
- Charcoal-filter safety mask
- Tile snap cutter (this is a cutting tool)
- Tile nipper (this is a trimming tool)
- Grout trowel
- Spatula
- Knives
- Sponge
- Rubber mallet
- Mixing paddles
- Cloths
- Rulers, tape measures, and other measuring devices
- Plastic dropcloths
- Thin-set adhesive (premixed or dry)
- Wood backing panel
- Grout (she uses a dry cement-based grout)
- Water sprayer
- Window scraper razor
- Tiles—all sorts, both industrial and studio made

- Velcro hanging materials (purchased from trade-show display houses)
- Books about installing tiles

Michener uses a good-quality plywood board for the panel backing. She chooses the thickness depending on the size of the panel. A 4' × 4' panel should be ⅝" thick and back-framed with 2" × 2" wood to reinforce the panel. She uses a ⅜" thick plywood board for this 1' × 2' panel.

SAFETY: Michener uses a dust mask when applying the bonding material and safety gloves when applying the grout. She works in a large, well-ventilated room and emphasizes the importance of the cleanup process to the health of the ceramist. She takes great care to follow directions for the safe application of bonding and grouts.

Creating a Mosaic Tile—Sally Michener

1. Michener first assembles her materials. She then shapes her tiles to fit the needs of the piece as it develops (Fig. 7-18A).

Fig. 7-18A.

Fig. 7-18B.

Fig. 7-18C.

Fig. 7-18D.

2. She begins to assemble the piece on a plywood panel. Ideas for the piece come to her as she moves the tiles around on the panel (Fig. 7-18B).
3. Michener works with the large areas first to establish structure and mood. She then begins to fill in the detail. She loves the different qualities that emerge from having a rich collection of material. She places every tile and mosaic element and rearranges the composition until she feels it is "working." She wants the piece to be interesting both up close and from a distance (Fig. 7-18C).
4. A closeup of the completed piece. She has applied a dry cement-based grout that she mixes with water. She uses grout for both practical and visual reasons. Grout serves to reinforce the bond of the tile to the backing. It comes in many colors and at least two textures and strongly influences the visual character of the work (Fig. 7-18D).

APPENDIX: SETTING UP A HAND-BUILDING STUDIO

Setting up a studio area for hand building can be easy and the demands in terms of space and expense are reasonable. You will need a wedging area, a work table, a drying area, a water supply, a glazing area, and a kiln. Except for the kiln and its ventilation system, you can make all these tools or convert them from tools created for other purposes.

The Water Source

Water is not only a necessity for hand-formed ceramic work; it is indispensable. Pieces must be joined together using water or slip. They also must be smoothed using wet sponges and kept wet with sprays of water or coverings of wet rags. The glazing process requires water as well.

Many ceramists manage to get by without having a sink in their studio, especially those who work in small spaces. They use a bucket of water and decant clay and glaze materials that settle at the bottom of the bucket. Although this system is not especially convenient, it does save money and you can recycle some of your materials. Many ceramists of course do use sinks and find them a real convenience. For those ceramists with a steady production of work, a sink is a necessity.

Situating the Kiln

Kilns can emit unhealthful gases. Therefore, you should place your kiln in a well-ventilated and fireproof area, preferably in its own space, isolated from your work areas. In a small space, this may be difficult to achieve. In a cramped studio, however, it is especially important to keep the kiln separate from the work space.

A Small Studio Area

Hand building lends itself to working in a limited space. You can create a great deal of work even in a small area. You will need:

1. A space two and a half to three square meters.
2. Good lighting.
3. A small but sturdy work table.
4. Wedging boards.
5. A water source.
6. A storage area for materials and supplies.
7. A shelf for drying your work.
8. A kiln.

A Larger Studio

For a larger studio, you will need:

1. A space five to seven square meters.
2. Good lighting.
3. A large and sturdy work table.
4. A wedging table.
5. A sink or water source.
6. An area for drying your work with shelving or drying racks.
7. A glazing area.
8. A storage area for clay and glaze materials.
9. Scales for weighing clay and glaze materials.
10. A kiln (in a well-ventilated space).

Optional equipment might include a slab roller, a workstand with a revolving top, and drying devices, such as blowers, heaters, or heat lamps.

GLOSSARY

Aggregates: Additions to the clay body that control shrinkage or warping and encourage workability and durability.

Ball clay: A fine-particled plastic clay. Used in clay bodies, these clays improve workability and plasticity. They encourage shrinkage and cracking, so their use must be carefully controlled and generally they are not used in amounts of more than 15 percent of the clay body.

Bisque firing: A preliminary firing of unglazed ware. While bisque-firing temperatures may vary widely, the most common are cones 08–04. The bisque fire prepares the work for glazing; the ware can be immersed in the watery glaze without cracking or breaking down.

Calcining: The process of heating a material in order to burn off organic impurities, water, or carbon (driven off as gases). Calcined materials are added to recipes to make them more stable. For example, in high-clay glazes, the plasticity of the clay may cause difficulties during firing; calcining will help diminish the plasticity.

Clay body: A compound of clay and nonclay materials chosen for their individual characteristics that, when combined, meet the specific requirements of the ceramist.

Colloids: Materials with a very fine particle size. Colloidal particles are useful to the ceramist because they encourage workability in clay bodies and good suspension in engobes and glazes.

Colorant: A mineral or compound of minerals used to color ceramic materials. The most common colorants are iron oxide, cobalt oxide or carbonate, copper carbonate, rutile (a compound of titanium and iron), and manganese dioxide.

Deflocculant: An alkaline material that encourages clay particles to repel each other.

Deflocculated: Lowered or entirely negated clay plasticity. Clay bodies that have been somewhat defloccu-lated (generally by alkaline melters in the formula) lose much of their plasticity. Clay that has been highly deflocculated becomes com-pletely nonplastic. Deflocculated clays are used in slip-casting to make high-clay-content bodies more liquid.

Engobe: Originally this term was related to the concept of an enve-lope—that is, an overall coating of slip. Slips used as engobes were almost always porcelain slips intended to disguise modest clay bodies so that they would look like porcelains. The term has come to mean a porcelain or semiporcelain slip applied in any fashion. Engobes have a clay content of 25 to 50 percent and a nonclay con-tent of 50 to 75 percent.

Filler: A neutral material. Clay body fillers are nonplastic and are added to recipes to increase strength and lower shrinkage. Their particle size varies from very coarse to very fine. Fillers added to slips, engobes, and glazes are finely ground, non-melting, nonclay materials that are employed to strengthen and stabi-lize the recipe.

Fillet: A coil of clay placed at the cor-ner joining two ceramic elements, such as two slabs. The fillet strengthens the bonds between the two elements, thus discouraging cracking at the join. Filleted joins are much neater than unfilled joins.

Fire Clay: A coarse, large-particled clay that contributes strength and workability. In itself it is only moderately plastic, but it may significantly enhance plasticity by encouraging particle-size differentiation. Fire clays tend to be buff, tan, or ocher as a result of their moderate iron (1 to 3 percent) and titanium (1 to 3 percent) content.

Flocculant: An acidic material that encourages the aggregation of clay particles. (For its opposite, see *Deflocculant*, above).

Flocculate: To cause clay-particle aggregation (which can encourage plasticity) by adding acidic materials.

Flocculated: A state in which clay particles tend to aggregate or clump together. The clay mass acts as a coherent, workable material that can be shaped and formed.

Flux: An oxide that causes melting. Fluxes include oxides of barium, calcium, boron, sodium, potassium, and silicon.

Frit: Manufactured compounds containing silica, alumina, and melters. While more expensive than many materials that find use in ceramics, they are highly valued and used widely for their stabilizing and strong melting powers. Sodium, calcium, and boron are the most common melting ingredients in frits. Any good ceramic supply house will stock a number of frits.

Glaze: A glassy coating especially formulated to fit over a clay form. Glazes contain silica, alumina, and melter.

Greenware: Finished ware that requires drying before it can be fired.

Grog: A coarse-particled filler for clay bodies. Adding grog to a clay body ensures that the body will contain a wide variety of particle sizes. Grog also impedes warping and encourages durability.

Ground silica (also called flint): A finely ground silica powder, free of impurities, which is an important source of silica in ceramic recipes (clay bodies, slips, engobes, and glazes).

Grout: A fine-particled mortar used to fill in the spaces between tiles or mosaics.

Inlay: A process in which clays of more than one color are worked together to create a multicolored clay piece.

Kaolin: Clay distinguished by its great purity and whiteness. Kaolins tend to be less workable than other clays, but its beauty and refined character compensates for its lack of workability.

Maquette: A small three-dimensional model.

Mastic: A paste-like cement used for gluing tiles or mosaics to a mounting board or a wall surface.

Maturity: When applied to clay bodies, "maturity" is the optimum point at which warping and brittleness are minimized and the absorption rate is reasonably low. When applied to glazes, maturity refers to the point at which the glaze produces a desired effect. Glazes are "mature" when they are fully melted in the fire and are glassy in surface.

Melter: A compound that causes melting, facilitating glaze formation. Melters include silicates, feldspars, and fluxes.

Modular: A construction in which the ceramist shapes the piece using modules.

Modules: Uniform structural elements.

Muriatic Acid: A weak solution of hydrochloric acid used to clean grout from the surface of tiles and mosaics.

Ornament: Imagery that is stamped, sprigged, carved (incised or excised), engraved, or cut (reticulated).

Oxidation: The combination of a material with oxygen.

Oxidation firing: A firing in which there is ready access of oxygen to the firing chamber at all times. Electric kilns in general are constructed in such a way as to fire in oxidation.

Plasticizing agent: An ingredient added to a clay body recipe to improve workability. The two types of plasticizers are organics and extremely fine particle materials. Organic plasticizers such as yogurt encourage bacterial action, which makes the clay more elastic and "slippery." Fine-particle materials such as bentonite and colloids increase the variety of particle sizes in the body. This encourages plasticity.

Porcelain: A pure white clay body that is translucent where thin. Porcelain bodies contain no more than half white clay; the other half composed of ground silica (flint) and feldspar. Because of their low clay content and nonplastic character, porcelains are difficult to work with; however, their beauty compensates for their limited workability.

Pyrometric cones: These narrow, three-sided pyramids mimick clay bodies and glazes and react to the combination of time and temperature (often called "heat work"). As time passes and the temperature increases, the cones soften and bend. The ceramist uses the deformation of the cone as an indication that the clay bodies are mature, the glazes are melted and glassified, and the firing is complete.

Reduction firing: Firing with a minimum amount of oxygen. In reduction firing, the ceramist interrupts the flow of adequate oxygen to the firing chamber of the kiln at certain crucial periods during the firing. This is most naturally accomplished in the fuel-burning kiln. Reduction firing strongly influences the character of clay bodies and glazes.

Refractory: Resistant to heat.

Silica: A crystalline material that, along with alumina, is one of the building blocks of all clays and glazes. The sources of silica are powdered silica, feldspars, clays, and silicates (talc and Wollastonite). Silica promotes plasticity and durability in clay bodies and glaze flow, durability, and a glassy melt in glaze formulas.

Slip: A mixture of clay and water. The word is used in two ways: (1) as a viscous mixture of clay and water used to hold clay pieces together and (2) as a mixture of clay (or clays) and water, with perhaps some nonclay materials, that is applied to the surface of the clay piece for decorative effect.

Soft paste porcelain: Traditionally, porcelain is fired to high temperatures, 1260°C or higher (cones 9–12). Porcelain fired to lower temperatures must contain strong melters (because of the refractory character of the clay content of porcelain); these strong melters, unfortunately, deprive porcelain of some of the dense and durable qualities for which it is so admired. However, the material is still quite durable and beautiful and worthy of use. These slightly softer, less dense, highly fluxed clay bodies are called soft paste porcelain to distinguish them from porcelain itself, which is fired to a higher temperature.

Stains: Calcined compounds of alumina, silica, and naturally occurring ceramic colorants that have been modified by additions of oxides, which affect their color. Stains offer a whole new color palette for the ceramist. The colors are brilliant, safe to use, and reliable. Stains are added to the glaze in varying amounts, usually 3 to 8 percent of the total recipe. While relatively expensive, they have certain advantages over naturally occurring colorants: they are predictable and reliable and their color is WYSIWYG (what you see is what you get). They may be affected adversely by an ingredient in the recipe, they must be tested before normal use.

Stoneware clay: A term used in the United States to designate a raw clay that matures at cones 8–9, is buff or tan in oxidation, and is plastic and workable. Their color is the result of a moderate iron content (1 to 3 percent) and titanium (1 to 3 percent). They are valued for their blend of workability and strength.

Stoneware clay body: A body that contains a high percentage of clay and a low percentage of nonclay materials (some stoneware bodies contain no nonclay materials). The clays used often contain some iron and titanium impurities (2–4 percent iron, 1–2 percent titanium). In color, stoneware bodies are buff, tan, orange, or brown. They have good particle-size variation and are workable and durable. They mature at cones 6–11.

Symmetry: Similarity of form on opposite sides of an object. Asymmetry: dissimilar forms on opposite sides of an object.

Talc body: A clay body that contains a significant amount of talc (usually 25 to 50 percent). Talc is a strong melter and is especially useful in low- and mid-fire clay bodies. Because of the "slippery" character of the talc, these clay bodies tend to be fairly workable even though they are low in clay.

Template: A pattern used as a guide for cutting or forming. Templates may be made from sheet metal, cardboard, or plastic.

Terra-cotta red clay: A high-iron clay. Because of its impurities, especially iron, this clay is valued for its rich, hearty color. The iron content often exceeds 6 percent. Iron serves not only as a coloring agent but also as a powerful melting flux. These clays, therefore, are often used as an ingredient to encourage clay body maturity. Terra-cottas mature at a low temperature; they are usually fired in oxidation to take advantage of their rich earthred fired color.

Tesserae: Small elements used with other tesserae to create a mosaic. Clay is a useful material for creating tesserae.

Warp: To twist or distort. Ceramic pieces may warp during drying or during firing.

Wedging: In kneading the clay, the ceramist forces one part of a lump of clay into another; the clay is rolled into itself. Wedging forces much of the air out of the clay and encourages a uniform moisture content.

White body: A clay body that contains only white and colorless clay and nonclay materials. Porcelain bodies are a type of white body; they are high fire and translucent; other white bodies may be opaque or intended for the lower fire.

White stoneware: An opaque white clay body. These bodies, like porcelain, must contain only white or colorless materials such as kaolins, ball clays, and non-iron-bearing melters. Unlike porcelain, they may have a fairly high clay-to-nonclay ratio and tend to be much more workable than porcelain.

INDEX TO ARTISTS

Page references in *italic* type refer to photographs.

Abbrescia, Sue, 59, *59*, 61, *61*
Akins, Lee, *64*
Anderson, Dan, 43, *46*
Arneson, Robert, 152, 174–175, *174*
Astbury, Paul, 183, *184*

Baldwin, Douglas, 152, 172, 175–176, *175*
Barringer, Mary, 125, 127, *127*, 152, 157, *162*
Barr, Marc, 62, *62*
Beard, Peter, 77, 89, *89*
Black, Deborah, 128, *131*
Brouillard, William, 128, *129*

Caplan, Jerry, 91–92, *91*, *92*
Cartwright, Roy, 117, 119, *119*, *143*
Cartwright, Virginia, *107*
Chabot, Aurore, 134, *135*, 152, 164, *165–166*, 166
Cimatti, Giovanni, 171, *171*
Cooper, Emmanuel, 184
Cummings, Ann, 41–42, *43*

D'Angelo, Milly, 103, *103*
Devore, Richard, 128, *130*

Ehrich, Lisa, 86

Forrest, Neil, 187, *188*
Frey, Barbara, 14, *14–15*, 85, 139–140, *139*, *143*

Gamble, David, 101, *101*, *102*, 132
Geffen, Amara, 66, *66*
Germanow, Jacquie, 154, *155*
Griffith, Roberta, 183, 184, *185*
Groover, Deborah, 128, *131*, *142*

Haniwa sculptors, 6–7, *7*
Hayakawa, Joanne, *167*
Hirsch, Richard, 152, *153*, 156, 177, *178*

Hofsted, Jolyon, 134, *136*
Holcombe, Anna Calluori, 34, *35*, 36, *191*
Höle, Nina, 164, *170*
Holt, Martha, *67*, 157, 160, *161*

Inskeep, Kate, *41*
Irwin, Jeff, 164, *168*
Ito, Itsue, *114*

Jurs, Nancy, 152, *154*, 168

Kell, Jeff, *115*
Kitaoji, Rosanjin, 8–9, *10*
Kokis, George, *64*
Kowalczyk, Susan, *192*
Krouse, Ned, 171, *172*
Kuo, Yih–Wen, 104, *104*, *170*
Kwong, Eva, 68, 69, 157, *162*

Laidman, Roberta, 164, *169*
LaVerdiere, Bruno, 52
Lee, Jennifer, 113, *114*
Levanthal, Robin, 125, *126*

MacDonald, David, *63*
MacDonald, Elizabeth, *192*
McHenry, Tim, *147*
McKinnell, James F., 12, *13*, *14*
McKinnell, Nan B., 12, *13*, *64*
Malta, Liliana, 164, *170*
Mangus, Kirk, 53–54, *54*, 128, *128*
Marcy, Ruth Dorando, 113, *115*
Marks, Graham, 152, *163*
Mason, George, 190, 199–202, *200–203*
Mathieu, Joan, *96*
Mellon, Eric James, *52*
Messina, Mitch, 152, 179–180, *179*
Michner, Sally, *118*, 164, 209–211, *210*
Molinaro, Joe, 85, *86*
Murdaugh, Cathie, *45*

Neely, John, 89–90, *89*, *142*
Nicholas, Donna, 90–91, *90*, 128, *130*

Ostermann, Matthais, 132, *133*
Ozdogan, Turker, *88*

Parry, William, 15, *16–17*, 109, 132, *133*, 134, 164, *167*, 171, *172*, 176, 180, *180*, 181–182, *182*
Pierantozzi, Sandi, *42*, 140–141, *140*, *141*
Powolny, Michael, *11*
Pozo, Angelica, 152, 177–178, *178*, *192*

Quackenbush, Liz, 65, *65*

Randall, Ruth, 9, 10, *11*, 12
Roberts, Ann, 152, 171, 172–173, *173*
Roberts, David, *63*
Roettger, Mary, *168*, *206*
Ross, Katherine, 183, 185, *185*
Salado people, 7–8, *8*
Salazar, Fiona, *63*, 125, *126*
Salomon, Judith, 128, *129*
Saperstein, Elyse, *169*
Schnabel, JoAnn, 112–113, *113*
Schneider, Christian, 8
Schreckengost, Viktor, 9–10, *11*
Scotchie, Virginia, 152, 156, 157, *157–159*, 159
Seawell, Thomas, 180–181, *180–181*
Selvin, Nancy, *191*
Sheba, Michael, *86*
Sherman, Paul, *162*
Stewart, William, 160, *161*
Strong, Leslie, *87*
Sullivan, Louis Henri, 8, *9*, 186
Sung, Dong Hee, *111*

Taylor, Bruce, 108, 176–177, *177*
Tubbs, Ann, 164, *170*

Valenti, Peter, *87*
Valkova, Ruska, 156, *156*

Vavrek, Kenneth, *30*, *114*
VisGirda, Rimas, *118*, *163*

Walker, Jamie, *62*
Walters, Karl, 9
Wilson, Lana, *143*

Xie, Margaret Carney, 4
Zakin, Richard, 15–16, 17–18, 34, 35, *103*, 203–204, *205*, *206*
Zheutlin, Dale, 193–195, *193*, *195*

SUBJECT INDEX

Page references in *italic* refer to illustrations, photographs, or caption information.

Absorption of clay bodies, 21–22
Aggregates, 21, 23, 24, 36
Air bubbles in clay, 24, 25
American ceramics, 9–10, *11, 12*
Ashlars (blocks), 8, *9*
Asian Ceramics in Alfred Collections (Xie), 4
Assembled sculpture, 37, *114, 168,* 171–176, *172, 173, 174, 175*
Asymmetry in ceramics, 4, 27
Atomizer, plant, for moistening clay, 31

Ball clay, 196
Banding wheels, 20
Baskets, 138
Bentonite, 24
Bisque firing, *96, 103,* 208
Blocks, clay (ashlars), 8, *9*
Bones as stamps, 47
Bottles, 138
Bowls
    coil–formed, 8, 137
    described, 137
    hand–forming processes for making, 8, 137
    nonutilitarian, 137, 144
    pillow drape forms, 106–107, *106*
    rigid drape forms, *96, 96,* 97–98, *97–98*
    technical aspects of forming, 144
    utilitarian, 137, 144
Braced forms, 152–154
Brushes, steel, 20

Calcining, 23
Calcium silicate, 196
Canvas, heavyweight, 19
Cardboard sheet as template, 34
Carved clay imagery, 43, *44, 45,* 49–50
Carving tools, 49

Casseroles
    described, 138
    structural integrity of, 28, *28*
    technical aspects of forming, 144–145
Cement, anhydrous, 154
Ceramic elements in mixed–media techniques, 120
Ceramic sculpture. *See also* Sculpture forming
    aesthetic aspects of, 149–150
    braced forms, 152–154
    clay bodies for, 150–151
    clay for, 149–150
    clay imagery and, 150
    described, 149
    large–scale, 152
    metal armatures in, 154, *155*
    mid–size, 152
    mixed–media, 179–182, *179, 180–181, 182*
    scale and, importance of, 151
    small–scale, 151
    technical aspects of, 150–151
Ceramic Sculpture (Randall), *11*
Ceramics, hand–formed. *See also* Guest artists; Portfolios
    American, 9–10, *11, 12*
    asymmetry in, 4, 27
    earliest, 4
    forming methods and, 27
    Haniwa, 6–7, *7*
    Japanese, 8–9, *10*
    mosaics, 8, 9, 207–211, *210*
    neolithic, 4–5, *5*
    Nigerian, 12, *12,* 32
    Salado, 7–8, *8*
    Shang dynasty, 5–6, *6*
    symmetry in, 27, 56
    wall thickness of, 31–32

Chamotte, 23, 36
"Cheese hard," *89*
Ciment fondu, 154
Clay
    air bubbles in, 24, 25
    atomizer, plant, for moistening, 31
    ball, 196
    for ceramic sculpture, 149–150
    consistency of, 24
    course, 36
    cutting, 24, 26
    with fiber, 203–204, *205, 206*
    fired, 36, 116–117
    kiln and, 20
    in mixed–media techniques, 120, 179
    with nonclay core, using, 110
    solid block of, using, 109–110
    structural integrity of, 27–28, *28*
    tesserae from colored, 208
    tools for working with, 19–20
    wedging, 24, 25
Clay bodies
    absorption of, 21–22
    assessing new, 22
    for ceramic sculpture, 150–151
    characteristics of desirable, 21–22
    color of, 21, 22
    de–aired, 22
    durability of, 21, 23–24
    firing temperature of, 21
    in hand–forming process, preparation for, 24–26
    for large–scale work, 24
    modifying, 23–24
    moisture content of, 21–22
    purchasing, 21
    recipes for specialized, 22, 90

Clay bodies, *cont'd.*
  for rigid drape forming, 94
  selecting, 21–22
  shrinkage of, 21, 22, 196
  stoneware, *89*, 90
  testing, 22
  for tiles, 196
  warping of, 21, 22, 36
  workability of, 21, 22, 23–24, 196
Clay elements in mixed–media techniques, 120
Clay imagery
  carved, 43, *44*, *45*, 49–50
  ceramic sculpture and, 150
  combed, 43, *46*, 50
  combining types of, 44
  complex, 8, *9*, 44, 49–50
  cut (reticulated), 43
  engraved (excised/incised), 43, 48–49
  of Haniwa ceramics, 6
  mosaics and, 208
  purposes of, 40
  relief, 150, 189, *192*
  repetitive, 112, *168*, *192*, *206*
  smoked, *92*
  sprigged, 41–43, *43*, 48
  stamped (pressed), 40–41, *41*, *42*, 44–45, 47–48
  for tesserae, 208
Clay Painting with Rabbits (D'Angelo), 103, *103*
Cloth sheeting, 20, 38
Coffee grounds as aggregates, 23
Coil forming
  advantages of, 56
  bowls and, 8, 137
  building with coils and, 55–56
  compound pieces, 58
  cylinder pieces, 57
  described, 55
  efficient methods of, 56, 57
  experimenting with, 57–58
  fabric and, heavyweight, 19
  forming coils for, 55, *57*
  guest artists, 59, *59–60*, 68, *69*, 127, *127*
  Haniwa, 6–7, *7*
  join–strengthening and, 33
  neolithic, 4–5, *5*, 32
  Nigerian, 12, *12*
  with pinch forming, 53
  portfolio, 61–62, *61*, *62*, *63*, *64*, 65, *65*, 66, *66*, *67*
  possibilities with, 56
  Pueblo, 32

Saldo, 7–8, *8*
  in sculpture forming, 156–157
Shang dynasty, 5–6, *6*
  thick–wall forms and, 32
  thin–wall forms and, 32
  vessels made from, 57–58, 125, *126*, 127, *127*
Colanders, 138–139
Colloids, 23–24
Colorants, grout, 208
Color of clay bodies, 21, 22
Combed clay imagery, 43, *46*, 50
Combs, 20
Complex clay imagery, 8, *9*, 44, 49–50
Compound pieces
  coil–formed, 58
  rigid drape forming and, 93
  solid–formed, 110–111
Cone 3, 39, *40*
Covers, vessel, 138, 145, 147–148
Cracking
  assessing, 22
  in large–scale work, 24
  in modular forming, 112
  in platter designs, 28
  problem of, 4, 36–37
  vinegar in preventing, 33, 37, 56
Crochet hooks, 20
Cups, 137, 144
Cut clay imagery, 43
Cut forming, 111, *111*
Cutting clay, 24, 26
Cutting wire, 20, 26, 111
Cylinder pieces
  coil–formed, 57
  slab–formed, 78–80, *79–80*

De–aired clay bodies, 22
Deflocculated slip, 89
Delaware River and Bay Authority wall piece, 194–195, *195*
Dog's–head wedging method, 25
Drape forming
  described, 93
  experimenting with, 93
  fired–clay drape forms, 94
  guest artists, 104–105, *104*, 132, *133*, 134
  hammock drape forms, 105–106, *105*, 107–108, *108*
  mixed wood and metal drape forms, 95–96
  pillow drape forms, 105, 106–107, *106*

plaster drape forms, 94–95
platters made by, *132*, 133
plywood drape forms, 95
portfolio, 103, *103*, *104*
rigid drape forms, 93–94, 96–101, *96*, *97–98*, *99*, *100–102*
soft drape forms, 93, 94
thick–wall forms and, 32
thin–walled forms and, 32
vessels made from, 96–101, *96*, *97–98*, *99*, *100–103*, 132, *132*, *133*, 134
Drawings, preliminary, 28, 29–30, *29*, *30*
Drying process, 36, 37–38, 56, 196
Durability of clay bodies, 21, 23–24
Dust mask, 210

Egyptian paste, 187, *188*
Electric kiln, 38
Elliptical pieces, *85*, 100, *104*
Engraved clay imagery, 43, 48–49
Engraving tools, 48–49
Excised clay imagery, 43, 48–49

Fabric, 19, 71–72, 117
Feet, vessel, 5, 28, *28*, 141, *141*, 145–146
Felt, heavyweight, 19
Fiber with clay, 203–204, *205*, *206*
Filler, 110
Finishing process, 38, *39*, 189
Fired clay, 36, 116–117
Fired–clay drape forms, 94
Firing process, 39, *40*, 196, 208
Firing temperature, 21, 39, *40*
Fixed wall pieces, 190
Flat tiles, 189, 196
Fluxes, 9, 196
Foil as stamps, 41, 44
Footed–jar designs, 28, *28*
Forced drying, 56
Forming methods. *See also* Coil forming; Drape forming; Slab forming
  ceramics and, hand–formed, 27
  combining types of described, 113
  examples of, *91*, *114*, *115*
  sculpture forming, 177–178, *178*

vessels made by, 134–139

cut forming, 111, *111*

finished piece and, 123

mixed–media techniques

ceramic sculpture, 179–182, *179*, *180–181*, *182*

clay in, 120, 179

described, 116

examples of, 120

materials for, 116–117

portfolio, *118*, 119, *119*

vessels, 134, *135*

modular forming, 112–113, *113*

pinch forming

with coil forming, 53

described, 52–53

experimenting with, 53

figures made by, *52*

guest artist, 53–54, *54*

in sculpture forming, 156

tools for, 53

vessels made by, 53–54, *54*, 128, *128*

problems with, 36–37

skills involved in, 51

solid forming

compound pieces, 110–111

described, 108, *109*

experimenting with, 108–111

rods in, 108, 109

in sculpture forming, 176, *177*

vessels made by, 109–111, *109*

types of, 3, 51

use and, influences on, 124

for vessels, 123–124

Four–sided slab pieces, 80, *81–82*, 83, 86, 88

Glass in mixed–media techniques, 116

Glazed tesserae, 207, 208

Glazes, 43, *45*, *86*, 113, *131*, *142*, *162*

Grog, 23, 36, 48, 94, *170*, 196

Grout, 199, 202, 208

Guest artists

coil forming, 59, *59–60*, 68, *69*, 127, *127*

drape forming, 104–105, *104*, 132, *133*, 134

modular forming, 112–113, *113*

pinch forming, 53–54, *54*

sculpture forming, 160,

161, 177–178, *178*, 181–182, *181*

slab forming, 89–92, *89*, *90*, *91*, *92*, 104–105, *104*

teapots, 140–141, *140*, *141*

wall pieces, 187, *188*

Hammock drape forms, 105–106, *105*, 107–108, *108*

Hand–forming process. *See also* Forming methods

appeal of, 3–4

for bowls, making, 8, 137

clay bodies for, 24–26

clay imagery and

carved (excised/incised), 43, *44*, *45*, 49–50

combed, 43, *46*, 50

combining types of, 44

complex, 44, 49–50

cut (reticulated), 43

engraved (excised/incised), 43, 48–49

purposes of, 40

sprigged, 41–43, *43*, 48

stamped (pressed), 40–41, *41*, *42*, 44–45, 47–48

described, 3

drawings/models for, preliminary, 28, 29–30, *29*, *30*

drying process and, 36, 37–38

evolution of artists' work in

Frey, 14, *14–15*

McKinnells, 12, *13*, 14

Parry, 15, *16–17*

Zakin, 15–16, *17–18*

finishing process and, 38, *39*

firing process and, 39, *40*

forms for

appropriate, 27, 28, *28*

inappropriate, 28, *28*

joins and, 33–34

kiln and, 20, 213

moisture content and, 31, 36, 37, 38

pictorial history of

American, 9–10, *11*, 12

earliest, 4

Haniwa, 6–7, *7*

Japanese, 8–9, *10*

mosaics, 8, *9*

neolithic, 4–5, *5*

Nigerian, 12, *12*

Salado, 7–8, *8*

Shang dynasty, 5–6, *6*

for platters, making, 136

problems with, 4, 36–37

structural integrity and, 27–28, *28*

studio for, setting up, 213–214

for teapot, making, 139–140, *139*

templates and, 34, *35*, 36

tools for, 19–20

uses of, 3

wall thickness and, 31–32

water source for, 213

Handles, vessel, 5, 146

Hanging vases, 137, 144

Haniwa ceramics, 6–7, *7*

Heat lamps, 56

Height guides, 71, 74

Held Under Wraps (Astbury), 183, *184*

Homage to Suizenji (Griffith), 184, *185*

Homosote, 20, 72

Imagery. *See* Clay imagery

Images (Zheutlin), 193–194, *193*

Incised clay imagery, 43, 48–49

Installation art, 183–185, *184*, *185*, *191*, *192*

Irregular contour coil-formed piece, 58

Japanese ceramics, 8–9, *10*

Jars, covered, 138, 145

Joins, 4, 24, 33–34, 112

Kaolin, 90

Kilns, 20, 38, 208, 213

Knives, 20, 49

Kyanite, *90*

Large–scale work

ceramic sculpture, 152

clay bodies for, 24

cracking in, 24

sculpture forming, 157, *157–159*, 159

warping in, 24

Leather in mixed–media techniques, 117

Leather stamps, 41, 45, 47

Lids, vessel, 28, *28*, 147–148

Lip, vessel, 146

Loading kiln, 208

Maquettes, 29, *30*, 104, 120

Mastic adhesive, 199, 208

Mechanical slab–rolling devices, 74, *75*

Metal armatures, 154, *155*

Metal in mixed–media techniques, 116, 120

Metal pedestal, 134, *135*
Metal sheet as template, 34, *35*
Mica, 23
Mid-size ceramic sculpture, 152
Mixed-media techniques
    ceramic sculpture, 179–182, *179*, *180–181*, *182*
    clay in, 120, 179
    described, 116
    examples of, 120
    materials for, 116–117, 120
    portfolio, *118*, 119, *119*
    vessels, 134, *135*
Mixed wood and metal drape forms, 95–96
Models, preliminary, 29–30, *29*, *30*
Modular forming, 112–113, *113*
Moisture content
    building process and, 36
    of clay bodies, 21–22
    drying process and, 36, 37, 38
    hand–forming process and, 31, 36, 37, 38
    slab forming and, 68, 70, *70*
Mortar, 199, 200
Mosaics, 8, *9*, *118*, 207–211, *210*
Mountain and Lake (Arneson), 174, *174*
Mounting large tile piece, 190, 199–202, *200–203*
Movable wall pieces, 190
Multiple pieces, simultaneously forming, 56
Muriatic acid wash, 202, 209

Needle tools, 20, 48
Neolithic ceramics, 4–5, *5*
Nigerian ceramics, 12, *12*, 32
Nonceramic elements in mixed-media techniques, 120
Nonclay core, using block of clay with, 110
Nonrigid backing on wall pieces, 190
Nude with Window (Caplan), 91, *91*
Nylon, chopped, 23, 196

Offshoot (Schnabel), 112, 113, *113*
Old Tomb Period ceramics, 7
On the Edge: Art Meets Craft (Cooper), 184

Oosphere (Kwong), 68, 69
Openwork vessels, 138–139, 145

Panel wall pieces, 190
Paper in mixed–media techniques, 117
Perlite, 23
Pillow drape forms, 105, 106–107, *106*
Pinch forming
    with coil forming, 53
    described, 52–53
    experimenting with, 53
    figures made by, *52*
    guest artist, 53–54, *54*
    in sculpture forming, 156
    tools for, 53
    vessels made by, 53–54, *54*, 128, *128*
Pitchers, 138
Plaster drape forms, 94–95
Plaster stamps, 41, 44–45
Plastic in mixed–media techniques, 117, 120
Plastic sheeting, 20, 37, 70
Plates, *101–102*, 101, 136, 144
Platters
    described, 136
    drape–formed, *132*, 133
    hammock drape forms, 107–108, *108*
    hand–forming processes and, 136
    rigid drape forms, 99–101, *99*, *101–102*
    structural integrity of, 28, *28*
    template to cut shapes of, 34
    warping in, 28
Plywood drape forms, 95
Porcelain, *156*
Portfolios
    coil forming, 61–62, *61*, *62*, *63*, *64*, 65, *65*, 66, *66*, *67*
    combined forming methods, *114*, *115*
    drape forming, 103, *103*, *104*
    installation art, *191*, *192*
    mixed–media techniques, *118*, 119, *119*
    sculpture forming
        coil–formed, *162*, *163*
        slab–formed, *167*, *168*, *169*, *170*, *171*
    slab forming, 85, *86*, *87*, *88*
    teapots, *142*, *143*
    wall pieces, *191*, *192*, *206*
Potter's wheel, 4, 21, 27, 51

Preshaping slabs, 76
Pressed clay imagery, 40–41, *41*, *42*, 44–45, 47–48
Public spaces, wall pieces for
    Delaware River and Bay Authority, 194–195, *195*
    Wang Laboratories, Inc., 193–194, 193
Pueblo ceramics, 32

Red stoneware, *107*
Relief imagery, 150, 189, *192*
Repetitive clay imagery, 112, 168, *192*, *206*
Reticulated clay imagery, 43
Rigid backing on wall pieces, 190
Rigid drape forms
    bowls made from, 96, *96*, 97–98, *97–98*
    clay bodies for, 94
    compound pieces, 93–94
    elliptical pieces made from, 100
    fired–clay drape forms, 94
    materials for, 93
    plaster drape forms, 94–95
    plates made from, *101–102*, 101
    platters made from, 99–100, 99
    spheroid pieces made from, 96
    wall thickness and, 93
Rods in solid forming, 108, 109
Rollers, 71–72, *72*
Rope in mixed–media techniques, 117

Salado ceramics, 7–8, *8*
Sand, 23
Saucers, 136
Sawdust as aggregates, 23
Scale of ceramic sculpture, 151
Scalpels, 19, 20, 49
Scoring tools, 20
Sculpture forming. *See also* Ceramic sculpture
    assembled, 37, *114*, 168, 171–176, *172*, *173*, *174*, *175*
    coil–formed, 156–157
    combined forming methods in, 177–178, *178*
    described, 154–155
    guest artists, 160, *161*, 177–178, *178*, 181–182, *181*
    large–scale, 157, *157–159*, 159

pinched–form, 156
portfolio
  coil–formed, *162, 163*
  slab–formed, *167, 168, 169, 170, 171*
  segmented, 37, *114, 168,* 171–176, *172, 173, 174, 175*
  slab–formed, 164, *165– 166,* 166
  solid–formed, 176, *177*
Scumming, 202
Seams, 4
"Seasoning" slabs, 70–71, 76, 93
Segmentation, 112, 187
Segmented sculpture, 37, *114, 168,* 171–176, *172, 173, 174, 175*
Segmented tile pieces, 187, 189
Shang dynasty ceramics, 5–6, *6*
Shaped tiles, 189, 196–198, *197–198*
Sheeting, cloth/plastic, 20, 37, 38, 70
Shrinkage, 21, 22, 24, 36, 196
Silica sand, 23
Sketches, preliminary, 28, 29–30, *29, 30*
Slab forming
  creating slabs and
    hand rolling, 71–72, *72*
    mechanical rolling, 74, *75*
    shapes of, 77
    thrown, 72–74, *73*
  cylinder pieces made from, 78–80, *79–80*
  described, 68, 70–71
  experimenting with, 78–80, *79–82,* 83–84
  fabric for, heavyweight, 19
  guest artists, 89–92, *89, 90, 91, 92,* 104–105, *104*
  hand roller for, 71–72, *72*
  mechanical rolling devices for, 74, *75*
  moisture content and, 68, 70, *70*
  portfolio, 85, *86, 87, 88*
  preshaping slabs and, 76
  in sculpture forming, 164, *165–166,* 166
  "seasoning" slabs and, 70–71, 76, 93
  tapered walls in, 71, 74, 76
  thickness of slabs and, 71
  thick–wall forms and, 32, 84

thin–walled forms and, 32, 84
three–dimensional pieces and, 76–78, *77*
throwing a slab and, 72–74, *73*
trays, 8–9, *10*
vessels made from, 78–80, *79–80, 81–82,* 83–84, 128, *128, 129, 130, 131*
Slab–rolling fabric, 71–72, *75*
Slab–rolling machines, 74, *75*
Slip, 5, 33, *131,* 207
Slip–cast forms, 4, 27, *114*
Slip–painted tesserae, 207
Slurry, *89*
Small–scale ceramic sculpture, 151
Smoked clay imagery, *92*
Smoothing tools, 33, 49
Soft drape forms, 93, 94
Solid forming
  compound pieces, 110–111
  described, 108, *109*
  experimenting with, 108–111
  rods in, 108, 109
  in sculpture forming, 176, *177*
  vessels made by, 109–111, *109*
Spatulas, spring–steel, 19
Spheroid pieces, 56, 57–58, 96
Spiral wedging method, 25
Sprigged clay imagery, 41–43, *43,* 48
Stains, *45, 92, 131, 142*
Stamped clay imagery, 40–41, *41, 42,* 44–45, 47–48
Stamps, 41, 44–45, 47
Stoneware, 13, 14, 36, *64, 162, 182,* 187, *188*
Stoneware clay bodies, *89,* 90
Stress points, reinforcing, 36
Structural integrity, 27–28, *28*
Studio for hand–forming process, 213–214
Symmetry in ceramics, 27, 56

Table sculpture, 151
Tapered walls, creating, 71, 74, 76
Tar paper as template, 34, *35*
Teapots
  described, 138
  guest artist, 140–141, *140, 141*

hand–formed, 139–140, *139*
nonutilitarian, 138
portfolio, *142, 143*
slab–formed, 85, *142, 143*
technical aspects of forming, 145
utilitarian, 138
white stoneware, 89–90, *89, 142*
Templates, 34, *35,* 36, 148, 195
Terra–cotta, 8, *9,* 65, 87, *113, 141, 175*
Terra sigillata, *5, 45, 63, 131, 141, 191*
Tesserae, 207–208
Testing clay bodies, 22
Textured material as stamps, 41, 47
Thick-walled forms, 32, 38, 84
Thin-walled forms, 32, 58–59, 84
Three-dimensional painted imagery, 189–190
Three-dimensional pieces from slabs, 76–78, *77*
Throwing a slab, 72–74, *73*
Tiles
  clay bodies for, 196
  designs of, 36
  flat, 189, 196
  making, 195–198, *197, 198*
  mosaic, 8, *9,* 207–211, *210*
  segmented/unsegmented, 186–187, 189
  shaped, 189, 196–198, *197–198*
  size of, 189
  wall-hanging piece
    creating, 203–204, *205*
    mounting, 190, 199–202, *200–203*
Tools
  carving, 49
  for clay, working with, 19–20
  engraving, 48–49
  for hand–forming process, 19–20
  needle, 20, 48
  for pinch forming, 53
  scoring, 20
  for slab rolling, 71–72
  smoothing, 33, 49
  templates, 34, *35,* 36, 148, 195
  toothed, 50, 56
Toothed tools, 50, 56
Trays, 8–9, *10*
Triangular slab pieces, 80, 83, *86*

Twin Span (Zheutlin),
194–195, *195*
Two–dimensional painted imagery, 189–190

Unsegmented tile pieces,
186–187
Use of vessels, influence on
forming methods and,
124

Vases, 136–137, 144
Vessels. *See also* specific
types
coil–formed, 57–58, 125,
126, 127, *127*
combined forming methods
to make, 134–139
covers, 138, 145, 147–148
details, 145–148
drape–formed, 96–101, *96*,
97–98, *99*, *100–102*,
132, *132*, *133*, 134
feet, 5, 28, *28*, *133*, 134,
141, *141*, 145–146
forming methods for, 123–
124
handles, 5, 146
lids, 28, *28*, 147–148
lip, 146
with metal pedestal, 134,
135
mixed–media–formed, 134,
135
openwork, 138–139
origins of forms of, 123–124
pinch–formed, 53–54, *54*,
128, *128*
slab–formed, 78–80, *79*–

80, *81–82*, 83–84, 128,
128, *129*, *130*, *131*
solid–formed, 109–111,
109
technical aspects of forming, 144–145
types of, 135
use of, 124
Vinegar for wetting cracks,
33, 37, 56

Wall–hanging tile piece
creating, 203–204, *205*
mounting, 190, 199–202,
200–203
Wall pieces
described, 186
finishing for, 189
fixed, 190
guest artist, 187, *188*
hanging tile
creating, 203–204, *205*
mounting, 190, 199–202,
200–203
installing, 199–202, *200–
203*
movable, 190
nonrigid backing on, 190
panel, 190
portfolios, *191*, *192*, *206*
for public spaces
Delaware River and Bay
Authority, 194–195,
195
Wang Laboratories, Inc.,
193–194, *193*
rigid backing on, 190
segmented, tile pieces,
187, 189

two- and three-dimensional
painted imagery, 189–
190
unsegmented tile pieces,
186–187
Wall thickness, 31–32, 93
Wang Laboratories, Inc.,
wall piece, 193–194,
193
Wareboards, 2
Warping
of clay bodies, 21, 22, 36
flat tiles and, 196
in large–scale work, 24
in modular forming, 112
in platters, 28
problem of, 4, 36
shaped tiles and, 196
*Water Cure: Contamination
and Cleansing* (Ross),
185, *185*
Water source for hand-forming
process, 213
Wedging clay, 24, 25
White sand, 23
White stoneware, 89–90, *89*,
142
Wiener Werkstätte crafts
school, 9, *11*
Wollastonite, 196
Wooden rollers, 71
Wood in mixed–media tech-
niques, 117, 120
Workability of clay bodies,
21, 22, 23–24, 196

Yang Shao ceramics, 32